WHAT I DIDN'T LEARN AT SCHOOL BUT WISH I HAD

C000219331

WHAT I DIDN'T LEARN AT SCHOOL BUT WISH I HAD

Jamie McIntyre

Co-author Leigh Barker
Accountant

21st CENTURY ACADEMY
EDUCATION FOR LIFE

First published in 2002
Reprinted in 2004
This edition published in 2005 by
21st Century NZ Pty Ltd
Level 20, ASB Bank Centre
135 Albert Street
Auckland, New Zealand
Telephone: (09) 358 7334
Facsimile: (09) 358 7332
www.21stcenturyacademy.com
Email: customerservice@21stcenturyacademy.com

Australian Mailing Address for 21st Century NZ Pty Ltd
PO Box 352
Tewantin, Queensland 4565

Copyright© 2002

ISBN 0 9581922 1 9

All rights reserved. This publication is copyright and may not be resold or reproduced in any manner (except excerpts thereof for bona fide study purposes in accordance with the copyright act) without the prior consent of the publisher.

Every effort has been made to ensure that this book is free from error or omissions. However, the publisher, the author, the editor, or their respective employees or agents, shall not accept responsibility for injury, loss or damage occasioned to any person acting or refraining from action as a result of material in this book whether or not such injury, loss or damage is in any way due to any negligent act or omission, breach of duty or default on the part of the publisher, the author, the editor, or their respective employees or agents.

Edited by Jana Rajnoch
Internal layout by Emigraph Creative
Printed and bound by Griffin Press

DISCLAIMER

The primary author of this book, Jamie McIntyre, is not a financial planner, adviser, registered accountant or financial professional.

The information presented in this book is based on his personal experiences as an entrepreneur, consultant, coach, investor, and others he has modelled in detail. You may have to modify them, do further research on them or adapt them to suit your personal financial situation.

Any information presented is given purely as an illustration and should not be construed as a specific investment recommendation.

The laws relating to investment, taxation, benefits, and the handling of money are constantly changing and are often subject to changes in government policy. Whilst every care has been taken to ensure the accuracy of the material contained herein at the time of publication and presentation, neither the author, presenter, promoters nor the publishers will bear any responsibility or liability for any action taken by any person, persons or organisations on the purported basis of information contained in this book.

Without limiting the generality of the foregoing, no person, persons or organisations should invest monies or take other action on reliance on the material contained in this book or any support material, but instead should satisfy themselves independently (whether by expert advice or otherwise), of the appropriateness of any such action.

Contents

When do you measure Education's Success, at Graduation or Retirement? The following facts exist for every 100 people at age 65.

DID YOU KNOW...

*** 25 ARE DEAD**

20 HAVE ANNUAL INCOMES UNDER $10,000
(Below Poverty Level)

51 HAVE ANNUAL INCOMES BETWEEN $10,000 AND $ 35,000 (Median is $ 18,000)

4 HAVE ANNUAL INCOMES OVER $ 35,000

YET 1 IN EVERY 100 IS A MILLIONAIRE

Today's average 50 year old has only $2,300 saved towards their retirement.
J. Urcivoli, Sr VP Merrill Lynch

Only 5% of the population can put their hands on $ 10,000 when they are 65.

When Social Security was started there were 16 people working for every one person on the program.

Today the ratio is 3:1

In the next 12 years

It is projected to be 1:1...
Source: "The Millionaire Next Door"

This book is designed to give you a 21st Century Educational System, way beyond that which is provided in 21st Century Schools and Universities.

MY EXPECTATIONS OF THIS BOOK

At the conclusion of reading this book, I expect to have achieved the following outcome:

To achieve this outcome, I am willing to commit to the following to ensure I achieve my desired results:

PREFACE

My belief is that if you are not just curious but committed to excelling in your life in the 21st Century, then what you will find in this book will be a real gift to you from someone who cares about helping you achieve similar things if you so desire. You can join the thousands of others who are applying these strategies and improving their lives immensely. I know I was extremely grateful when I first learned this information – an education for life. In this book you will learn:

- How to develop the mindset of a millionaire
- Why most people fail
- The history of money and how the systems control it; why you must understand this
- A real life "21st Century Modern Day Education" that enabled me to excel financially, more than what I learned at school or university
- How to rewire your subconscious mind for financial success
- How to generate instant cashflow, even if you have little money to start with
- How smart investors earn $35,000 per year from investment property — Tax Free
- What you should have been taught at school, but weren't
- The 4 key skills you must master to succeed in the 21st Century, and how others have used these to earn over $100,000 pa
- The 5 key components of a 21st Century Education, that should be taught at school
- How smart investors are replacing their income in 90 to 180 days or less by using a unique renting strategy
- 8 ways investors raise money to start investing immediately, even if they have no money

- How to easily develop the mindset of a millionaire and think like a winner.

To accomplish these objectives, I believe it is important to share parts of my story to make it more relatable and also spend time on developing a solid foundation of understanding on the big picture of money and how to change our thinking to be more effective at implementing these exciting strategies.

FOREWORD

If someone told me nine years ago that this is how my life would be, then I would never have believed them, especially from where I was starting. I share the following with you, not to impress you but to impress upon you dreams do still come true. They did for me, I believe they can for you.

I still pinch myself being able to sit in my outdoor hot tub on the deck of a multi-million dollar mansion, overlooking the pool and waterfall which flows into the extended lounge room of my luxury Noosa waterfront home. The reality of my life today sinks in when I glance out over the water, looking at a gleaming brand new luxury sports cruiser boat. I am planning the next overseas holiday to include a stay with some of my closest friends and family in our brand new luxury winter home in the mountains overlooking Queenstown, New Zealand. It is comforting to have the feeling that despite still being only in my twenties, I never have to work another day in my life unless I choose. I reflect with immense gratitude on my life and can hardly believe that some of my wildest dreams are now a reality, like having a farm to escape to the solitude of nature, with its own personal airfield for a private plane to land. Or to have a beautiful apartment overlooking the world's most beautiful harbour (Sydney), in my opinion, to entertain friends when visiting this beautiful city, or to be able to stay in a luxury chalet in one of the world's top ski resorts in Whistler, Canada. What is even more exciting is to have the thrill of having enough money to sponsor a whole school of children in a third world country and experience the happiness this brings to their faces.

Being able to also help our own Australian teenagers transform their lives by donating teenage scholarships to educate them with a real life education, unfortunately not taught in our schools yet.

I love being able to travel regularly to some of the most beautiful places in the world like Monte Carlo, Portofino, Venice, Prague, Africa,

Majorca, the Caribbean, Canada, Machu Picchu in Peru, Aitutaki in the Cook Islands, to name just a few magical places in our beautiful world.

Even more important than just the wonderful material things I am blessed with today, is being surrounded by like minded friends and having the freedom to do whatever I want, whenever I want, with whomever I want, as much as I want, and importantly spending quality time with family, taking them on exotic holidays.

What touches me the most is to know that I get to live my life's purpose, serve my creator and contribute and impact on so many people's lives in such a positive way. There is hardly a week that goes by that I am not touched deeply by someone sending me a card or present or an email, thanking me for the difference I have been able to make to their lives or their teenage childrens. Also getting pulled up in restaurants and thanked profusely by people who have recognised me from a live seminar where I have been asked to share my strategies, concepts and ideas with fellow Australians and thanking me for how it has changed their lives.

I share none of this to impress you as I said, as I am humbled by my life today and you will understand why when I share my story. However, I share it more to impress upon you that what my attempt and intention is to do by writing this book is to share freely with you the ideas, strategies and concepts that have transformed my entire life over the last eight years. This includes my health, relationships, my emotional fulfilment, and especially my finances. Here I went from sleeping on a mate's couch (mate means 'friend' if you are not an Australian), $150,000 in personal debt, no job, no income, no assets, not even $20 left in my wallet, virtually bankrupt, to becoming a self made millionaire in a little under four years, and creating an extraordinary quality of life for myself and others.

My belief is that if you are not just curious but committed to excelling in your life in the 21st century, then what you will find in this book will be a real gift to you from someone who cares about helping others achieve similar things, if you so desire. You can join the thousands of others who are applying these strategies and improving their lives immensely. I know I was extremely grateful when I first learned this information, so I commend you in advance for taking action and developing a 21st Century education, an education for life.

I would be honoured if you would consider me as a friend, a coach, working together through this book step by step creating and redesigning your life, with an emphasis on improving your financial results until you produce the results you ultimately desire. Let us begin shall we, as it is an exciting journey you are starting on.

If only I had learnt this education at school, how much easier life would have been for me, and no doubt many others. My dream is this type of education will soon be available in all Australian high schools, especially if I get my way.

INTRODUCTION

When I was a kid people would ask me, "Jamie, what do you want to be when you grow up?" Now, some people may want to be doctors, nurses or lawyers (well maybe not lawyers). But perhaps astronauts, policemen, actors, actresses and so on — it is different for different people.

I did not know exactly what I wanted to be, so when people would ask me that question at a young age, I would answer, "When I grow up I want to be rich." I do not know if it was from watching the American TV show "Dallas" too much, but that looked pretty good to me because J.R. Ewing did not seem to work too much, drove around in expensive cars and lived on nice ranches, if you recall. Or it could have been from playing too much Monopoly with my brothers, or perhaps it was just in the back of my mind that I linked being rich to being above average and going for it in life.

I grew up in a small country town on a 2,000 acre farm which my family still have to this day, in a small town called Glen Innes, which is in Northern New South Wales, Australia. If you go there in winter you will never forget it, it is rather cold, however quite warm in summer and usually nice and green. Growing up with a farm background, the two things that were conditioned into me from an early age were that life was hard work and a struggle. In order to do well in life and make money, you had to work really hard. That is what my father had done and what my grandfather did when he was alive. And the second part of the equation for the "ultimate success formula" was that you needed to go to school, study hard to get really good grades and with those really good grades, hopefully one day you would get a really good secure job. Then, on the proviso that you worked hard for 40, 50 or 60 years of your life you would get to retire to the "good life". Now I often wonder in the 21st century how that formula is going for people. Has anyone ever bothered to check that out?

Going through school, like most people did, I just coasted along. I was not at the top of the class, or at the bottom. I preferred to play sport rather than apply myself academically because I quite liked the idea of becoming a professional rugby league player. But unfortunately for me, there was no mention of professional football when my teacher gave me his recommendation on what to do as a career. He said, "Jamie, if you want to make a lot of money when you grow up, you should go to university and become an accountant." Now some accountants find that rather humorous, but I did not know the reality back then. So I stuck to my teacher's game plan and went off to university, just like many other young people do. I started to pursue a career without knowing if that was what I really wanted to do with the rest of my life.

I soon discovered that accountancy was not my passion and eventually got to a point where I was disillusioned with what I had learnt at school and university. I can remember asking my mother, after I had spent all my hard earned savings to fund my way to university, "Why is there not a university that will teach me how to be successful in life?"

I felt that many things I had learnt at school and was learning at university were never going to be helpful in achieving my dreams in life, let alone excel in the 21st century. I felt the education system was failing me and many others and it was then that I started to become restless and looked for an education that would serve me for life.

It is interesting to note that nearly all millionaires I have since had the fortunate opportunity to study were high school or college dropouts and now employ those who were apparently smarter and gained a higher HSC score or university degree.

At the time, I felt like a failure because I could not just settle for what I was being taught at university. It was like peer group pressure, and this sense of fear that if I did not get a degree, I would be a failure in life. That was the real reason I and I believe many others were there.

I did not know at the time, but as I later realised out of all the successful role models and mentors I would study in the years ahead on what it takes to have an extraordinary quality of life, not one of them said, Jamie, you need a university degree or otherwise unfortunately you will not make it in life. Actually, many of them stated that a university degree can be a major hindrance, and what is taught in our current education system is mostly useless and is why most people fail miserably in life (more of this later in the book). However, this was the exact opposite to what I had been conditioned or convinced into believing all my life.

(Author's note: If you are at university, I do not suggest you quit as it teaches many valuable things, however, it also fails to teach many things which are so necessary to excel in the 21st century. In my opinion, one needs more than just a university education to achieve one's dreams in the 21st century.)

About this time I heard an interesting statistic from a wealthy gentleman. He said, "Did you know that over 70% of people that become rich in this country do so by owning their own business?" At this point in time I knew nothing about making money or anything like that, so I thought, "OK, I am not rich yet and I want to be rich one day, so this must be the true secret to becoming wealthy! I simply need my own business and because I have been working for someone else, that is why I am not rich. I need a business — that will bring millions to my door!", or so I thought.

My first challenge in owning my own business was where I was going to get the money to start it. You need money to make money, right? Well, that is what I had always been taught growing up. I do not agree with that any more but that was my old way of thinking. A bank appeared to be the logical answer. I mean that is what banks must be for, right? — to give money to people that really desperately need it. However, I later figured out the only way to get money from banks was to prove to them right up front that you do not need it in the first place, and then, they seemed to just send it to you without asking in pre-approved credit cards and lines of credit, etc. Unfortunately, I did not meet the bank's criteria at the time and they would not give me any money. But I did not want to give up my dream of being rich by owning my own business, so I got creative and came across a thing called credit cards. Have you discovered credit cards yet? I was able to develop multiple relationships with credit cards. Using credit cards, I was able to acquire around $16,000 in cash to launch my first business, even though I did not have any idea of what business I should be in.

I thought owning a business that made lots of money would be handy. So I did some "in depth" research. A friend of mine had a mobile phone and I could see that more and more people were using them. I came to the conclusion that by the year 2,000 most people would own a mobile phone, therefore the telecommunications industry was definitely the industry of the future. As you can see a lot of planning went into this new business venture — a whole 30 seconds of research!

However, surprisingly within nine months of starting my business with no real business experience, just a dream and lots of courage, I was making more money per month than I used to make in a whole year working for someone else. This led me to believe that business was simple, success was easy and there was nothing to it. My business was turning over large amounts of cash so I thought, "Ahah! Another secret to becoming wealthy must be simply to make lots of money."

I find many people to this date that I coach still think that making lots of money is the main key to becoming wealthy. (Please note, this is a major wealth myth.)

However, as my income increased, the expenses and overheads rapidly followed behind and then my expenses actually overtook my income. I discovered a new experience, how to get into debt fast, I was spending more than I earned and I quickly became an expert at creating debt.

Soon I became weighed down with debt and lost my enthusiasm for life. No one had ever taught me how to manage this thing called money and it was creating major havoc in my life. I do not know if you were ever taught at school how to manage this thing called money. My teachers at school could only teach me what they knew and nobody had ever taught them. So I, like a lot of people, had to figure out money management the hard way.

After a period of time I started to link more pain to money than pleasure. My debt was spiralling out of control and I thought that if I could just earn more money then everything would be all right. Subconsciously what started to happen was that I began to link pain to money from the stress of not having enough and not knowing how to manage it. I was living up to the good work ethic that my parents had instilled in me of working really hard, putting in long hours and then struggling to cover my bills. It eventually got to the point where I was saying, "I am not interested in making money. Money is not important". I thought, "There has got to be more to life than just working for money." I looked around me and found that most people's day to day activities were very similar to my own, they too were focussed on going to work, and to work for money. Is this what life is meant to be like? Is this what I have to put up with for the next forty years? There has to be more to life than just working for money.

I decided I could not stand being in business any more and wanted out. I wanted my life back. I had initially decided to get into the telecommunications business to get a life. In hindsight, I had given my life to the business. (Years later I learned that many others could relate to this as they had started their own business or career to get a life, but they too had found that it consumed their life.) Later still I learned that you need to be careful what you ask for. But at this point in time I did not care how I got my life back, I just wanted to be out of the business and a few months later I was out of the business — in fact, I could have been declared bankrupt! In hindsight, I should have said that I wanted to get out of the business by selling it for a nice profit and be financially comfortable until I decided what I really wanted to do. But I forgot to mention that and I lost the business and my entire company. As a result, I now had my time back, but I had no money, which was not what I was really after. I was owed several hundred thousand dollars from the service providers I was dealing with. Yet, because I was too trusting I fell victim to their foul play, whereby many service providers deliberately delayed paying commission to smaller businesses, like mine, that connected mobile phone customers to them, so virtually forcing small businesses like mine to bankruptcy. When businesses like mine go broke, the service providers save paying out all their commissions, but still retain all their new customers the small businesses worked hard for years to create. They also avoid paying out the airtime commissions (percentage of customers' mobile phone calls which is money that would come in while you sleep if you owned a successful telecommunications company and one of the reasons I originally thought of it as being a great business).

In fact, one of the service providers I was dealing with, a supposedly reputable company in Australia deliberately switched off all my mobile phone customers for several hours. They phoned my customers direct, told them that my company had not paid the phone bills and my company was going broke, and they should sign up direct with them.

They failed to mention that I was only going broke because they refused to pay the commissions. A reason they wanted to get my customers to sign up directly was that they did not want to pay out their agreed commissions.

Obviously, you could imagine I was not a very happy young person when I found out. Not only were they doing something highly illegal but they were attempting to destroy my credibility, which hurt even more.

Many people said I should sue them, take it to the courts, however, that takes enormous money and time which without the commission payments I did not have. Since that time over eight years ago, I have been informed that many of the mobile phone companies in Australia are still up to their dirty tricks and driving small dealers to the wall and quickly replacing them with the next victim. Hopefully, one day they will be investigated and someone will stand up for small Australian businesses being destroyed by the large, mostly foreign companies.

However, I had more pressing problems to face. Not only did I lose my entire income and my business was destroyed, I owed over $150,000 in personal debt accumulated to cashflow my company whilst waiting for commission payments which never came.

I was facing bankruptcy, my dreams were shattered and I was feeling sick in my stomach from stress.

What I was really after was to get control of my life and also a thing called LIFESTYLE. In essence, Lifestyle is really TIME plus MONEY. Now it sounds very simple, but it can be a difficult equation for most people.

For most Australians the way they try to get lifestyle is to take their time, which we all have 24 hours of in a day, and then they try to sell that time in exchange for some money. Some people get really good at that, they often have a better education than others and they can sell their time at a higher price. The name of the game is to sell that time for as much as they can per hour or per week. The challenge is that because we need both time and money to have lifestyle, we often sacrifice our time for money.

Of course there is always the other side of the spectrum where people will say that money is less important to them than their time. Instead, they sacrifice money for time. I was holidaying in Byron Bay once (a beautiful part of Australia), and I witnessed many examples of this — people with lots of time on their hands, but not much money. (No offence to Byron Bay.) So the challenge is to find a way to have both time and money and to ensure the correct balance of both. Imagine if we could have both together. That was something I thought would be ideal but I did not have a clue how to do it. I do not think I was the only one.

So there I was with no lifestyle and $150,000 in personal debt, which at the time I thought was a lot of money. Plus, I had company debt on top of that and no income, no job, nothing. Lucky for me one of my friends, working for me at the time, let me sleep on his couch because I could not afford to pay rent — that is how bad it got. At this stage, no money, not even $20 to my name, I only really had two options. Either I could retreat to the family farm with my tail between my legs and become a farmer like my father and his father before, or I could stay in Sydney and try to turn this mess around.

I vowed that one day I would become so wealthy I would buy the telecommunications company that sent me to the wall, walk into their offices in Sydney and fire the employees that ruthlessly enjoyed seeing my business destroyed for the sake of their increased profits. Some say success is sweet revenge, however I had to let go of the hurt and anger I initially felt in order to actively become a millionaire.

This was a major turning point for me in my short life because for the first time I took a good hard look at myself and asked what it was that I really wanted to do with the rest of my life. It eventually became clear, what my purpose was. I will share the process I went through to work this out later in the book. It was then that I realised I needed to go out and seek teachers and role models to help me achieve that purpose. Not traditional teachers that teach theory like many do at school or university, but teachers that had real life experiences. I realised that my education in the past had been based mainly on theory. You know, university, school etc. — I do not mean to be critical of those education systems, but they are often based on theory, not actual experience, and that was when I realised I had to produce some real life results — the things that actually made a difference in my life.

I also realised that if I was going to live my dreams I needed to change as a person. You or someone you know may have read a personal development book or attended a seminar, the concept being that if we grow as people we are more likely to live our dreams. So I started to do that. I also realised I needed to develop different areas of my education and I started to seek out mentors in these particular areas. No doubt you may also be looking for mentors. What I found was that I needed mentors that had produced phenomenal results in their life. I thought that perhaps I could learn from a multi-millionaire, surely someone like this would know more about money and success than I did.

A lot of people ask me where I got my role models or mentors from and I often jokingly say to them, "Well you can be lucky and your local multi-millionaire could knock on your door one day and say, 'I hear you want to do well financially and I am your local multi-millionaire here to give you some coaching.'" Or you may need to do as I did and go out and search to find and do whatever it takes to develop relationships with people who have produced the results that you want in your life or easier still, read books they have written.

My wealthy mentors shared information with me that proved to be very valuable which I will share with you in this book. But it was not the information alone that made the difference. The information age allows people to access information via seminars, books, tapes and the internet. I used to think knowledge was power until I learnt that I actually had to act on that knowledge, nothing ever just happened. I had wealthy mentors (my millionaire mentors as I refer to them), who were patient and caring enough to help me, not only to understand but also apply these skills and strategies. Once I had learnt how to apply this information to my situation, my life started to improve rather rapidly.

I was able to learn how to make money with no money. I thought it would be great to learn how you make money with no money, because I had none and I was hoping that would work. I also learned how to eliminate debt rapidly. And that was important as I had lots to practice on. However, if I had just followed what most people do, I would still be paying that debt off. Instead, I followed the strategy my millionaire mentor recommended that one of the ways to be financially successful in life was to simply find out what most people are doing and then to do the exact opposite. I call it the law of opposites. In other words, I consistently look at what most people do in a particular situation and then I generally do the exact opposite. And I usually find I am heading in the right direction — even if I have no idea of what I am doing! This also explains why many people never succeed because one of their excuses is they do not know what to do. However, successful people in the beginning do not either. They just get started and go on faith that they will learn what is necessary on the way.

These strategies started to work well for me and over a short period of time, I was able to firstly get an income and then increase my income. In fact, my income went through a massive transformation where it increased fifteen fold in less than twelve months from an above average income in the first place. Jot down what your current income is, multiply it by fifteen and imagine it increasing to that figure over the next year. That is, if you were earning $50,000 per annum x 15 = $750,000. Would you be happy if that was the case? Most people would be happy if their income increased by only 10%. To dramatically increase my income like this I had to learn strategies that enabled me to do that which I will expand on further in the book.

My millionaire mentor also asked me how many forms of income most Australians have. I thought, probably one, or maybe two if they had a second part time job or part time business. He told me he had dozens of forms of income and most of them were coming in while he slept. I liked the sound of making money while you sleep so I thought I would try that as well. I learned how to build multiple forms of income, while keeping the one focus, which was important. The strategies my millionaire mentor shared with me were so simple that anyone could apply them — even a young farmer's son who some said was a dreamer, that was too trusting and often overly optimistic!

I also learned that being financially successful is not just about making money, but what you do with that money is what's important. I had to learn how to keep money, how to manage my cashflow and how to turn that money into more money. In other words how could I get it to come back to me, and ideally while I was sleeping. Because once I could do that I could free my time up and have the thing I wanted most — **LIFESTYLE. The freedom to do what I want, whenever I want, where I want and with whomever I want sounded great to me, even if it was hard to believe.**

Today I get to live the lifestyle I have always dreamed about. But I share my story with you not to impress you but to impress upon you that there were certain things I had to learn that made a huge difference and turned my life around from being one of hard work and struggle into a life that is definitely not hard work and not a struggle. Today I pinch myself to think that my dreams are now a reality.

If someone had said to me eight years ago that I would have the lifestyle I have right now, be earning the income I do, by impacting on the amount of people I do in a positive way, by driving nice cars, travelling the world, owning a multi-million dollar Noosa waterfront home and a dream winter home overlooking the beautiful lakes and mountains in Queenstown, New Zealand, having a farm with its own personal airstrip, having a successful share and property portfolio, amongst other things, I would have said, "Yeah right — impossible!" But I have found that amazing things can happen if people are willing to be open-minded and committed. The things I treasure and value the most are the great friendships I have developed, the amazing people I have met, but most importantly living my life's purpose, serving my creator and contributing and adding value to so many people's lives. I decided to measure my success by what difference I make to the world and how many people I help rather than using material things as a measure.

Today I get the chance to travel extensively and one thing I have noticed about fellow Australians is there is only a very small percentage of people like myself who are actually willing to learn with an open mind. No wonder so few people ever live their dreams.

Eight years ago not being open-minded was a major part of what was holding me back. When I changed from someone that was very closed minded to a sponge, open to any idea or concept that could improve my life in some way, my life changed too. So I really respect you if you have read this far, you must be open to learning and I admire you for picking up this book and taking some time out of your busy schedule to read it.

The other thing I recommend is the concept of giving. Now I do not know if you can relate to this, but I used to make enough money to only get by. And sometimes I could not even manage to do that. My millionaire mentor who was an Australian multi-millionaire said to me, "Jamie, don't you think you are being a little bit selfish just making enough money to take care of yourself?" This gentleman was earning forty times more than he could ever possibly need and I replied, "Aren't you the selfish one? You are rich! You must be selfish."

He said there was a different way of looking at it and that he deliberately made thirty to forty times more in net worth and income than he needed. He said, "I do not do it because I am greedy, I do it because it puts me in a position to help other people." He went on to explain that if you just make enough money to take care of yourself, then you are the one being selfish because you do not have the time, the money or the energy to help a lot of other people as you are too overtaken with your own financial problems to consider helping others.

For the first time, by shifting my focus from myself to helping other people I was able to look at creating wealth in a different way. **I REALISED THAT INSTEAD OF FEELING GUILTY ABOUT MAKING MONEY I WAS OBLIGATED AND MORALLY RESPONSIBLE TO BECOME WEALTHY TO HELP OTHER PEOPLE.** It was this alternative way of looking at things that made a big difference to me as unfortunately many people feel that they can not be spiritual and rich at the same time. I realised I could be committed to helping others and become rich at the same time.

Now, I am happy to share many wealth creating strategies with you over the course of this book. All I ask in return is that if your income or net wealth increases as a result, that you will consider giving a percentage of that increase to a favourite charity. If you do not have a favourite charity, I am sure you will find someone in your circle of friends who will volunteer for this role. Just joking.

Today I still work to create wealth, not because I need it to survive as I have a lot more income and a lot more net worth than I need to live the lifestyle I always dreamed about. I do it primarily because I am driven to serve other people. To me money is a tool. Money is a tool to serve. Imagine what you could do in your life, not just for yourself or your family, but for other people, if you could master this mysterious thing we call "money". I link massive pleasure to helping people which highly motivates me to work, which means I earn even more money due to putting passion into my work.

To master money was a goal of mine and I am glad I have achieved it to a level that produces better results than I ever expected. There are many people in this country that are financially wealthy (or so you would think), they have lots of money but they live in fear of losing it. You probably know some people like that who live in fear of losing money. I learned how to develop what I call an ideal mindset. If I lost the wealth I have been able to create in the last eight years, I would be lying if I said it would not bother me. I would probably be upset for a day or two, but I know with certainty I could create it back faster and easier without the need to work hard. To me that is real freedom. Who would not like to have that freedom? That is more valuable than having wealth alone because it is something that can not be taken away. We do not have to live in fear of what is going to happen because we can have a sense of certainty about our future. And I think that is what most people want. I will cover practical ways throughout the book to achieve this mindset. I also personally enjoy facilitating seminars on behalf of The Financial Education Institute and the *21st Century Academy*, a multi-million dollar Australian education organisation that teaches the skills and strategies of a 21st century education which includes overcoming fears, which is what holds most people back.

As part of the *21st Century Academy*, they run follow-up support seminars and whenever I attend these sessions I am blown away by the phenomenal success stories I hear from graduates from all walks of life who have successfully applied these strategies. I share this with you to help you understand that what I am going to be sharing with you is not theory. They are real life strategies I have personally used myself and strategies I have modelled from some of the most successful people on the planet.

One of their recent graduates, a middle-aged gentleman, was going nowhere financially. He had a high-paying senior management role in a multi-national company, but he had no idea how to manage his cashflow to the point where he was heading towards bankruptcy. The truth of the matter was that he could not determine the difference between an asset and a liability. Once he applied our debt reduction and cashflow management strategies he was able to eliminate 50% of his debt and save for the first time in his life. These two simple strategies alone have completely impacted his life and he is no longer a victim of financial stress. He now enjoys a better quality of life and can look forward to a great future.

Another story I heard was from two teenage brothers who have created a monthly cashflow of $1,600 extra without needing to work by using some of the simple strategies covered in this book. In order to earn the equivalent they would normally have to work 230 hours, (about 6 weeks, working 8 hours a day) as a casual employee at a hamburger restaurant such as McDonalds. So you can image how exciting their futures have suddenly become.

Other graduates have made $5,000 to $10,000 per month within 90 days of implementing some of these strategies and have been able to leave their jobs.

Since applying these strategies, one individual found a Residential Investment Property at $15,000 discount with 100% finance. She also re-negotiated her partner's loan and released $200,000 in equity to use for the strategy you will learn later in the book.

Yet another person created enough cashflow from her investments to take her family on a long overdue five week trip to visit her son in Switzerland. They travelled around Europe through their investments. It is great to have this new mindset which allows them to share these experiences.

Since applying these strategies one person has managed to increase his active income to the maximum. He has given all his customers guarantees for his computer programming service, doubled his fees and his customers keep coming back.

At the *21st Century Academy*, they teach people to start with the end in mind — just as the founder of IBM did long before he ever opened the doors for business. I mention *21st Century Academy* because the strategies in this book have already been utilised successfully by thousands of ordinary Australians who can testify to their results. You are going to get access to many of these strategies that normally you would have to pay thousands of dollars to access in seminars.

All *21st Century Academy* graduates are taught how to design their lives down to the smallest detail and are shown how to create action steps to ensure their dreams become a reality.

One of the guest speakers at one Advanced seminar last year, Australia's leading direct marketer, knows first hand the impact designing your life can have. When he first immigrated from the Czech Republic, he had no money, could only speak basic English and he and his wife lived in an apartment with no furniture. Several years later, after struggling financially, he created a vision statement of what a day in his "ideal" life would be like and wrote it out no less than twice a day. Within six months, he had completely turned his life around and the life he created in his vision statement began to appear before his very eyes, including massive financial success and plenty of time to spend with his growing family in their new dream home.

By writing his vision each day, not only did he reinforce it, but it kept him focussed on what was really important in his life and gave him something to strive for. Now, I am not trying to tell you that he just wrote his vision out daily and did not take any action. Obviously to achieve such dramatic results in such a short period of time requires dramatic action. By using the strategies of designing your life, combined with RPA (Results Purpose Action), shown in this book, combined with the best financial strategies I know, you too can create your ideal life much sooner than you expect.

You may notice that the layout of this book is a little different to many other books you have read before. You should use it like a workbook and a reference guide to look back on after you have finished reading it. For you to get the most out of this book you will need to become involved, so when you come to the exercises in the book I suggest you commit to doing them, as it will come down to your level of personal commitment to how well you apply these strategies.

So, if you think that learning how to make money while you sleep, or reducing debt, or creating your ideal life sounds like something that you are committed to do, then you are definitely ready to get started.

But, before you learn all these exciting cashflow and lifestyle strategies and how to excel in the 21st century, we need to discover why it is that we live in one of the wealthiest nations on earth but so few of us achieve the riches most people desire. In fact, nearly 96% of the population never achieve financial independence according to the Australian Bureau of Statistics. To find out how to become part of the 4% that excel financially, then you will need to know…

SECTION ONE

"I LIVE IN ONE OF THE WEALTHIEST COUNTRIES ON EARTH — SO WHY AM I NOT RICH?"

CHAPTER ONE

WHY DO MOST PEOPLE FAIL?

After I made the decision to stay in Sydney and turn my financial crisis around, I began to ask myself some valuable questions. The first question being, "Why is it that most people do not make it?" After all, the World Bank once considered Australia to be the wealthiest nation on the planet. Unfortunately, now the standard of living for many Australians is dropping rapidly, despite our politicians trying to convince us otherwise. With all the wealth that still exists, why is it that so few Australians get to share in it? What is going on that limits us to sharing in only a fraction of this country's wealth, and what can we do about it?

The other thing I was very curious about was why there are some people that start with nothing and become millionaires, some people even in their early 20s, and there are a lot of examples of that in Australia right now. Some people in their 30s, 40s or 50s — there is no age limit for financial success. But there are other people who seem much more intelligent, often with a higher education, that in terms of achieving financial success, fail and their lives are filled with hard work and struggle. What is the difference between the two? Is it luck that has some people acquire wealth, perhaps they buy more lotto tickets? Do they marry into money, or inherit it? Or is there a bit more to it?

Let us then look at the "success formula" that most people have been following. That of going to school, getting a good education and then working long and hard until retirement. It is interesting to note the people following this formula, which is nearly *96% of the population*, are the ones who generally by the age of 65 end up dead, dead broke, on a pension or need the family to support them. I have been dead broke before and at one stage I thought that "dead" would have been better and I am glad I did not take that option, but some people do.

4% of the population become what we call "Financially Independent" (FI) which means that at age 65 they are able to stop working and continue to live a comfortable lifestyle. It does not mean they are rich. It just means they have enough money coming in to support them, usually around $42,000 per annum.

1% of the population at age 65 will become what we call "rich". The Australian Bureau of Statistics classifies "rich" as having a net worth in excess of $1 million dollars. A million dollars used to be a lot of money years ago, but by todays standards, it is not that much. In the future, most people will become millionaires just by paying their house off over 20 or 30 years. There are about 200,000 millionaires in Australia, but even then, do these people necessarily have lifestyle? Remember, what we are trying to learn is how to achieve lifestyle, and lifestyle = time + money. There are many people that become millionaires but still lack time and money. In other words, they need to keep on working. They become what we call asset rich and cashflow poor. You probably know some people like that — maybe even intimately. Becoming asset rich and cashflow poor is really not the idea. Having money stuck away that can not be used is pointless. There are many people who die with it and there is not a lot of lifestyle in that. Sadly, the percentage of people that actually have the quality of life they would really like is very small.

Exercise 1

At age 65 in Australia

96% D ________________

3% F ________ I ________

1% R ________________

For those of you into detail, imagine you had 100 classmates. Out of 100 of your classmates, despite their best intentions, 71 of them will end up broke at age 65 and sadly 25 of them will be dead — now you may say you can not blame money for that — or can you? A lot of doctors talk about a thing called cancer of the wallet. Do you know what that is? It is financial stress and is usually not caused by having too much money but a lack of money.

Now, let me ask you a question. When you were leaving school, did your teacher ever say to you, "Who would like to volunteer to go out into the world, get a job that you do not really like and work really hard for 45 years? You will work Monday to Friday, (and some of you will need to work Saturday as well) to pay the bills and never get to do the things you really want to do because you will not have enough time or enough money. Then at age 65 you will get to retire and within 2.7 years you will drop dead." What percentage of students do you think would have volunteered to do that? Maybe one or two up the back of the class who must not have been paying attention and missed the question.

Alternatively, how many do you think would volunteer to learn how to set themselves up financially, so that from age 25 to 30 onwards they never had to work another day in their life unless they chose to? Instead they would get to spend quality time with family and friends, travel to all the places they ever wanted, establish a career that they believe in and live the life of their dreams. My guess is nearly 100% — except for the ones up the back who must not have been paying attention and missed the question again.

So, 25 of your classmates have unfortunately passed away. What about the ones that retired broke. How broke are they? 20 of them will have incomes of less than $15,000 pa at age 65. That, by the way, is below the poverty level! 51 of them will have an income between $10,000 up to as much as $35,000 (with an average of about $18,000) — that is not crash hot either! Only four of them will have annual incomes of over $35,000 and only one of them will be classified as a millionaire.

It is clear now that this formula definitely is not working for most people. We could look at this as evidence that it is highly unlikely that we are going to succeed and we could say, "What is the point of really trying? The people making it must be really, really lucky."

Instead it is probably a good idea to take the advice of my millionaire mentor who said, "Jamie, if you want to succeed, you need to figure out what most Australians are doing and do the exact opposite." I believe that anyone can follow this philosophy if we keep it rather simple.

Have you heard the phrase that success leaves clues? I have found in my experience that failure leaves more clues. Usually when things are not working we tend to look within. When I was turning my life around I had to be completely honest with myself for the very first time. I had to take a good look in the mirror, and find out what it was that was holding me back.

Denial

I used to say, "I am not interested in money — money is not everything." Until my millionaire mentor told me that I was in denial. I could not figure out what he meant by this. He said, "Jamie, do you think if you say you are not interested in money then that is going to help you become financially successful?" and I thought, "Well, no, maybe not."

Then he said, "You know most people would agree with you that there are other things more important than money. A lot of people say they are not interested in money, but can you guess what the people do who usually say that? They go and work for it because they are just like you Jamie. You go off and work your whole life for money and the whole time you say you are not interested in it. Would you not say that is a classic case of denial?"

For the first time I was actually honest with myself and I said, "That is true." My millionaire mentor also said, "If you want to become wealthy, you must not make money your god. Instead you have to learn to master money. If you can learn how to master it and have it work for you as opposed to you working for it, then money will no longer be an issue. Those things that are most important to you like family, health, career and relationships will always be your top priority." I thought, "Well that sort of makes sense."

So I went from denying that I was interested in money to admitting that I was very interested in money because I loved my family dearly and valued my time and wanted to control my life. I decided right then that I was prepared to make the effort to master money, because if I did I could have the freedom I wanted. I learned subtle shifts make a big difference to what is going on inside our heads and this became a huge turning point for me.

Blame and Excuses

The other two important qualities you need to have in order to be in the 96% of people who fail financially, (I will call them 96 percenters) is the ability to blame everyone else for your problems and to create elaborate excuses. I became really good at blaming other people when things were not working for me. Not only did I blame other people but also the circumstances. I would blame the companies that would not pay me. I used to blame my business partners who took advantage of me and I used to blame my parents for not being rich. I would have blamed the dog if I had one! What I realised was that I was taking the power away from myself whenever I blamed other people. If you still want to blame something then blame excuses!

I used to have lots of excuses like, "I am not interested in money, or you need money to make money, or if I did not have all this debt, or if I could just find the right job or the right career, or if someone would help me out, then I would make it." All of these excuses were not doing me a lot of good. ***"I heard once that you can make excuses in your life and you can make money, but you can not do both at the same time."***

One of my favourite excuses was, "If I could just get back all the money that is owing to me then I could turn my business around." When my millionaire mentor heard this he said, "Jamie, you could focus your energy on your past and try to collect all this money that is owing to you, that is called 'old money'. Most people live in the past and they devote their energy to the past. If you want to become wealthy you need to devote your energy to your future. That is called new money." Then he gave me another pearl of wisdom. He said, "I guarantee if you take that energy and dedicate it to the future you will be a selfmade millionaire well before you ever collect the money that is owing to you."

At the time, I did not realise it, but by letting go, moving on and forgetting about it I was creating the space for a lot more new money to come into my life. In the same situation, many other people would have been tempted to hang on and be upset, angry and peeved off about what happened to them. I am not the only person that has been taken advantage of financially in one way or another, probably half the population has. For those who have not, what do you think is likely to happen in the next 10, 20 or 30 years? The question is how will you deal with it?

So should we let those things stop us? Some people say, "I invested in the market once and I lost a lot of money, therefore I am never going to invest ever again." Instead they should be taking a look at what they did, and what could be done differently so they do better next time. I know someone who bought a property and lost money, as a consequence they have never invested in property again. And then there are some people who never touch anything or do anything. They think this is a risk proof strategy. Is it really?

I have covered the qualities that a 96 percenter possesses in abundance, but what attributes do you need to develop to put yourself in the 4% bracket of the financially independent.

Accountability and Action

Until now I had been making excuses and shifting blame. Once I applied the Law of Opposites, I discovered that if I was going to make it financially and in any other area of my life, I needed to be accountable. Once I accepted I was responsible for my mistakes, I was able to reclaim my personal power.

Along with accountability comes action. Now, that is pretty profound. How many people do nothing different and wonder why nothing changes in their life? When I first learned I had to take some action, I thought that meant all I had to do was go out and take any sort of action and I would be successful. Unfortunately, my actions were not always intelligent or consistent. Eventually I realised there was no point in being motivated for only a few weeks at a time. As well as consistent action, I learned to ask myself quality questions about the action I was taking. I call this intelligent action.

For example, at the time I was sleeping on my friend's couch and I was $150,000 in debt and I was not sure what to do to turn my situation around. I asked myself what most people would do faced with the same situation, and the answer was — become negative and settle for a low paid job for the rest of their lives! Getting a job and working hard, yet not thinking about things sometimes is the easy solution to the problem and most people opt for the easy way out in life. But when you think about it, it is not the easiest solution because I would have needed to work at a job for around 25 to 30 years just to pay off my debt. So using the Law of Opposites I knew the financially intelligent thing to do was not going to be to just settle for a job. The intelligent action I took was to invest in my real life education. Obviously this was not an easy thing to do because I did not have any money at the time! I will later share in detail the major obstacles I had to overcome and the sense of commitment that was required of me.

Gratitude

The other thing I had to develop was gratitude. At the time when I was waking up on my friend's couch freaking out about how I was going to get out of my financial mess, my millionaire mentor said to me, "Jamie, if you want to be successful, here is what I recommend you do. Every morning when you wake up, find five things that you can be grateful for in your life." He said, "You may need to train yourself to focus on what you can be grateful for, because without gratitude you will never have true wealth."

"You can become a millionaire and lose your gratitude, so are you really wealthy? Obviously, the answer is no," he said. "In order to have more of what you want, you need to accept the wealth you already have."

But what I was focussed on at that time were my obstacles. I know that what we focus on in life is what we get — that is common sense. So once again I had to apply the Law of Opposites and slowly began to focus on what I had, rather than what I did not have and immediately my life looked and felt better.

At first I really struggled to find anything to be grateful for. I would wake up each morning and ask myself, "What am I grateful for?" In the beginning I said, "Nothing!" I was ungrateful and angry. Then I thought, "Hang on a minute — I am alive!" If I wake up breathing is it more likely that I can become a millionaire as opposed to if I do not wake up breathing? I said, "I live in Australia!" Is that a great place to live to create wealth? Australia is definitely a great place for lifestyle.

Especially since the September 11 attacks in America, Australia and New Zealand have been rated two of the safest countries in the world, with both USA and UK citizens flooding our embassies for visas to come and live here, along with thousands of boat people.

In this country we are all incredibly wealthy. Do you think anyone in Australia in their right mind would want to trade places with someone in Bangladesh or Ethiopia? We have a tremendous amount of wealth already and I had to start to recognise that. In fact we already have everything we need to be successful. And that is a lot to be grateful for.

Exercise 2

96 percenter

D ________________

B ________________

E ________________

Exercise 3

4 percenter

A ________________

A ________________

G ________________

So when I added DENIAL + BLAME + EXCUSES, I got the perfect ingredients of the mindset of a 96 percenter — I was becoming one of the people that retire either dead or dead broke and are headed for financial disaster!

Whereas, once I decided to have a combination of ACCOUNTABILITY + ACTION + GRATITUDE, I started to develop the mindset of a 4 percenter and inevitably move towards becoming financially independent.

My millionaire mentor pointed out to me that the thing that was stopping me from having wealth was my thinking. He told me that in order to live my dreams I would need to master two things. MINDSET + STRATEGIES. Both are important, but most people only want to know about strategies and they neglect their mindset.

Mindset and Strategies

Imagine for a moment that there was someone who was willing to give you:

(a) a million dollars in cash; or

(b) alternatively teach you to develop and create the mindset of a millionaire.

Now, if we asked most Australians what they would prefer:

(a) the million dollars cash; or

(b) taking the effort to develop the mindset that is necessary to have the success they want in their life.

What do you think they would go for? I believe most people would take the cash. The reason I believe this is because about eight years ago that is what I would have chosen. I used to be in business purely to make money. I have nothing against making money and making a profit, but it is the intention and energy behind it that really makes the difference. I did not have a higher purpose behind why I wanted to make the money (another big success clue).

I found most people go to work for money. They have been taught at school to get a job to work for money. So if they have not already become wealthy enough to live their dreams by working hard for money they try other alternatives — they can gamble, try to marry into it or wait until their parents die to inherit wealth. That is a strategy, unfortunately, some Australians are using.

Did you know you can go to seminars that will teach you how to marry into wealth? Seriously, they have them in New York and 90% of participants are female for some reason.

Or the most common one is to buy a lotto ticket. If you invest in lotto every month, you may live in hope (but unfortunately die in desperation). And that is how most people plan to become wealthy. So let us assume someone is lucky enough to win lotto. How well do you think they are doing three to seven years later? Are they better off financially or are they worse off? Statistics show us that in fact they are worse off! Even if an average Australian wins a million dollars in lotto, research shows they will be worse off 3 to 7 years later. Can you believe that?

Would they have been better off with the cash or the mindset? If you can understand that simple concept you can do the opposite to most people. So what I had to do was take my eyes off the cash, I used to say to my millionaire mentor, "...this makes sense, yeah, yeah, yeah, I know all this stuff, just show me the money! I just want the nitty gritty, you know, the strategies because I just need to pay some rent next week."

That is where my thinking was. I wanted to get to the point, and my mentor would say, "Jamie, this is the point! **If you do not develop the mindset and convince me that you are willing to work on it, then I am not going to waste my time sharing the strategies with you.**" He said, "Because if I do, you will most likely stuff them up as you will have too much fear and too much doubt, or you will think it sounds too good to be true because it is simple. And success, you will think, can not possibly be that simple, when really it is unbelievably simple."

I thought success had to be hard work and a struggle. To me hard work and struggling made sense. In other words my mindset was in the way of my success and fear kept me paralysed from taking action. My millionaire mentor said, "Mindset represents 80% of success. Strategies only equal 20%. Therefore, if we neglect mindset it is going to hold us back from financial succcess."

Exercise 4

Success =

80% M ______________

20% S ______________

I often believe that the reason why I have excelled financially in the past eight years of my life, where many other people around me who have had the same opportunities have not, is because I developed my mindset. My world has changed mainly because I have changed. That is exciting because the faster we change our mindset, the faster we will create the things we want. So how do we change our mindset around money right now? Have accountability, that helped me, have gratitude and take lots of action and you will be well on your way, along with the powerful processes I am going to suggest you do later in this book. With mindset and no strategies you will still make it, you will figure out a way, but with just strategies and incorrect mindset it is virtually impossible to apply the strategies.

When it comes to wealth creation, mindset is an internal factor and is very much under our control. In other words, we can do something about it. There are, however, many external factors that we do not necessarily have any direct control over, that affect our finances and can prevent us as everyday Australians from ever living our dreams. However, once we know what these external factors are and how they affect us, we can learn to make them work for us, rather than against us.

We need to discover where money comes from and who controls it.

One of the most common myths about financial success is that working hard is the key to success.

Let me clarify this for you now to ensure you do not fall into the trap of believing this myth like I used to.

My millionaire mentor said, **"WORKING HARD AND MAKING MONEY HAVE NOTHING, I REPEAT NOTHING, TO DO WITH EACH OTHER IN THE 21ST CENTURY."** Allow me to explain what he meant.

I will use my Dad as the first example. He started off with nothing and today is worth over a million dollars. He is like most farmers. He believes hard work is the key to success and that is why he believes he became a millionaire.

But I explained to my Dad that hard work did not guarantee or actually play the major part in him becoming a millionaire.

You see, my Dad is a millionaire because his farm is worth more than 1 million dollars. But when he bought it many years ago, he acquired it for less than $50,000. Despite the fact he has worked hard on this farm for decades, this has not made him wealthy. Farm incomes have actually dropped and he would never save a million dollars from his farm income in three lifetimes.

His wealth was created by buying land at a low price and it increasing in value over a period of time.

Actually, his wealth was created while he was sleeping, almost without effort. Now it is true that a good work ethic and some hard work in the beginning helped but this most important key was investing his money and letting his money work for him, not just working hard himself. He made more money while he slept at night from the capital growth of the farm than he did by working hard during the day on the farm for decades.

I will use my Mum as a second example of working hard versus working smart.

She had always wanted a coffee shop in a town called Glen Innes in Northern NSW where I grew up.

I did not realise until many years after she bought the coffee shop that she was offered the opportunity to buy the building in which the coffee shop was located as well. However, she did not buy it because they had already borrowed nearly $100,000 for the business and did not want to borrow another $100,000 to buy the building.

She worked hard for many years, often not paying herself a salary, (another big mistake, my millionaire mentor warned me, "You must always pay yourself first to be wealthy," he said). Often she struggled to simply pay the rent on the shop, working hard for little result. Sound familiar?

Here is the key. If she had borrowed another $100,000 for the building, she could have:

1. Charged her business higher rent. Even if the business still struggled but only managed to pay the rent, it would have paid off the $100,000 loan for the building.
2. The building would have increased in value making her more money without working, plus her charging higher rent automatically makes the building worth more.
3. She could have then sold the business and kept the building. To make it easier to sell the business, she could have offered vendor finance and the new owner pays her off for the business. All she needed was the business owner to meet rent payments, making my Mum money while she sleeps. No need to work hard at all. Actually working too hard prevented my Mum from thinking about how to become wealthy by working smart. If the new business owner was not successful and did not meet her commitments, my Mum could simply re-sell the business again to another owner as she is not responsible for their success — they are. She can only help them succeed; if they fail she can always sell it again, for which she gets paid again. In the business, the key is to simply ensure the new owner meets her rental obligations, and ideally her vendor finance obligations.
4. If she wanted to still work, she could consult or work part time for the new business owner and pick up another income and enjoy her work because she does not have to work long hard

hours. She works because she enjoys it and it is a choice, not an obligation.

5. Which debt becomes the greatest risk, the $100,000 for the building or $100,000 for the business? Obviously the business as it can become worthless quickly, where the building is likely to increase or maintain its value.

I hope this explains why working too hard can often be detrimental and is not the key to wealth creation where working smart is.

Chapter 2

THE WORLD OF MONEY

Things you will learn in this chapter:

- Why, if you have been conditioned for hard work and struggle, you will attract "more hard work and struggle", instead of becoming rich, and ways to change this
- How to change your wealth conditioning
- Why how you feel about yourself can determine your income
- Do you charge enough for your time and services?
- How to be spiritually comfortable being rich
- Why you should avoid the cheap and discounted products and only buy quality if you want to be rich
- Why as children we can grow up thinking it is bad to become wealthy
- Why if you are negative you will repel money

When I first started looking at how to overcome my financial situation I came across the work of an English gentleman. His work taught me some very valuable lessons in mastering money. He shared some esoteric concepts that improved my ability to have money attracted to me in my life. His belief is that it is not necessary to become a millionaire, or become immensely wealthy, but it is important to have enough money to go through the physical plane to buy those experiences that you need for yourself and for your loved ones. Like my millionaire mentor, he also opposed the concept of working hard, struggling and forcing money into one's life. The way he taught me to understand esoteric money was simply to raise my energy, to have more life force, more power. He says:

"... when you do that people will be pulled to you. People will show up. They are going to crawl over the walls and under the doors, they are going to lower themselves in through the ceiling. They will be there. And when they show up, what you have to do is bill them. You have to have a way of billing these people so you can basically make money and that means being organised, having a product or service, or something that you can give to these people when they show up in your life."

Although it was a different and humorous way to explain wealth creation, after a while I realised it made sense and it was not very different to what my millionaire mentor had been teaching me. If you raise your energy and have all these people showing up and then you have no way to bill them, then obviously you will not have the abundance you want in your life.

He said that when you look at the universe, or physical plane you can understand that it was not designed for people to be rich. If we divided all the wealth up in the world, among all the people, in fact, everyone would be a millionaire. The system has been designed so that only a few people have the wealth. To pull yourself out of the system you need to put in a certain amount of transcendent energy. An interesting point he brought to my attention was:

"Imagine if you could go to work and in one week could earn $2 million dollars. And you think, Friday, ah, I think I will retire from here on. The system is not designed like that. The way it is designed is that if you work really, really hard it will spit out just enough cash to keep you just above what I call the revolution level. You know, where you are not out in the street tearing the system apart, but they have fed you just enough to keep you going so that you do not blow away the system."

He believed just a few people, somewhere between 500 and 1,000 families, own the world. These families also own the governments, the societies, the banking systems, and all the financial institutions. I could not understand or believe it at first but I now believe it is possible and you will discover later that there is a lot of compelling evidence to show exactly that. They decide virtually everything for you and they also decide how much money the average man in the street will have. If you own a small business then you are trading in an energy pattern of control and restriction. These controls ensure that the average person will not become too self-empowered and start to take away control from these families. If the people around you are in the same situation, of only earning just enough to survive and you can only earn money from the energy of those people, then they are not going to have any disposable income to buy your product. So you can see how everybody is affected by the system. He reminded me that:

"The world is not designed for the people. It is designed to keep the institutions up, it is designed to keep the philosophies up, and it is designed to support the governments. You as the ordinary working people are always sent the bill. You get to pay for everything. If there is a mistake you get to pay for it. If there is some kind of disaster you pay for it."

Let us consider changing our Wealth Conditioning! I learned the only way you can get out of the system and its conditioning is to have a force of will that is stronger than the force of will that is trying to control you.

He went on to tell me our societies do not teach us power. We are conditioned to believe we are weak, and we should have guilt. We are supposed to support everything else, by sending money to everyone else, and that if we do too well, we will be considered evil, greedy and corrupt. That simply is not true. The universe is absolutely abundant. It will give you anything that you believe in and more. A story he once told illustrates this:

"You only have to look at nature, you can look at a cherry tree, or an apricot tree and it has more apricots on there than you can ever eat, it has more cherries on it than you can eat. And when you look at it, it has that splendid abundance naturally. If a man designed an apricot tree, it would have two iddy biddy apricots at the top of the tree and they would be out of reach and a little stale. You would have to have permission to climb it and a certificate for when you got it and then a third of the apricot would belong to somebody else and eventually you would wind up with just the pith and a little bit of apricot. And that is how the system is designed."

You can see he has an elaborate way of explaining things but it helped me grasp the world of money in a whole new light, causing me to see the bigger picture of the way money works.

I could relate to what he was saying because I would experience first hand, being in this circle of activity, when my business was going broke. The fighting, kicking, clawing and the ripping off others was in a bid to make money! Now, I believe as he does, that making money should be a more fluid and simple activity by moving into a pattern that allows wealth to flow to you naturally.

Where you scratch and bite to get money it is almost like your wealth means someone else's poverty. On the other hand, if you choose the more fluid approach you allow others in the universe to share your energy and from your wealth they become richer.

There is no limit on how much is out there, nor is there a limit to how much money you can have. There are millions of opportunities for cash at no effort at all. Your wealth is not going to financially constrain anybody else, because we are not living in a finite world. There is always an ever-expanding amount of wealth.

Why many children grow up feeling guilty about becoming wealthy

He believes:

"The way we teach our children disengages them from money. It discourages them from having wealth because we condition them that it is wrong to be wealthy. Our language is made up of hundreds of proverbs that illustrate this conditioning, for example, 'The meek will inherit the earth'. But of course, that is not true, the universe is neutral, it is not emotionally involved with how much money you have or do not have. If you are doing well financially then your wealth will help others because you will be contributing to the community, spending money and hiring people. You know you are actually helping the world by becoming powerful."

He says:

"So if you imagine a small baby and it is lying there, constantly recording information and it has been born to parents who think working hard is

honourable. Then you can see that this small child begins to record the belief patterns of its parents and it has no volition to stop it. In other words the baby has no control over what information they record. So if the mum and dad are fighting over the rent, that is in their subconscious mind. If the mother is into saving and clipping little coupons and there is a big stack of them in the kitchen, what is going on inside the baby's mind is, 'If I do not save coupons, there will not be enough to eat.' Now, I am not saying that you should waste stuff, because I do not agree with that, but the main idea is we take on the concepts of our environment. This is because often our fathers and mothers came out of a generation when there was a depression, when there was a shortage of money and food, so they are not able to express a more fluid understanding of money.

Today, we are living in one of the largest and most fast moving capitalist societies in the world. There are millions and billions of dollars circulating at any one time and we still take on these ridiculous beliefs that have been handed down through the ages. You know the sort of thing like, 'A stitch in time saves nine, and a penny saved is a penny earned.' We take on that mentality and then we wonder why as we go out as young adults into the workforce, we begin to resonate these thoughts and feelings into the universe. Once we resonate this to the universe it begins to reflect to us exactly what we believe. Now if we had been conditioned that we need to work hard and struggle, it gives us back hard work and struggle."

He explained what we needed to do to break free of these negative energy patterns surrounding us:

"For you to get out of that energy pattern you have to push against it. You have to literally force yourself to allow yourself to be in control of the money that you make and to master the money. And the mastery of money for me is, as I said, not necessarily becoming very, very wealthy, but being in control so you spend less than you earn and you earn enough to buy yourself all the experiences that you are ever going to want on the physical plane."

Why you can be spiritual and rich at the same time

He also pointed out to me that very often we are taught that you can not have money and also be spiritual. It is interesting though that when you meet a person that is truly spiritual they will have a lot of energy, and so automatically they will have a lot of money. He said:

"In the olden days, say in 500 BC, it was fine for a person to withdraw and go up the mountain and sit under the Ban Yan Tree to contemplate upon the light of God. But you were not born then. You are here, you are in commerce, travel and making things happen. It is a totally different society. I feel you could transcend by pulling out and sitting on a mountain top, but once you had the power, you would have to come back down into the physical plane and do something with it. So the philosophies that came out of poverty and seeing it as beautiful and seeing it as righteous, came out of a time when there was not anything to do."

Why if you are negative you repel money

In essence, we need individuals that are preparing to push against the system without confronting it. As he says:

"The system will never look after you. It is not designed to."

He says:

"The feelings you are resonating can change moment by moment. If you feel negative, you begin to create energy that pulls to it the same type of energy. So if you are negative you will pull to you someone else who is equally negative. If you are negative you will pull to yourself energy patterns that are disastrous. It may start as something small, like the car will not start, or the handle comes off the bathroom door. But over time suddenly the whole energy pattern begins to break up around you and things become much worse until your whole life collapses around you."

"Unless you are resonating this everlasting supply from within yourself and resonating it powerfully and strongly, then what happens is you get into the habit of holding your energy, holding that power to yourself and it is the same way with money. If you feel confident about it, it begins to be there. It becomes natural."

"But you can not come from a state of limitation and poverty to instantly resonating absolute abundance. You need to allow yourself the patience to go beyond your old conditioning and begin to resonate in your feelings the

abundance that you are a part of. But you need to be careful, because a lot of people begin to think, "Oh, yeh, all I have to do is act abundant, act powerfully, act transcendent, buy a lot of stuff, buy a lot of fancy clothes and abundance will come to me." In fact what you have got to do is begin to see abundance in the things that you already have. It is not a matter of going out and spending a lot of money on imported clothes, then being in debt, because the very fact that you are in debt is going to pull you backwards. Instead, we need to see beauty and abundance in what is around us already. As you begin to become more and more confident, and you have more and more surplus income, you will begin to create affirmations of abundance in your feelings that actually affirm that you are doing well. Then you can go out and buy a good suit or dress and a fine pair of shoes."

Why you should buy quality not cheap discounted products

As a result of what I was learning, I always knew to buy the very best I could possibly afford but buy less of them. He shared a great story that underlines this strategy:

"If you go for the cheap and the cheerful and the discount it always has that energy. I remember my wife once bought this vacuum cleaner; it was from a used machinery shop, you know one of those places where they sell used appliances. She was all proud of herself because she got this thing for $15! So she wheeled in this vacuum cleaner and it looked like a $15 vacuum cleaner. In fact, to me it looked like she had been ripped off at $15. She plugged it in and there was this limp little bag hanging on the back of this thing. I mean it was just holding on for grim death and I said, "Don't you think that bag is supposed to be full of air and abundant and pleased with itself?" and she said, "Yeh, I think you are right." So she started vacuum cleaning this room and the vacuum cleaner made a decent kind of noise, but you could see that nothing was coming up off the carpet. As it went over dust and pieces of paper it just jumped up and then went back down again. I thought, "This is not a real effective way of vacuum cleaning the carpet." Then as she was wheeling this stupid thing around, the wheel came off and as it came off it created this sort of very, very gentle curve as it went around the carpet and came in to this semi circle around the other side of

the room. As the wheel went round the room it did pick up a little bit of dust on the wheel, that was natural. And I looked at it and thought, "Oh, this is how this vacuum cleaner works! It fires little wheels that pick up microscopic bits of dust." The morale of the story is that, "If you buy something at a discount, if you buy the cheap and cheerful that is the only energy you will ever have."

What if how much money you make was linked directly to how good you feel about yourself?

Another great concept I learned from him is that the amount of money you make, is directly linked to how you feel about yourself. Since we were born we have vied for love and attention and acceptance from the people around us. When we translate this need into the marketplace we have a tendency to charge less for our products and services, or not charge anything at all just to win peoples' acceptance. If you do not want peoples' acceptance then you just go about your life and what other people think about you is their problem, you can begin to charge what you like for your services.

If you sell your products and services with energy and love you are selling a higher ideal and there is no limit to what you can charge. I know when I first started in business, I worried about charging my clients too much until he pointed out:

"So often you will do an incredible job for someone and they will come up to you and say, 'How much do I owe you?' You will say, 'No, no I do not need any money. 'But, what you are really saying is, 'If I do this for absolutely nothing will you love me?' Or you have said, 'Yeah, ok it should normally be $100 but just give me $20 and that will be enough.'"

"This is a way of expressing that you are not feeling confident about yourself when you sell something to somebody. When you give them a service or do something for them in a commercial act, you are actually loving them. For example, if you are a hairdresser and you do someone's hair for them, then you are saving them from actually doing it themselves, you are helping them feel good about themselves and probably listening to all their problems at the same time! When you transfer goods and services to people it is a way

of loving them. So if you love them, is there anything wrong with them loving you back by giving you their money?"

Do you charge enough?

How much should you charge? He says:

"If you have come out of energy and dedication and you have come out of service there is not any limit to how much you can charge within reason. I do not believe in rip off or overcharging but I certainly do not believe in undercharging."

So many people do not charge enough. They do not charge enough for their labour and they do not charge enough for their products. This comes from self-image that people have of, "Oh gosh I am not really worthy of all of this so I really should not charge that, or they are not going to love me if I charge so much." But in fact when you can see the transactions that you are involved in as energy then you are not involved in the emotions of how much something costs. The fact is, the more quality that you put into something the more you can charge. At the top end of the scale you can charge anything you want. The aim is to put yourself and your energy into your commercial endeavours.

I know personally I have been into a shop or hotels and the whole energy of the place is flat. Nobody seems to want to serve you. Nobody really cares. You do not really want to spend your hard-earned money in such an establishment. But when you are served by a person that is enthusiastic and happy and they are willing to put their heart and soul into the product, I do not mind, I feel the energy and that inspires me.

"Isn't it so true! As you go out into the world you find mediocre restaurants, mediocre hotels, mediocre airlines, mediocre everything. You walk in the door and the staff can not even be bothered with you. They are not organised and they are not interested in what you want. You get this feeling of 'I am not a customer, I am not a person' and as a result you do not buy or limit the amount that you will buy. There is not anything more required than just performing an act of service. When you can subjugate your ego and put yourself in the mind of the customers, then it is not difficult to figure out what they are going to want.

"Almost invariably, your customers are going to want to be comfortable. They are going to want you to serve them quickly. They are going to want your product or service to work. They are going to want value for money and they may want more than one way of paying for your product or service."

He talks a lot about the systems that control us. So if we are going to master money then we will need to understand the history and origin of money and how the systems play the game. Because if you do not, you will just keep on playing the game the way the systems want you to play. At the time I had no idea what systems he was talking about.

He also told me that these systems were never designed to have the average person become incredibly wealthy. In other words, if we follow the masses and do what the systems condition us to do, we will end up in financial disaster, dead or dead broke at age 65. I am not necessarily saying that is deliberately designed that way, however it does not matter as the result is the same. So, how do we change that? First of all to change it we have to look at how the systems play the game and why most people are not going to make it, then we can see what to do differently and you will see how simple it can become.

Up until now, you have been taught by certain systems that the only way to get money is to work for it. However, there is another side to money that most of us have never been taught. The reason you have never been taught this is because it is not in the best interests of the systems and organisations that control money to tell you the truth about it. That truth is that money is simply an idea. I often say to people that the cows, the horses and the sheep on our farm could not give a damn about money. It does not mean anything to them. It only means something to you and I as humans. The value of money is only an idea that you and I have accepted. In other words, whether you believe it or not, money is literally made out of thin air.

To demonstrate what I am talking about, we will take a look at the history of money, where it comes from and the systems that control it. The information and ideas you will learn in this chapter will show you how everyday thin air is turned into cash.

Do you believe in scarcity or abundance?

If you have ever studied economics at school or university, you would have learnt about what is called the scarcity or poverty model. When I was taught economics at university I was told it is the study of scarce resources. Essentially, there are two different ways of looking at the world. Most people look at it through the scarcity model hence why they lack things in their life. In the beginning of this chapter you were introduced to a story about the apricot tree and the reality that there is an abundance in the world. If we look once again at the 'Law of Opposites' and realise that most people in the world see life through the scarcity model, then we can see immediately that the abundance model is the mindset we should adopt. I look at the world in abundance and that is probably why I have an abundance of things in my life. Isn't it interesting?

But that was not always the case. I used to think that for someone to be rich, they must take from others, in other words, they win and someone else loses. I thought, "I am not like that, I want to help other people, but still do well at the same time." If I was going to become wealthy I wanted to feel good about it, not become wealthy from being someone who rips people off.

At this time, my millionaire mentor said, "Jamie, the secret to success in the 21st century has nothing to do with working hard and everything to do with helping others become wealthy in some way. That has always been the key to creating wealth." The other thing he talked about was that if all the wealth on the planet were divided equally, everyone would be worth close to 3 million dollars right now, including people in third world countries. I know it is hard to believe. Would you be happy with 3 million dollars as a start? Who would not be? I often say to people that if you are not worth 3 million dollars right now, then basically you are being ripped off.

If 3 million dollars is not enough for you, then you can rest assured knowing that every couple of hours there are several billion dollars being created out of thin air. In fact, a trillion dollars is created in the world over one weekend! So if you have not acquired your 3 million dollars yet, let us find out how you are being possibly ripped off and how you can get some of your money back.

Most people are not aware of the abundance theory and they think that the real reason people on this planet are starving is a lack of food. In reality, there is enough food to feed everyone on the planet several times over. So if it is not the amount of food available, what is it? It is the distribution of food that is the problem, just like money. If you do not have enough, it is not because there is not enough for everyone in the world to be comfortable.

It is the distribution of money and who controls it. There are three major systems that play their part in the control and distribution of money. These are:

1. Government System;

2. Banking System;

3. Education System.

They all play a part in conditioning us about money that is often detrimental. Once you start to look at the systems you notice some inherent problems. If we know that nearly 96% of people end up dead or dead broke, then it is obvious that these systems are highly ineffective at helping the average person attain financial success. The second is that as these systems were designed in a time that no longer exists, the world is changing so rapidly that the systems just can not keep up and they are outdated. Thirdly, there is a lot of evidence to suggest, and I challenge everyone to make up their own mind about it, that many of these systems were never designed in the first place for you and I to become incredibly wealthy. So if these systems can not or will not help us to become wealthy, we need to set the agenda to become wealthy for ourselves, because nobody will set it for us.

If we continue to allow the systems to control us, we will end up dead or dead broke and heading for financial disaster — that is where most people are headed. We could look at these systems, and say, "That is not fair, why don't they change them?" Let us look at these systems and see what we could do to improve them. When it comes to the government system, you could say, "Enough is enough," and vote for a different political party, but has that ever really changed anything? Or, to get your voice heard down at the bank, you could maybe run a protest rally outside one! Unfortunately, none of it is probably going to make a big difference, especially if you are broke and sleeping on a friend's couch like I was. We can conclude that there is not a lot you can do to change these systems right now. Maybe one day if enough people become wealthy with the right intention, these things will change automatically. I am currently writing a book that covers the history of money and exposes one of the world's greatest financial scams by the US Federal Reserve, the IMF, and the World Bank, which continues to this day. It shows exactly how these systems were established, especially the banks and their immense control over the world. It is highly controversial and already there are attempts to prevent the general public from finding out this factual evidence. But for the purposes of this book, we need to look at areas where we have the control to make a difference right now. It is imperative we begin by regaining our power.

The third system is the education system which is pretty difficult to change while you are at school, but you can change it when you leave school. If you have not already read a book called, "Rich Dad, Poor Dad," by Robert Kiyosaki, then I highly recommend you get yourself a copy. I am sure most people would agree it is a good start on the subject of money. What Robert talks about is a concept that school is designed to teach us how to work for money. In other words, we are taught how to get a job. **Nowhere in our school life are we taught how to have money work for us.** Isn't it interesting. In other words, we are taught only one part of the equation and not the other. The basic concept of how to have money work for us could be taught to 10 year olds at primary school in probably a one hour session. It would make a big difference in their life. Robert also says, "The other thing to understand is, our education system has planted seeds of failure, frustration and financial disaster in our societies." Unfortunately, we see evidence of it everyday. He wrote a best selling book before "Rich Dad, Poor Dad" called, "If you want to be rich and happy don't go to school". Although the title may suggest otherwise, Robert is not against education. In fact, being the son of a teacher and being a teacher himself, he is all for education. By writing the book, he was really challenging people to question the education system and ask, "If the education system is so phenomenal, why then do most people end up as dismal failures in the financial area of their life?" Would you not agree that it is a fair enough question? Robert also identified that our education system is outdated. It was designed two hundred years ago in the 19th century. So immediately we can see a challenge with that. If most people have an outdated education how do they expect to excel in the 21st century?

In this chapter, we have learned how money is just another form of energy; we have also learned about the major systems that control the money supply. Now we need to know how these elite families control the world's money supply and how that affects you.

To assist you further with the strategies being taught in this book I am making available to you FREE, a 3 hour Video/DVD, valued at $97.00. To have this sent to you complimentary, simply phone the number below or go online to order. The video/DVD will explain many strategies in even further detail than this book, to ensure you learn even more. I am donating 100,000 of these for free. After that they will cost $97.00 each, so take advantage of it while you can. 50,000 have already been requested. So be quick. Also feel free to go to www.21stcenturyacademy.com, click on Discussion Forum, and join our online forum for free.

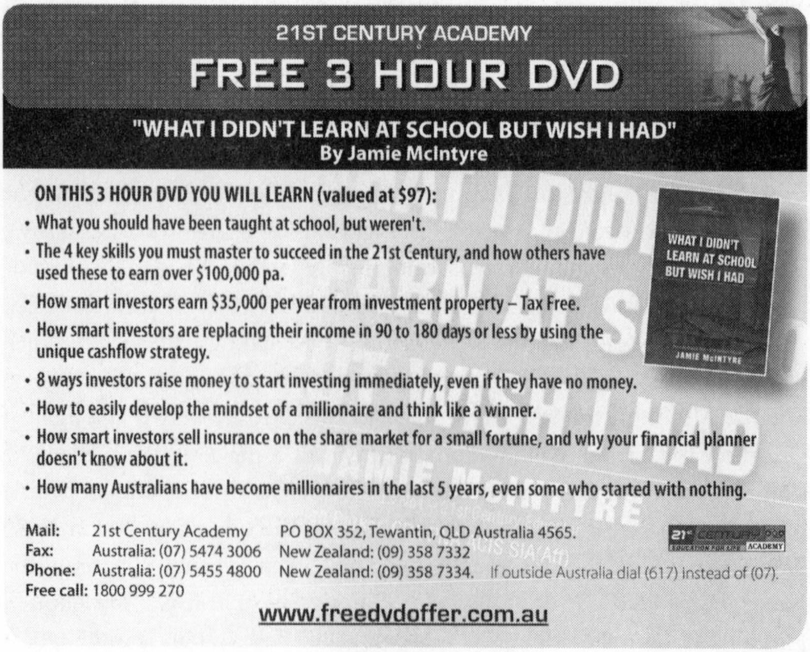

21ST CENTURY ACADEMY
FREE 3 HOUR DVD
"WHAT I DIDN'T LEARN AT SCHOOL BUT WISH I HAD"
By Jamie McIntyre
ON THIS 3 HOUR DVD YOU WILL LEARN (valued at $97):
• What you should have been taught at school, but weren't.
• The 4 key skills you must master to succeed in the 21st Century, and how others have used these to earn over $100,000 pa.
• How smart investors earn $35,000 per year from investment property – Tax Free.
• How smart investors are replacing their income in 90 to 180 days or less by using the unique cashflow strategy.
• 8 ways investors raise money to start investing immediately, even if they have no money.
• How to easily develop the mindset of a millionaire and think like a winner.
• How smart investors sell insurance on the share market for a small fortune, and why your financial planner doesn't know about it.
• How many Australians have become millionaires in the last 5 years, even some who started with nothing.
WHAT I DIDN'T LEARN AT SCHOOL BUT WISH I HAD
JAMIE McINTYRE
Mail: 21st Century Academy PO BOX 352, Tewantin, QLD Australia 4565.
Fax: Australia: (07) 5474 3006 New Zealand: (09) 358 7332
Phone: Australia: (07) 5455 4800 New Zealand: (09) 358 7334. If outside Australia dial (617) instead of (07).
Free call: 1800 999 270
www.freedvdoffer.com.au

CHAPTER 3

MONEY IS JUST AN IDEA

FRACTIONAL RESERVE BANKING

We have covered the major systems that control money, but where does the money actually come from in the first place. Previously, one of my mentors mentioned that 500 to 1,000 families control most of the world's money supply. When I first heard that I thought, "That can not really be true! Could it? I mean, how could that be possible?" Sounds like a conspiracy theory. When I did my own research into the history of money and how money is controlled, I realised how it was actually possible for a small minority of people to virtually control the wealth of the entire world. It is so critical if we are going to master this thing called money that we know more about it than what most people are taught at school and university or by our local media.

Many people believe that governments print money, which is true. Governments do print some of it. However, most of us would think that is what the government is for — to create money. When we look into the history and study money, the facts are that governments only print a very small fraction of it. In fact, you would be amazed at what really goes on. The banking system creates about 99% of the world's money supply. The Government only creates a fraction of the money supply. So how does this affect you?

The few families that control the world's money supply can determine what we pay for virtually everything. Ranging from the

T-shirt you wear to the fuel that goes into your car, even how much you pay for your mortgage!

If this were true, how is it possible for a select few families to have this control? Simple! Throughout history, these families have controlled the money supply and my research found that they maintained control over governments and citizens. One example was the Rothschild family. By the early 19th century, they and their allies used fractional reserve banking techniques to dominate the central banks in the UK, USA and France.

However, the concept of fractional reserve banking did not start there, it began in medieval England around 1024AD by the money-changers. They were not considered bankers as such but were generally goldsmiths. They started storing other peoples' gold for them in their vaults. On receipt of this gold, goldsmiths issued gold deposit receipts to the owners. This was the advent of paper money. Paper money became popular because it was more convenient and safer to carry than gold. People then no longer needed to visit the goldsmith regularly to collect their gold to purchase something.

To simplify the process, the receipts were eventually made out to the bearer making them easily transferable, without the need for an endorsing signature. This broke the tie to any identifiable deposit of gold. Over time the goldsmiths became aware that most depositors never returned for their gold. At this time they started to lend out some of the gold that was entrusted to them and kept the interest earned from the loan themselves. They then started to print more gold deposit certificates than gold they had in reserve. They discovered they could lend out this extra paper money and charge interest on it as well. This was the birth of fractional reserve lending or in other words lending out more money than reserves you have on deposit.

Really, it was the beginning of an elaborate scam that continues to this day. If you and I sould commit such acts, we would be jailed for fraud.

Would you agree then, that it is definitely in the bank's best interest for you to deposit your money with them? Remember at school, not only were we conditioned to work hard, but also the bank came around to our school to encourage us to open an account and regularly deposit money into an account. Now I have got nothing against savings, but is it not interesting that at a young age I was conditioned that the safest place to put my money is in the bank. Let us look at whether it really is the best place for us to put our money.

Modern day fractional reserve banking works in the same way as when the goldsmiths first started it. For example, if we put $1,000 in the bank tomorrow, the bank is legally able to loan out a lot more than the $1,000 you have deposited. The amount of leverage it can get depends on the type of bank you deposit your money into and its liabilities ratio. Since 1984, trading banks have been able to loan out 18.3 times the money they have on deposit, and savings banks and building societies up to 32.8 times. Therefore, for each $1,000 deposited, the bank is able to loan out $32,000 plus. From this example, you can see how money is created and expanded. Not all banks do this, usually just the larger central banks. Some banks just buy money off other banks at one rate and sell it at a higher rate. If the bank loans your $1,000 out 32.8 times at 10% they would earn $3,280 pa. This interest rate could vary anywhere between 5% and 10% for a mortgage and up to 16% for a credit card. The interest you would get in return would be around 3%–6%. For this example, let us be generous and say you earned $60 on your $1,000, ie., 6%. You then pay tax to the government and you are left with about $45. In essence, the bank has risked nothing and earned $3,220. So you can see that the money is usually made by the bank, rather than the depositor. Would you not like to be a bank?

So who sets the bank's liability ratio? Generally, there are rules and regulations that to some degree are set by the government. Most people would assume that the government, seeing that it is designed to represent the people, should regulate that figure in the best interest of the people. However, there is a tremendous amount of money at stake when it comes to 'fractional reserve banking' and the Centrally Controlled Banks (CCB) can wield a lot of influence over individual politicians or the entire government to have the regulation set at a level that they would prefer.

If the banks have only a small fraction of reserves, what then would happen if everybody wanted to withdraw their money? The truth is, if everyone demanded their money, the banks would run out before they had even paid out 3% of their customers. This is because the account holders funds no longer physically exist as they have been loaned out so many times. The banks have little or no reserves. Essentially they are giving you fake money but because everyone accepts it, they can keep creating more of it, without actually earning it like we have to. Through the Fractional Reserve System, they effectively create counterfeit money and get away with it, yet you and I would go to jail if we did the same thing. Is it any wonder the banks own the tallest buildings in every city.

So how does a small minority of the world's population gain control of the money supply and why is this of concern to us. There are two major players in the money game. The first is what we call a Centrally Controlled Bank (CCB). CCBs are owned and controlled by a small number of families and individuals. The second player is the US Federal Reserve. Now with a name like the US Federal Reserve you would think it was a government organisation designed for the people. The interesting thing is, if you ask the average American if the US Federal Reserve is a government organisation, what do you think they would say? Most would say yes of course. However, if you look it up in the Yellow Pages, guess where it is listed? It is not listed in the Government area, it is listed in the commercial area where all commercial businesses are registered, because it is a private organisation and not a government organisation. The US Federal Reserve is a private organisation designed to make maximum profit and does not answer to the US Government or the citizens of the USA. The US Federal Reserve is a deliberate name designed to fool people into thinking it is a Federal Government organisation. The US Federal Reserve was actually formed out of deceit when the US Federal Reserve Act was railroaded through a carefully prepared Congressional Conference Committee meeting. The meeting was scheduled when most members were sleeping, on Monday 22 December 1913 during the unlikely hours of 1:30am and 4:30am, during which time 20 to 40 substantial differences in the House and Senate versions were supposedly described, deliberated upon, debated, reconciled and voted upon in a near-miraculous four-and-a-half to nine minutes per item, at that late hour.

At 4.30am, the Committee's prepared report was handed to the printers. Senator Bristow of Kansas, the Republican leader, stated on the Congressional Record that the Conference Committee had met without notifying them, and that Republicans were not present and were given no opportunity either to read or sign the Conference Committee report. The Conference report is normally read on the Senate floor. The Republicans did not even see the report. Some senators stated on the floor of the Senate that they had no knowledge of the contents of the Bill.

At 6.02pm on 23 December, when many members had already left the Capital for the Christmas holiday, the Bill was hurried through the House and Senate. President Woodrow Wilson signed the Federal Reserve Act of 1913 into law.

The act transferred control of the money supply of the United States of America from Congress to a private banking elite. It is not surprising that a bill granting a few national bankers a private money monopoly, was passed in such a corrupt manner. (Source: Anthony C. Sutton). This is a perfect example of how governments are only puppets for CCBs.

So, you may ask, "If governments only print around 1% of the money supply, where do they get their money?" The answer is often the International Monetary Fund (IMF), which is largely controlled by the US Federal Reserve, which is the face of many of the CCBs. You often hear about the Federal Reserve through Alan Greenspan making certain decisions that are going to change the interest rates and you would probably realise that American interest rates have an effect on Australia and the rest of the world. So, you can see that decisions made by the US Federal Reserve can affect how much we pay for our credit cards, our mortgages and virtually everything because interest rates affect the whole economy.

The IMF loves to loan as much money to governments as possible. Why might they do that? If you were a CCB and your agenda was to make a lot of profit, do you think that, say the Australian government would be a good organisation to loan money to? It would be, would it not? Most governments would be. Governments have a choice, including the Australian government. We can print our own money debt free and back it up by our own reserves and not have to pay interest overseas, or we can borrow money. If the governments want to borrow money, the IMF is only too happy to loan it because, firstly it will be guaranteed security from the taxes imposed on its citizens. The IMF knows that the government can increase taxes to pay back that loan. So the IMF knows it is fairly certain they are going to be repaid. Secondly, if the country can not get enough money from its citizens, they know that a country has assets. If a country can not afford to meet its interest repayments it can then be forced to sell its assets. Now, of course this would never happen in Australia, or would it?

If we look at what the government has done over recent years you will see that it is now selling off what was the last remaining asset of any significance in Australia. Of course, that asset was Telstra. The Government's promise as part of its re-election platform was that in return for being allowed to sell Telstra it could completely wipe out the government debt.

At first it sounds smart does it not? If they can do that and wipe out the debt, the repayment money can then be used to virtually bribe voters to ensure they win the next election. I am sure if you are old enough to vote then you may know that during an election, governments find out what different sections of the community want and then offer it to them as an inducement to vote for them. In fact, governments tend to promise voters whatever it takes to win that next election. So you can see these decisions are often made for short-term gain. **Short-term pleasure, however, often leads to long-term pain. The result being that if we cash in all our assets to wipe out our debt, which virtually has already happened in Australia, and the debt habit has not changed then the whole country is in financial trouble.**

Unfortunately, governments are in the habit of getting into more and more debt. Let us relate back to yourself so it makes more sense. If you had a profitable business that brings you in money without you needing to be there and you had a credit card bill which is getting bigger, should you sell your business and lose your income in order to wipe out your debt?

In the short-term, it looks great because you have eliminated the debt. Only now you still have the same habit of getting into debt, so you run up a huge bill on your credit cards again, however, now you have got nothing left to sell to wipe out the new debt. The result being, that you are now going to have to work harder for someone else to earn money to pay it off. However, if you are the government you simply send the bill to someone else in the form of increased taxes. Guess who that someone else is? Generally the middle class, everyday Australians as that section of the community gets the biggest tax bill in Australia.

Australia has been quoted as being one of the highest taxed nations in the world. If taxes go up in a country then there is less wealth for the individual of that nation and their standard of living decreases. Running a country is in some ways very similar to running a business. If that is the case then, you can see that politicians need to understand how to run a business successfully because they need to have the same mentality to run a country. Unfortunately, many of our politicians have no real-life experience at running a successful business.

Let us look at the challenges this situation creates. We will use Australia as an example as it affects us if we choose to live here. What happens if the government borrows a lot of money? Firstly, the country becomes impoverished because of the higher debt, this leads to higher taxes to pay back the debt, with lower wealth for citizens and the sale of national assets like Telstra. This then results in the need to encourage investment in Australia by foreign companies, leading to excessively high levels of foreign ownership.

Recently, I was skiing in Whistler, Canada. Whenever I go to a new country I like to read the newspapers to study the economics of other countries as it fascinates me. In Canada, the government controls the majority of newspapers and foreigners are only allowed to own up to 25% of them. Is that the same as in Australia? Australian newspapers are mainly foreign controlled, despite technically being Australian owned. The interesting thing is that in Canada foreign ownership levels have increased from about 22% to 27% and Canadians are getting a little bit nervous. They are beginning to think that maybe foreign ownership is creeping up too much. The mentality is, "We do not mind the money but we do not want to sell off our whole country." In Japan, the USA and the UK foreign ownership levels are all less than 11%.

What surprised me was that these countries are worried about the level of foreign ownership. Then dare we ask the politicians of Australia, how high our foreign ownership level is? These figures are actually meant to be published regularly, but for some strange reason they have been hidden over the last four or five years. Could it be possible then that the government is a little bit concerned about the average Australian finding out how much of their country has actually been sold?

Many experts are stating that foreign ownership is now between 70% and 90% and by the year 2005 it is predicted that Australia will be virtually foreign owned. Not that there is anything wrong with controlled foreign investment, but should we be concerned at this excessively high level? In the short-term foreign investment means our standard of living increases, because there is an influx of money flowing into the economy. Foreign investment creates jobs, Australians get to work for the foreign owned companies and take home a wage. But where do the profits go? Do they stay in Australia or do they go back to the companies that invested here? Obviously, if foreign companies are going to invest in Australia they are going to expect to make a profit and there is nothing wrong with that, but these profits mostly go offshore virtually tax free.

As a result, the standard of living in Australia in the future may start to fall. We are now only rated the 30th wealthiest nation in the world and we used to be rated number one. There are countries that were once rated as third world countries that now have a higher ranking of wealth per capita than Australia, i.e., Singapore. **I am amazed that a tiny country like Singapore with no natural resources can buy out large Australian companies. It is a classic example of Singapore outperforming Australia as investors and savers.**

There is another country that used to be as wealthy as Australia that has dropped to 33rd wealthiest country and is now classified as a third world country. You may have heard of Argentina. Now, I am not suggesting that we have their problems but we must not become too complacent living in Australia that we will not face serious financial problems in the future. Luck may be running out for the "lucky country", unless of course we all decide to do something about it. Hopefully, this book will help achieve that, at least in some way.

So, what has this got to do with you? I believe that if Australians were educated about these challenges they would want to help overcome them and ensure the long-term future of our country. The best place to start is with our own financial wealth. We need to take a look at what we are doing in our own lives. Are we running up excessive bad debt and then cashing everything in to wipe out the debt? And then repeating that pattern? In Australia we tend to think everything is fine and we have not yet felt the full effects of the decline in our standard of living. But once we run out of things to sell, there will be no fallback position. **The wealth of a nation is determined by the wealth of the individuals of that nation.**

The Government has already sold off most of our last remaining assets such as Telstra. This could explain why the government had to introduce a new tax system called the GST. If the Government knows that we can not sell much more to raise the revenue, the only place left to get the revenue is from the people. The GST is a broad-based tax designed to target the Australian people. But, will it tax the rest of the wealth in the country like the foreign owned interests? Well, that is a different question.

To run Australia as a business it costs $160 billion dollars a year, (ABS Statistics 1999). Australia is a very profitable business. So when we are told the economy in Australia is going really well, that is great, but it is a pity we do not own most of it so that we can share in it. Australians now only own approximately 9% of corporate Australia. Do you think that as we only own 9%, it would be fair that we only had to pay 9% of the tax and the remainder should be paid by the foreign interests that potentially own the other 91%? I mean, if they make most of the money, is it not only fair that they pay most of the tax? The reality of the situation is quite the opposite. **Australians actually pay the majority of the tax. Companies mainly owned by foreign organisations contributed less than 9% — less than $8 billion of the total $160 billion in tax revenue.** I hope this helps you understand why Australians pay such a high level of tax. Someone has got to pay the bill, and they know where you live so to speak; that way you get sent the bill.

But it is not all doom and gloom! The good news is that you can become wealthy despite the current tax system and the country's foreign debt and economic challenges. It does not matter what they are doing in Canberra; you can still get the results you want. The important thing to remember is not to be disempowered by what the systems are creating. However, in understanding that, we can take control of our own financial situation and eventually change those systems to make them fairer for everyone else in the future.

A number of other solutions to solving some of the world's finance problems that I discovered are to firstly increase the cash reserves in the banks by at least 50%. This would reduce the spiralling debt of many countries and could be done at say a 1% increase over 50 months. These cash reserves could then be used to wipe out third world debt. Once the third world debt is gone, the individual country debts could be extinguished. The consequences of not implementing some type of solution to escalating levels of debt is that the CCBs will continue to do what they are doing, which will create such poverty that it could lead to a major economic collapse. As nations become poorer and poorer, they will have less and less money to spend on products and services. These countries will become so poor and impoverished that they are not going to be able to buy products to sustain their people and everyone will eventually lose. **Repeatedly, there have been times in our history where this has happened.**

The second solution is to completely reform the world's monetary system to remove the power of the monetary system from the private bankers, for example, from the IMF, back into the hands of the nation (that is, governments elected by the citizens of the nation). This may mean the complete elimination of the IMF, the World Bank, and the World Trade Organisation, or at least some major restructuring and transparency so they are accountable to individual citizens of nations. I would not be the first or last person to suggest such major changes.

Central banking could still continue as it provides competition to the government having complete control over money, however, some benefit is that they must be controlled and accountable to the individual citizens of nations. After all, it is collectively our money and wealth they are taking.

It also comes back to personal solutions for ourselves for which we can take control. We have the power to change our own situation. After looking at the bigger world solutions, which we may or may not be able to directly influence immediately, the question I had to ask myself was whether I have ever been guilty of running up a lot of bad debt like the government does. I realised in the past I have been guilty of that. What we have to look at are the areas under our control. If we are getting into a lot of bad debt, then we are contributing to the debt of the nation. We are contributing to the wealth declining in our country. **On the other hand, if we become wealthy and manage our debt, then our nation becomes wealthier.**

So I often say to people, "If you do not have enough reasons to become wealthy for yourself, then just know your entire country depends upon your decision to become wealthy." In other words, if you fail to become wealthier and your wealth decreases, then everyone is worse off, especially yourself. We are all linked. If there are people in our country or in the world suffering, it means we will all suffer to a degree. The terrorist strikes in the US have shown this in a major way.

Another area that the CCBs use their power to influence is the media. In fact, a few years ago in the USA, three quarters of the majority stockholders of ABC, CBS, NBC and CNN were banks. The power to influence the media has however been reported since early last century, as evidenced by the following example from the USA Congressional Record (Vol. 54, 9 February 1917, p. 2947). "In March 1915 the JP Morgan interests were steel, ship-building and powder. Their subsidiary organisations got together 12 men high up in the newspaper world and employed them to select the most influential newspapers in the USA, and a sufficient number of them to control generally the policy of the daily press. They found it was only necessary to purchase the control of 15 of the greatest papers. An agreement was reached; the policy of the papers was bought to be paid for by the month; an editor was furnished for each paper to properly supervise and edit information regarding the questions of preparedness, militarism, financial policies and other things of national and international nature considered vital to the interests of the purchasers."

Another interesting example of media control comes from John

Swinton, the former Chief of Staff of the *New York Times* and "the Dean of his profession". He was asked to make a toast before his peers of the New York Press Club. He responded with the following statement: "There is no such thing as an independent press in America, if we except that of little country towns. You know this and I know it. Not a man among you dares to utter his honest opinion. Were you to utter it, you know beforehand that it would never appear in print.

I am paid one hundred and fifty dollars a week so that I may keep my honest opinion out of the newspaper for which I write. You too, are paid similar salaries for similar services. Were I to permit that a single edition of my newspaper contained an honest opinion, my occupation — like Othello's — would be gone in less than twenty-four hours. The man who would be so foolish as to write his honest opinion would soon be on the streets in search of another job.

It is the duty of the New York journalist to lie, to distort, to revile, to toady at the feet of Mammon, and to sell his country and his race for his daily bread — or, what amounts to the same thing, his salary.

We are the tools and the vessels of the rich behind the scenes. We are marionettes. These men pull the strings and we dance. Our time, our talents, our lives, our capacities are all the property of these men. We are intellectual prostitutes." (Quoted by T. St John Gaffney in *Breaking The Silence*, p. 4).

If you would like to do some of your own research into who controls the world's money supply, I highly recommend a website www.themoneymasters.com or email: customerservice@21stcentury academy.com.au, and order the video called *The Money Masters*. It is highly factual and will change your perception of the world immediately and help you understand why certain things are currently happening in the world such as terrorism and anti-American sentiment. Another video I recommend is called, "Australians for Australia" presented by myself to highlight to Australians the economic challenges we are facing that our politicians are hiding from us.

You can see how difficult it is to convey accurate information in our society. **One vehicle assisting with freedom of speech and the accurate dissemination of information is the Internet.** The Internet is one source that the major systems have not yet figured out how to control. However, as I write this, the Government is now trying to come up with ways of doing just that. Nevertheless, the Internet has already created massive change in the 21st century and I believe will continue to do so.

I have shared a brief insight with you on the world's monetary system to assist you in the bigger picture of how you fit into the world structure. I could write a whole book on this topic also (I am actually in the process of it), but for the purpose of this book, I just wanted to give you a brief idea of the way money works in a global sense.

Now you know where money comes from and how the systems create it out of thin air. To tap into this thin air for yourself and excel financially in the 21st century, you will need to gain some new 21st century skills and strategies. In order to do this you will need to find out exactly what a 21st century education is and how to go about accessing one.

World Solutions Institute

One of my new projects is establishing a non-profit organisation called World Solutions Institute. This will be to educate people about the world's greatest challenges and educate the public about potential solutions.

If you are interested in learning more about this or contributing to help make the world a better place, then email, customerservice@21stcenturyacademy.com regarding World Solutions Institute and we can update you further. A website at www.worldsolutionsinstitute.com will soon be ready to access.

CHAPTER 4

WHAT IS A 21ST CENTURY EDUCATION?

The object of this chapter is to highlight the five crucial components of a 21st Century Education including how to become financially intelligent.

Now you understand the concept of how money is made out of thin air by the systems and how the families that control the money do this every day. These concepts are important stepping stones to a 21st century education. When I first began to understand these concepts, I started to say, "Maybe if I want to excel in the 21st century I need more than a school or university education I received in the 20th century (which was actually created in the 19th century)." **Common sense told me that to excel in the 21st century one needed an education designed for today's world, that is what I called a 21st century education.** It is obvious those who have a 21st century education are probably more likely to excel than those who do not.

What I started to look for was solutions and different ways to take back control of my finances and my life. Many people want to change the world, but we can never change things on the outside, unless we first change things inside ourselves and then our world automatically changes.

When I first looked at the idea of getting a 21st century education, I had a couple of challenges with it. My first question was, "What exactly is a 21st century education?" and secondly, "How do I go about getting one?" Now you can ring your local TAFE college and say, "I am reading a book at the moment that has suggested to me that in order to excel in the 21st century, I need to have a 21st century education. Can I please enrol as a matter of urgency in the next 21st century education course?" They will probably say, "What are you on? What are you talking about? We are still in the 19th century here, please do not rush us — you will need to take a number!" In other words, how do we get this 21st century education?

To be honest, the investment over the last eight years, for me to acquire a 21st century education, has been rather tremendous — in excess of $100,000, though the return on that investment has been phenomenal! Now, I am not suggesting that you have to invest $100,000 to develop your 21st century education. With the advent of the information age, these days it is much easier to do that. However, I will say that yes, I was worried when I was attempting to borrow $25,000 to start acquiring a 21st century education, when I did not even have the money to cover the rent the next week, but I was focussed on developing a millionaire mindset and developing a real life education. If you get that first, then the rest will fall into place.

In this chapter, I will give an overview of the components that make up what I call a 21st century education. Then the following sections in the book will cover each of these areas in detail.

There are five major components of a 21st century education:

1. **Emotional Intelligence**
2. **Financial Intelligence**
3. **The four key skills**
   - **(i) creative thinking**
   - **(ii) negotiating**
   - **(iii) communicating**
   - **(iv) marketing**
4. **Results, Purpose, Action (or RPA)**
5. **Designing Your Life**

What is Emotional Intelligence?

How do you define emotional intelligence? Rather than reacting to life as most people do, emotional intelligence is the ability to consciously respond to a situation rather than react under the influence of our emotions at that time. Unfortunately, we can not control everything that happens in the world. However, I have found that most people do not consciously respond to life, but subconsciously react to it driven by their habitual emotional patterns. In other words, whatever happens in their life they will react to it, keeping in mind that they are probably not resonating positive energy patterns and therefore probably not attracting positive energy into their lives.

You may have heard before that **"emotion is created by motion"**. One of my mentors, Anthony Robbins, explained to me that every emotion you feel has a very specific physiology connected to it. What I mean by physiology is your posture, breathing, facial expressions and patterns of movement. The problem is that most people limit themselves to only a few habitual patterns of physiology that result in them experiencing no more than say 10 different emotions on a weekly basis. These physiology patterns, after a while, run automatically and begin to dictate the emotional states we live in. Unfortunately, most of the ten emotional states we live in are negative and will not serve us on our path to success, for example, doubt, fear, uncertainty, worry, frustration, anger, disappointment, anxiety, stress.

So if we are going to be emotionally intelligent human beings and improve our chances of being successful in the things we want most, rather than reacting unconsciously, we want to once again do the opposite. We want to make a conscious decision on how we will respond to a situation.

Unconscious Reaction versus Conscious Response is the essence of what emotional intelligence is at a basic level. For example, have you ever experienced in the past, being madly in love with a special person, yet when the relationship ended, for a time you were emotionally distraught and perhaps devastated at the loss? Most people would have experienced a relationship break up at some time in their life. When that happens you can be emotionally devastated. I know it happened to me in the past and I lost all my motivation. This particular relationship did not work out and I was really upset about it. It was over. My heart was shattered into a million pieces. In that state of mind I was definitely reacting to what was happening. But looking at that same experience, say five or ten years later, what I thought was a crisis at the time turned out to be the best thing that could have happened. For instance, if my old girlfriend did not dump me way back then, as devastated as I was, I would never have attracted more ideal relationships. Actually, now I am glad and happy it happened, even though at the time I thought my life was virtually over and I could not imagine overcoming the loss.

This is true for relationships, jobs, businesses and even a financial crisis. The question is, **"What has happened for us to change our perspective of that same event?"** Initially we have reacted, we may have been devastated by it in the moment, and you meet people where that has happened and they stay in that state for a month, a year, some people for the rest of their life; they never recover from it. Others however, over a given period of time, look at things differently, through different sets of eyes. Applying emotional intelligence means you do not need to wait twelve months, or five years or a lifetime to be able to look back at a particular experience, look at it differently and choose a different response. Emotional intelligence shortens the gap.

When a crisis strikes in our lives, we do not really want it to happen but it does. Instead of reacting and being devastated by it, what if in that moment we could choose to look at it differently? **It is not what happens to us in life, it is how we react to it and what meaning we associate with the particular event.** Some people say the reason they are not successful is because of a particular event that happened in their life. Whereas a different person may experience exactly the same event, yet that has become the reason why they are successful today; the same experience but two completely different outcomes.

Everyone, no doubt, would remember exactly where they were the moment they heard about the planes crashing into the World Trade Centre Towers in New York on September 11, 2001. That was a tragic event that caused massive reaction worldwide, understandably. I, like most people, initially went into a state of shock. This soon then tends to change to a state of denial. We think it can not be true, it must be a movie or a hoax we are watching on television, hoping the next day we wake up and everything will be fine. If we are not careful we can then go into a state of fear and/or become paralysed, creating tremendous doubt and uncertainty about the future of the whole world, which is understandable. But these are all reactions, no doubt natural reactions for humans.

Then what will tend to happen after that is that we will begin to attach meanings to what has happened. Some people will begin to attach a meaning that the world is over, this is the beginning of the end and be paralysed by terror and refuse to go to work, refuse to even fly ever again, just sit at home and go completely into their shell. But if we are going to be emotionally intelligent, even though it is not easy, reacting in that way, mainly in that state of fear and terror is giving our power away. It is actually a state of selfishness about how we feel instead of perhaps that of more intelligent individuals who after they initially go through the shock and denial and natural terror begin to say; what can we do, what are some things we can do immediately to try and do our best to help the people who have been affected by this situation. Can we give blood, can we send donations and can we pray for the people?

Then what is important to be emotionally intelligent is what meaning we now attach to the situation, do we now attach a meaning that life as we know it is over and the world is doom and gloom and we can never live life as we know it. Or, do we attach a different meaning about what has happened, why has it happened and what can we do about it? I think the greatest danger is that many people feel helpless, that they can not do anything and that is not a good state to be in. I think the state should be a state of what can we do. Initially we can donate blood and help people in that way, but then we have to look at the bigger picture and I guess the key is what meaning do we attach to it?

A very important step here is getting the right perspective, because if we look at the media, the media has blown this totally out of perspective. It is tragic that some 3,000 people were virtually murdered on that day, but if we put into perspective what is happening in the world, the world's media is so focussed on that particular event, but in other parts of the world more than 3,000 people die every single day from other tragic events. But because we are not focussed on that, we are not aware of it and we do not feel the immense pain of that situation, despite that fact that there are people starving and cruelties occurring in the world, but it is where we focus that we notice.

The ability of focussing on a particular event can always distort our perspective and the media, unfortunately, is very good at this and distorted what happened, even magnified it. We must put things into perspective and the question is what can I, or you as an individual do about this situation? Are we going to be disempowered by this for the rest of our lives or are we going to say this has happened and now I am going to be more committed to being a better person and enjoy my life while I can and help make a difference so that this may never happen again? I think some of the great things that came out of this unfortunate tragedy were that the world united as one, they all felt the pain and united on what to do to eliminate terrorism and what we had possibly done that could have indirectly contributed to this. Are there people suffering in the world that maybe we have overlooked or have not paid enough attention or perhaps done enough to try to assist? It made people look differently and realise that there are people starving and suffering under regimes and dictators that are cruel to the people of their countries. Then, ultimately if they are suffering we are all going to suffer unless we can help to change that, as difficult as that may be.

I know myself I decided rather than be disempowered about this, I became more committed and I asked myself what I could do to help improve the world's monetary system. Realising that poverty and the economic hardships that are caused by our current monetary system have a big part to play in this what can I do to attempt to influence that more and create positive change. What can I do to give more to charity, what can I do to reach out and contact people and let them know how much I care about them while I am actually alive and have that opportunity. Also, to really appreciate the freedom and wonderful things I have in my life which, prior to that tragedy and situation in the World Trade Centre Towers, many people had taken for granted. Do we go into fear and never fly again? Many people said to me, you are crazy for getting on a plane and still flying. I happened to be in Africa at the time and then London shortly thereafter, where there was a lot of fear and panic in London as it was possibly a target to be attacked. If we give away our power and give into terror, then that gives the power to the terrorists when we do not want to give into terror. We want to go about living our lives and that is what George Bush said, and I certainly agree that we need to get on with our lives. The best thing we can do to help is going about our normal lives, get on a plane and do not cancel things as it just makes the situation worse. If we allow ourselves to be controlled by terrorism it will only become worse. We must stand up to it and that is one of the best ways to deal with it.

So, the question for yourself is how did you react to that, did you choose to put it into perspective and choose what we call emotional intelligence. In other words, did you react to that in a way that is going to empower you to be more, become more and assist more in a more positive way. If there are enough people on the planet doing that, then we are collectively all better off.

While we are on this topic I would like to share a story, which was relayed to me by Tony Robbins, one of the world's leading success coaches and presidential advisors. He was sharing a story how at the time he heard about the planes crashing into the World Trade Centre, it was about 4am in Hawaii where he was conducting his Life Mastery seminar events. It is an event I attended many years ago, which I highly recommend to anyone, and I coached and assisted at these events for several years. I was not at this particular event, but Tony was at the beginning of the second day of a nine-day event, quite a long event. The second day is on this topic that he teaches, where I first learnt about this concept of emotional intelligence. He was saying it was quite prophetic that the first day of the seminar, the day before the towers were struck, he started the seminar by mentioning to his audience, how would you live your life differently if you knew you only had days or weeks left to live? When you think about what you would do differently in your life and to determine what is most important, who would you call, what would you appreciate, how would you value your life differently?

He talked about this the whole night and a particular lady stood up in the seminar and said, "You know just hearing what we have been talking about here tonight and what you are saying Tony, has made me realise something. Just before coming along to the seminar my long term boyfriend had asked me to marry him and because I have lost my husband under tragic circumstances many years ago and I was not over that yet, I told him no. I felt like he was putting too much pressure on me and I was not ready and did not want to commit to marriage at this point in time. I was going away to Life Mastery in Hawaii to really focus on myself. He had made an ultimatum to me that if I was to go away to Life Mastery then that was it, it was over between us." So they parted, as quite often happens in a heated dispute. She realised by what Tony had been talking about what was most important to her so she made a decision that she wanted to accept his proposal and agree to marry her long-term boyfriend whom she loved dearly. So after the seminar that night, she phoned. Obviously it was a different time zone back in New York where he lived and all she got was his work voice mail, so she left a message saying she had been doing some thinking and wanted to let him know how much she loved and cared for him and that she would be delighted and happy to accept his proposal to get married, and that she could not wait until she got back. And, the very next morning was when the world trade towers where struck by the two planes. She obviously found this out the next day. There were about 500 people in the seminar alone who were actually from New York and many people had workmates, family and friends working in the building when the disaster struck. And she shared her story the next day, obviously extremely devastated about what had happened. The morning that her boyfriend had gone to the World Trade Centre, and had just arrived at work, he checked his voice mail and heard her message. He was so happy he phoned back but she was not available because of the time difference but she received a voice mail back from her boyfriend. He was expressing how unfortunate it was that they would probably never see each other again. He said, "You may not be aware that the building has just been struck by a plane and is on fire, and it does not look like we will get out of here. I would just like to let you know I received your message and it meant so much to me that you agree to marry me and love me. It is the happiest day of my life and I will die a happy man knowing that you have said yes."

Quite a tragic story, but it really makes you realise how much we take life for granted knowing that we may only have hours, days or weeks or years left to appreciate it.

Another example I will use is my financial crisis. People who have gone bankrupt and have been in a lot of debt have jumped out of windows and killed themselves because they have linked massive pain to staying alive and facing their reality. Yet, I have been in a very similar situation; I had two options to choose from, dead broke or dead, and at one stage dead was sounding attractive, or at least a whole lot easier.

I chose to look at it in a different way and not use my financial crisis as an excuse but a reason to be successful. I had to become a lot more emotionally intelligent and with the help of my millionaire mentor I began to look at my situation differently. As difficult as it was at that time, I actually had to ask myself what was great about my situation? I look at it now and I am so glad it happened, because if it did not then I would not be where I am today.

So, often things that we think are bad turn out to be good. Have you ever noticed that in life? What we need to look at is how we take control in the moment to respond to something rather than react to it. We can not control what happens out there in the environment around us, but we can control what happens inside of us. So what we are looking for is how to create certainty in our lives. **The way we want to do that is by taking control of what meaning we attach to events. Whether it is a good thing or a bad thing is all interpreted by our choice.**

There is a story of a man called Victor Frankel who survived the WWII concentration camps. He talks about how being locked up in a concentration camp is one of the worst things that could ever happen to a human being. However, he realised that although he could not control the conditions surrounding him such as virtually being beaten to death, starved or being taken outside in the freezing snow, stripped naked and left there, one thing he could control was his emotions and what meaning he attached to them.

When many people were hoping to die because they could not handle the pain, he looked at it differently. He believed that no matter how much he was beaten into submission, that inside he chose to remain free and therefore his freedom could never be taken away. That took a lot of courage and a lot of power and he survived that better than many others. Victor Frankel took charge of the resources he had, despite how bad it was inside those concentration camps. Hopefully, most of us will never have to go through that. However, we will endure other crises in our lives. So are we going to live with a sense of certainty or live with the fear of something bad happening one day?

We do not want to live in fear with the mentality of, "I do not want to put the effort into a relationship in case it ends, or become wealthy in case I lose it, or what is the point of trying as the world as we know it may end." We want to have a sense of certainty no matter what happens.

Today, I live with a complete sense of certainty that it does not matter what happens or what is taken away from me, I know what I have within me is everything I need to succeed. And that inner sense of certainty is something that can not be taken away unless I allow it.

So this is what I mean by emotional intelligence on a higher level. We are going to respond, as opposed to react to life by asking different questions. It does not matter what happens, we choose how we interpret it. We need to ask, "What is great about this situation?" So it does not matter what happens, even the worst thing could happen but we will still find the good in it. I can not stress enough the importance of mastering emotional intelligence. There is a lot to understand which is why I have dedicated an entire section in this book to help you develop the millionaire mindset. With your newly acquired emotional intelligence you will be more than capable of putting any financial strategy into practice, along with mastering other areas of your life.

What is financial intelligence?

Financial Intelligence is something that Robert Kiyosaki, author of "Rich Dad Poor Dad", talks about. Without it, we are forced to follow the path that most people take that we have seen very often leads to financial disaster. So, if we are to become financially intelligent we need to know exactly what it is and how to go about it. I am going to suggest that if you want to excel in the 21st century you need to have money work for you, not just work for money. That is an important part of our education. Who would have gone to a lesson on financial intelligence if they taught it at school? If the teacher had said, "Instead of having our usual lesson today on Algebra, we are going to have a lesson on how to have money work for you, so when you leave school, if you do not like working for someone else, you do not have to." Most people would have gone to that lesson and I know that would have been one lesson I would have actually paid attention to.

The following example illustrates the depth of financial intelligence in the Australian population. If we gave every Australian $10,000 right now, what would happen to that money in twelve months time? Statistics show that 80% of Australians would have spent all the money and have nothing left, because this is what most of us have been taught to do. 16% of people would have turned the $10,000 into $10,500. Where do you think they would have put it, to get such a handsome return? Of course, it has gone straight in the bank! Now, we can not call either of these categories financially intelligent and those figures make up 96% of the population! Less than 3% of the population would turn the $10,000 into as much as $20,000 inside twelve months. If you can do that you would definitely be considered financially intelligent. In fact, if you can do that, there is probably no dream on the planet that you could not afford to buy one day, that is up to 100% return on your money! The remaining 1% of the population can turn that $10,000 into as much as $1,000,000 inside twelve months.

Exercise 6

Financial Intelligence in 12 months

$10,000	________	80%
	________	16%
	________	3%
	________	1%

Only a small percentage of people reading this book will develop the mindset necessary to one day be able to consistently do that, turn $10,000 into $1,000,000 or more. However, the incidence of that happening is becoming much more rapid because of the internet and dotcom billionaires. And that is exciting, but for most people, it is not realistic, at least in the short to medium term.

In order to become financially intelligent, there are a few basic words we need to understand. I call them financial words. Imagine we are back at school and we have to understand how to make money work for us, instead of working for it. At school we have a thing called income, which would be our pocket money and then we have expenses. I know back then, my expenses were things like the school tuck shop or canteen. **Expenses are monies that go out of our pockets.**

There are also things called assets and liabilities. Now, the interesting thing here is if we apply for a loan at the bank, a credit card, home or car loan, etc., what are some of the things they let you put down as an asset? You can put down a car, house or furniture. You can also put down your clothes, CD collection, hi-fi and even your television. Let me ask you another question, not that we are picking on banks here but do banks make record profits in this country? Yes. Does the average Aussie make record profits in this country? No. In other words, is it a good idea to follow what the banks let us believe are assets and liabilities if we want to do well financially? I would dare say, no. But you need to make up your own mind. There is no right or wrong here. Remember, it is what you choose to believe that is important! I used to say "Well, that is not right!" and my millionaire mentor used to say, **"Do you want to be right, or do you want to be rich? Make up your mind."** I am glad I forgot about who is right and who is wrong and just decided to become rich.

So what I am going to suggest is that we need to create a new definition as to what the banks allow us if we want to do well financially.

The definition that I like to use for an asset is something that makes me money while I sleep, without working. Do you think that would be a good asset if it did that for you? What I wanted in the back of my mind was lifestyle. I wanted the end result. I did not want to get caught up in becoming asset rich and cashflow poor. **I could have created**

$10,000,000 in assets but have been cashflow poor and still not had the lifestyle I desired, or I could have just $500,000 making me cashflow while I slept and be wealthier in quality of life than someone who is worth $10,000,000 or even $100,000,000, yet has no cashflow. I believe we have to think smart in the 21st century. Access to cash and cashflow is important for lifestyle.

If you do not like my definition of an asset, you could borrow Robert Kiyosaki's definition of an asset and that is, **something that will put money into your pocket without the need to work for it.** What would happen if you stopped working right now? Do you have things that will continue to put money into your pocket? If so, you can put these items in your asset column. **A liability then will be the exact opposite. A liability would take money out of your pocket.** It maybe a harsh criteria, but if you can understand that, at least it is going to set you up for a great lifestyle.

The great Australian dream is to own your own home. Which one of the systems sells that dream by the way? Of course, it is the banking system. Obviously there is no agenda behind that — or is there? We are going to look at some strategies later where banks are going to love us because we are going to make them lots of money. But you will be on the winning side too, because these strategies will generate plenty of cashflow for you too.

I believe a WIN/WIN relationship is the way the universe works best. There are people that think win/lose is the way to win, but I do not see how that can work long term. In understanding that a bank has a different opinion of an asset consider the following. If you own your own house, you are living in it and paying it off. Under the bank's definition they will call your home an asset, but under the new definition would we call it an asset or a liability? Unfortunately, I would call it a liability. Obviously, we term it as a liability because it is not making us any money while we sleep, in fact, it is taking money out of our pocket, is it not true? Under that new definition it would not be an asset, we would put it in the liability column.

Now, if you manage to work very hard and pay that home off and you are still living in it, is it an asset or liability under our new definition? Unfortunately, it is still a liability because it still is not putting money into your pocket. I know it is a tough definition, you do not have to use it, but let us face it, a house will take money out of your pocket if it just sits there. **This typical scenario is exactly why most people, even if they do really well, become asset rich and cashflow poor.**

The other area we have to look at is debt. Once I had dug myself out of debt, my goal was to never, ever be in debt again. When my millionaire mentor heard me say this he said, "Jamie, I can understand why you say that, but if you want to do really well financially, you might want to consider that not all debt is bad." At first when he told me this I didn't want to listen and I said, "There is no way you are going to convince me to go into debt." He said, "Well, let us see, do you want to make more money while you sleep?" I said, "Yes" and he said, "You might want to consider a thing called good debt." There are two thought forms to debt. One is bad, most people are familiar with bad debt, this includes purchases that depreciate and have no tax benefits. The classic bad debt that most people have that drops 20% in value as soon as they drive it out of the showroom is of course a car. Obviously, good debt is the opposite. It is debt that will go up in value, instead of down and ideally has tax benefits. Therefore, we have to become comfortable with debt.

Some people say, "They will never go into debt again." But that is a 19th century belief. It is essential if we are to excel that we look at debt differently. There is also something I term 'super duper' good debt and that is debt that you do not have to work hard to pay off. Money can come while you are sleeping to pay it off. Or better still, imagine a debt where you never, ever have to pay it off. Would you agree that is a good debt to have? We will look at this type of debt in Section 3.

Since this talk with my millionaire mentor, I have increased the amount of debt I have gone into rapidly. I have increased my debt loading in excess of $10 million in recent times whereas I used to be concerned about being a hundred and fifty thousand dollars in debt. In the near future my goal is be able to increase my debt loading by many more millions and continue to grow that every year.

I estimate 50% of people reading this book will be in a position to take advantage of the strategies I am going to share with you in Section 3 and could within 90–180 days, if they applied them successfully, be making more money while they sleep than while they work. I base these estimates from 10,000s of my seminar participants, which represents a typical cross section of Australia and New Zealand, predominantly the baby boomer 45 to 55 age group.

The other 50% of readers are quite capable of implementing the strategies too, it just may take them a little longer. I have had *21st Century Academy* graduates replace their income the very next day from just one strategy, after attending some of our intensive programs. Stories such as that are real to me, but due to society's conditioning it is not reality for most people. However, if we understand by having a different mindset and a different understanding of money, it becomes possible. If we use the mindset that most of us have been taught — that of working hard, then becoming financially free becomes almost impossible. Most people who work hard and are wealthy believe they got wealthy from working hard, but in fact the wealth has really come out of thin air. A lot of farmers, like my dad's example, are worth a lot on paper, and they think it is from hard work, but the increase in the value of their property has come from guess where? Thin air — the capital growth of their properties while they were sleeping, whether they worked hard or not.

For those of you who have not read Robert Kiyosaki's book, I highly recommend his work. He is a very good teacher on the subject of money. What he covers is something I had to learn, which was cashflow management. He breaks the population down into three classes; poor, middle-class and rich.

THE POOR

The poor are told to get a job. If they are lucky they will, and that will bring in cashflow. But what they also have are expenses and most of us learned how to spend money rapidly at an early age and at the end of the week or month our pay cheque is gone. I used to live pay cheque to pay cheque, which would put me in the category of the poor. That is where many Australians are financially.

THE MIDDLE CLASS

Then there is the middle-class. The middle-class generally earns a higher income, usually they went to university, etc., and the reason most people go to university is so they can get a higher paying job. With that extra income also comes a major expense called tax. In other words the more they earn, the more tax they pay to the government. (Did you know income tax was created by the communists. It is interesting why in a so-called free country we are slugged with it. The removal of income tax would solve a lot of societies financial problems.)

The government and banking systems know all about making money out of thin air. The middle-class also tend to have bigger expenses; the golf memberships, the clubs, they eat at better restaurants, etc. The other thing is the middle-class believe what the banks tell them are assets and liabilities. The banks tell middle-class Australians that their house is an asset and that is not a lie because the house is an asset, but whose asset is it really?

The banks forget to mention to middle-class Australia that it is actually the bank's asset not theirs.

It is the bank that gets money coming into its pocket every month while it sleeps, and they have complete security over the property. From their angle it is a pretty good asset.

The middle-class start acquiring things that are really liabilities. In other words, these purchases start taking out their cashflow. After a while they buy a bigger house in a better suburb and that usually costs more. To go with that bigger house, there is one thing that often happens. They can either become wealthy, by just doing the fundamentals of good investing, which is not perceived to be sexy or flash, or they can appear to be wealthy. For many people, first appearing to be wealthy is actually easier because they can do it straight away.

Many people get caught up in appearing to be wealthy, instead of becoming wealthy.

These people get caught up in appearing to be wealthy and often they will have a nice car that goes with the nice house. Often that nice car is financed, so there is more cash going out. These days anyone can get credit cards, but Mr and Mrs Middle-class are VIP clients of the bank. These are the people they make most of their money from. These VIPs are sent pre-approved credit cards. After all, they have always promised the children they will take them to Disneyland for their holidays, so when the Gold Visa card arrives, they book the family holiday to Disneyland and whack it on the Gold card, with the intention of paying it off with the next pay rise.

So, you can see how most of the middle-class do not have a lot of cashflow left over at the end of the month. It does not matter how much is earned, most people think the answer to their financial problems is to earn more. I know people who come to me who earn $1 million a year plus and they fit into this category. When I point it out to them, they are not really impressed because sometimes the truth hurts. In other words, they spend more than they earn so they fit into the middle-class definition. If we want to become wealthy we obviously need to change that.

HERE IS WHAT THE RICH DO DIFFERENTLY!

On the other hand, in the beginning the rich will get any job, instead of focussing on income, they are not into status and will do whatever it takes to get started. They will focus on real assets, things that make money while you sleep, or put money into your pocket. The first way to build up assets is by saving money. The reason I live my dreams today is because I became one of the best savers in the country. You do not have to be very good at saving to be one of the best savers in Australia. Australia is not a nation of good savers. We have one of the lowest savings rates in the entire modern world. One of my goals is to change that.

With these savings, we need to learn how to turn these assets into making us money while we sleep. In other words, our assets will be able to draw out cash, or generate cashflow from our asset column, which will come in as our income. That means the money comes in without working, you no longer have to rely on a job. Most of us need to focus on our asset column more. There are three areas the rich get rich from, these are business, property and shares. I call them the 3 Pillars of the Rich and consistently focus on all three to become wealthier.

The other area the rich understand is taxation. The rich earn, then spend their money and lastly pay tax on what is left, that is, they run themselves as companies. Companies pay tax on what is left after expenses at a lower rate than the middle-class. The poor and middle-class earn money and get tax taken away immediately and then they get to spend what is left and try to create wealth out of that.

I am Australian and I believe in paying tax and as a result volunteer to pay tax in this country. I am not into simply offshoring money, although I know that has become popular. I think every Australian should pay a fair amount of tax. The operative word though, is fair. What is a fair amount of tax? I do not agree with the amount of tax that most Australians have to pay, especially middle-class Australians and especially if you know about credible taxation alternatives other than the GST that would lower your tax rates massively by taxing every dollar in the economy. This would mean all multinationals would have to pay their fair share of tax. You may have heard of debit tax, e-tax and other credible taxation alternatives which seem never to be allowed much public debate in our country.

In section 3, we will cover some tax minimisation strategies, but initially we will look at Bill and Mary, our average Australian couple and see if we can help them generate an extra $10,000 to $30,000 out of thin air. We will also help them to go from making no money while they sleep now, to making $4,000 per month in passive income. We will also cover property and other strategies, looking at these areas to see traditionally what people are doing and how we can improve upon these strategies by once again using the 'Law of Opposites'.

4 KEY SKILLS

1. Creative Thinking

Of the four key areas that I have worked on during the last eight years of my life the first is the ability to think. This may sound obvious, but you would be surprised at how few people actually do think creatively. In the 21st century the ability to think will be invaluable, but we must learn how to think creatively. What I mean by thinking creatively is having the ability to solve challenges.

Unfortunately, most people have been taught not to think and how to have someone else do it for them, like their boss or spouse.

2. Negotiating

The second area we need to nurture is the ability to negotiate. In life to get what we want we have to know how to negotiate. As children, we are very good negotiators, is that true? But when we start to get rejection as we get older we start to take 'no' as an answer. If you want to be successful, the secret is to never take 'no' for an answer.

3. Communicating

The third skill is the ability to communicate. To communicate effectively is not something we are taught at school. It is just not good enough knowing something beneficial. If you can not communicate a benefit to someone else so they can understand it, then you are not communicating effectively and will not achieve your desired results.

4. Marketing

The fourth area is the ability to market or marketing. I do not mean you need a marketing degree like you would get at university. I am talking about results focussed marketing. In other words, how do you take an idea or concept and communicate that message in a business format to the marketplace to make it a reality?

All these skills can be learnt rapidly and they are what we call generalist skills. In the 21st century those who are generalists will excel, those who are specialists will suffer. For example, not that many years ago approximately 100,000 people were employed in the vinyl record industry in the USA. When the CD was brought to the market, that industry was virtually wiped out overnight. Now, if these people had developed the four key skills and had a generalist education, they could have gone to another industry with their communication, negotiation, marketing and creativity and problem solving skills, and been successful. However, because they had specialised in their knowledge, that knowledge was no longer required, or had very little value. This caused these specialists a tremendous amount of uncertainty and financial desperation.

Now you may say this was a one-off occurrence, but when you think about it, what is the likelihood of industries and companies coming and going at a rapid rate in the 21st century. I believe that businesses will change even more rapidly the further we move into the information age. So you can see the importance of a 21st century education and the four key skills. These skills are so critical to have, and fun to learn.

RPA

The fourth area we will cover is RPA. That simply means Results, Purpose and Action. **Being results focused, purpose driven and action oriented.**

One question everyone seems to ask today is, "How do I turn my dreams, my goals, my desires into reality?" The RPA Planning Process is a proven system for taking anything you can envision and making it real. It not only teaches you how to organise, but how to actually think differently from those who become muddled in an ocean of activities.

There are three simple steps to the process. The first is to ask the question that all people who succeed ask — "What do I want from this situation? What is my result?" The word result is the 'R' in RPA. So do not ask yourself, "What should I do?", but, "What is the result I am committed to achieving?" Until you are absolutely clear about what you specifically want, any "to do" lists or plans you create will be generalised and ineffective.

Secondly, you must know why you are doing what you are doing. You must know the purpose, represented by the 'P' in RPA. Having a sense of real purpose, compelling reasons, will make this result or outcome happen. There is a major difference between simply having a dream and achieving a worthwhile goal. There are many ways to achieve a result, but you must know why you are going after it so that if your first plan or attempt fails you have the necessary drive to follow through.

And lastly, once you know the exact result you are committed to achieving, why you must achieve it and what it will give you emotionally, physically and psychologically, then you are in the state of mind to begin creating an action plan. Begin by asking yourself what you must do in order to achieve this specific result. That action plan is the 'A' in RPA. The sequence in which you determine these three elements is the difference between success and failure. For example, you may know all the individual digits in a person's telephone number, but unless they are in the right sequence, the numbers are useless. Similarly, knowing all the numbers to a combination will not open the lock if they are not in the correct order.

If you wish to succeed, always start with the end in mind. Successful people are totally clear about the final result they are after. They have accessed the Power of Why; they have a burning desire to achieve their result and it is tied to a clear specific goal. Creating the action plan is simple when these first two elements are put together. When you have developed a results-focused, purpose-driven, action-oriented plan for your week, your day, your month, or for any project or goal that you are committed to achieving, you will have created the certainty of knowing that your dream is about to become a reality.

I use RPA to design my life to a 'T'. In other words, the life I live today is no accident. When I was on my friend's couch I fantasised about the things that I wanted. I wanted to earn in excess of $1,000,000 a year. I wanted to travel, see the "Leaning Tower of Pisa" and different places around the world. I wanted to lay in the Caribbean, go to Hawaii and America. In short, I wanted to do whatever I pleased, whenever I pleased. I also wanted to plan what sort of home I would live in and the sort of people I wanted to associate with.

In the future, do you want to be surrounded by people who are uplifting, caring and who respect you, or do you want to be associated with people who take away from who you are and hold you back? Those things are critical. What do you want to do on a daily basis? Do you want to do something that when you wake up you can not wait to get to work because you love it? Or do you want to have to say, 'Thank God it is Friday!' **Is it not interesting that most people that die of a heart attack have it between 8.30am and 9.30am on Monday morning? 86% of Australians have a job they are dissatisfied with.** So I am sure you would agree it is imperative we learn how to design our lives and design them well to ensure we choose a career we love!

I have covered the components of a 21st century education. Once we have learned to apply these critical areas, our lives will undergo dramatic changes. There will be a lag time between applying the principles and having your dreams show up in your life. However, if you persevere, the rewards will be unbelievable. So if you want to make a start on your mindset you will need to turn to Section 2, to discover the secrets of emotional intelligence.

SECTION TWO

HOW TO DEVELOP YOUR EMOTIONAL INTELLIGENCE

CHAPTER 5

HOW TO RAISE YOUR ENERGY LEVELS FAST!

TO ATTRACT MONEY AND SUCCESS INTO YOUR LIFE

In Chapter 2, I briefly mentioned that in order to be successful, you need to raise your energy, to have more life force and more power. But how do you go about raising your energy? In this paragraph, I wish to explore this concept with you, as it is a key step in achieving millionaire status fast. Let us imagine a graph where 0% represents no energy and 100% is maximum energy. If someone is at 0% energy, then we can probably assume they are dead. I dare say many people are living just above 0% energy. Not to be critical, but many people are living in a state of death warmed-up.

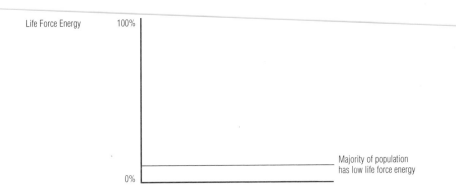

At the other end of the scale is 100% and that is an extremely positive energy. If a person moved up the scale, they would have more of a fulfilling life because they would be vibrating and evolving at a higher level. They would be more spiritually connected where they can think a thought, attach emotion to that thought and then manifest it rapidly, as their life force is flowing more powerfully and is not stagnant or blocked like many people's.

One of my goals always was to have a loving, fulfilling relationship. My millionaire mentor said, "Can you see that if you want a loving and fulfilling relationship, then having a very dense or a low level of energy could make that goal very difficult to achieve because you are only going to manifest the same energy you are projecting? In other words, you will manifest into your life someone who also has a low, dense level of energy. In essence, your relationship will result in a competition for energy."

He referred me to a book called the "Celestine Prophecy" by James Redfield. It talked about a concept called 'Control Dramas'. It is a great way to illustrate a competition for energy. If you grew up with brothers and sisters like I did, you will probably relate to the following example. He said that when we are little babies, we think we are the centres of attention. If we cry we get attention, we get love and we get energy. Then as we grow older, we have to start competing with our brothers and sisters for that energy because they also want our parents' love too. Now there is competition, so we get into what are called control dramas. These are used as a tool to control and manipulate people around us, often subconsciously. Therefore, we often do not realise we are doing it.

My millionaire mentor said, "Most people want energy, without even being aware of it. People think they want money, but what is money? What is love? What is having an exciting life? All these things are just another form of energy. Everyone wants energy. When you can figure this out, you can see the whole world differently. So we start to run control dramas to get that energy, even if we have to steal other people's energy. Let me explain."

"There are many different control dramas. There are some people who use the 'poor me' drama. Their way of getting energy would be to get your sympathy by telling you all about their tragic circumstances and their catchline is, 'You just do not understand how tough it is for me' or 'You do not realise how much has happened to me'. They want you to know how bad things are so that you will feel sorry for them. You probably know some people like that." I certainly did.

He went on to explain to me that others are into confrontation, they might be what we call 'intimidators' or 'interrogators'. You may know some people who are rather intimidating and interrogating and they like to confront people. They are often rude and abrupt. To get their energy they deflate others and literally take their energy if they are allowed. They possibly learned at a young age to compete with their brothers and sisters or other people around them to get attention.

Some people are 'aloof'. They seem quiet and shy, and often do not fully participate in an attempt to be different. That way, by being different, they attract some much desired energy.

After my millionaire mentor shared this with me, I thought to myself if we have these patterns as children, is it possible that we may continue these patterns into our adult life? Unfortunately, often that is exactly what happens. People sometimes come to tell me how bad things are (poor me). It is not that I do not care for them, but the last thing I want to do is give them sympathy, because that is their pattern of how they get energy. That is what they think they need, but it is not really what they need. That is why I realised it is great to have a coach or a mentor as that makes a big difference; I know it did to me. I could tell my friends my hard luck stories and they would sympathise with me because misery loves company, so they say. They would embrace my negative situation and share with me that they knew my business venture would not work because it backed up their reference of "why even bother because nearly everyone fails". I later realised subconsciously they were possibly comforted by my setbacks, as it made them feel more comfortable now that I was no longer more successful than them. Often people who are insecure become uncomfortable if someone is successful as it highlights to them what they could be doing if they were more committed to their life. This often explains the tall poppy syndrome that occurs a lot in Australia where often society wishes to pull down the successful people back to the level of everyone else.

On the other hand, I learned that a mentor or coach is emotionally unattached to my situation. They would look at my situation objectively and see where my improvements lay in my life today. So when someone comes to me with financial problems the last thing I do is feel 'sorry for them'. At the time they think I am too tough and that I should not be like that. It is because I care deeply about people that I will not allow myself to be caught up in their control dramas as **I would only be supporting them where they were at, instead of supporting them to change and become what they are capable of.**

Have you ever had an argument? Silly question. I know everyone has had at least one argument in his or her lifetime. But what is an argument really? What I referred to as an argument, is really only a competition for energy. It is two people using control dramas to compete for energy with one another. In most cases, the intimidator or interrogator usually wins, they will get the energy and the other person will lose the energy if they allow the intimidator or interrogator to upset them. They give away their power to the intimidator or interrogator type personality.

I later realised if we can raise our life force energy, we will start to feel ourselves pulling out of the negative energy surrounding us. The energy in our environment is often pulling us down and we have to look at how we can build up our energy. Often I found after attending an inspiring seminar my energy level naturally increased because I was surrounded by the group's combined energy. But when I left that uplifting environment and went back to my normal daily routine, that higher energy level often dissipated. This was a major challenge for me as it was for others.

I had to learn to condition my energy to maintain and resonate, or vibrate at a consistently high level of energy. Once I could maintain my energy I could use that energy to uplift other people. My mentor talked about the concept of becoming wealthy by raising your life force energy and then you take some of that energy and help other people raise their own. Once I understood that concept it became part of my purpose to raise the life force energy of every person I met. Today, when I meet a total stranger, I make the effort to uplift their energy, even if it is as simple as giving them a smile or being warm and friendly.

Just as an experiment why not try walking along the street to practice how your energy affects others. Walk along and in your mind project love to a complete stranger. **Try sending love to someone that maybe is having a bad day and is not looking happy. You can project an intention or an emotion and you can see an impact it has on people.** They will not even know where it is coming from, all of a sudden they will feel better. We are truly amazing human beings. You might be thinking, "But is not that manipulating people?" Maybe. However, I believe it is better to project love than to project anger. **We are manipulating people everyday, often unconsciously, so if you are going to manipulate someone, would you not agree it is better to manipulate them in a positive way by sending love or acceptance rather than anger or judgement?**

If we are always projecting energy, then who we are as a person is going to affect other people. Have you ever noticed how scattered the energy tends to be on forms of public transport like trains or buses? There tends to be, more times than not, a dense level of energy. I do not like travelling on public transport for this reason, because you have to continually try and maintain your energy and not let it be affected by the energy of fellow commuters.

Right about now, if you were like me, you may be saying, "Is this not hokey, pokey stuff? Just show me the money!" that is what I said to my millionaire mentor. **However, if you can understand this, then we can raise our energy and help other people raise theirs, which will improve our relationships, finances, career, health and all areas of our lives.** After all, do you want to be rich and miserable or rich and happy? **I can promise you that making a million dollars is easier than being consistently happy and fulfilled in life.**

If you have a low level of energy, what do you think happens to your health? Sadly, you can develop diseases. **Disease is another word for disharmony.** If people have diseases in their bodies, their energy is in disharmony or not vibrating in harmony. In other words, there is a wound, blockage or a breakdown in their energy flow. You will notice the energy of a newborn baby is very pure. The baby has a pure energy field flowing around it. What can start to happen though, is that energy does not stay pure. As the baby grows, things happen that cause disappointment, which causes anger and upset. In short, these occurrences begin to take the child's energy. When that happens an energy leak is created. So you can imagine if there is a hole in one's energy field and energy starts to pour out, it starts to leak away or disappear. As the child goes through life, there is the possibility of being wounded or traumatised again. For instance, a teenage relationship may end in heartbreak. The energy starts to lower and more and more negative things start to happen.

I was fortunate enough to learn that one of the keys to avoiding these leaks and wounds is to learn to heal ourselves. If we can resolve our past emotional issues we can heal our wounds. This is definitely a major part of emotional intelligence. I found that the thing that gets in the way of a lot of people's future is their past. If we can deal with our past effectively and accept that we are human and we all have different experiences, we can start to heal these wounds. Then our energy will start to vibrate at a higher level and we will continually evolve as human beings. Part of healing is forgiving ourselves for our mistakes and learning to love and accept ourselves for the greatness we are.

If we do not heal these wounds, you can probably guess what they turn into? Unfortunately, it leads to diseases such as cancer. There is so much credible evidence now that many doctors will agree that cancer is often simply the result of unresolved emotional issues. A lot of people who do not deal with their issues will pay a price down the track, which is very sad. There are very few people in our country or in this world who simply die of old age. In other words, most people die through disease or poor health before they need to, and that is a shocking cost. We have a lot at stake in becoming emotionally intelligent.

I work with some amazing people who have the ability to help people resolve their issues and they have had people with cancer whose cancer has disappeared in a very short period of time after the issue has been dealt with. Amazing you may say, and yes, it seems like a miracle, but if we understand energy fields, it is not such a miracle; it is just part of the laws of nature.

I have had people attend my seminars that have had chronic illnesses. One lady in particular had severe back problems and she could not sit or stand for a long period of time. During the seminar she went through some processes where she had the opportunity to deal with some issues from the past and let them go. A short while later she was walking fine, by the next week she could not believe it. She said to me, "I do not know what you did Jamie, but I have not felt like this for 20 years." I replied, "I did not do anything. You did!" The truth is, we all have the amazing ability to make sure our heart beats every second, non stop, without us thinking about it, so do you think your body would also have the ability to heal itself? It is all within us. If we start to tap into this infinite intelligence you can see how we can do these sort of things. **All of a sudden making a million dollars is like a piece of cake if we focus on the necessary steps.**

I have also looked into Reiki and other energy healing techniques, which are continually raising my energy. It also assists me a lot in business dealings as my perception and awareness of others is much greater.

So let us look at how I raised my energy and was able to manifest and draw to me the things I desired most. Firstly, we need to take a look at some practical ideas we can implement right now to raise our energy.

Let us start with a list of things that drain our energy. Environment can play a very big part in boosting our energy, but unfortunately it often tends to do the opposite and drain our energy. I used to work in an office in Sydney over eight years ago and the inside of the office was grey. The walls were grey, the desks were grey, there was fluorescent lighting, air-conditioning and in short, the environment was not really uplifting.

At the time I was passionate about building my career, learning lots of things and studying from my mentors. So, what I would do is go on a holiday at least once every couple of months, to get away from my working environment. Every time I would go away on a holiday I would come back really uplifted and energised. I would go to a nice coastal town and come back vibrant, on top of the world and motivated. **But within three or four hours of being in that office, I felt like I needed another holiday. I was completely drained! This happened for nearly a year before I finally figured out that if I want to be empowered and do empowering work then I need to be empowered not just once in a while but on a day to day basis.** I realised that when I sat down at my desk in a slouched state, surrounded by grey walls, air conditioning, fluorescent lighting and computers, and trying to work and be creative, it just was not effective for me.

Obviously, if my environment was draining my energy I needed to do something about it. One of the things I did was, instead of coming directly into the office in the morning, I would spend an hour to two walking along the beach first. To me, there is nothing better than walking along the beach and listening to the sounds of the waves crashing. Bare feet in the sand, breathing in the rich ocean air. It is like you breathe in and you can feel the energy expanding inside. I would sit down on the rocks by the ocean and I found this was where I could tap into my creativity. I did not have to do anything and the ideas would just flow to me. It was like the universe would open up and bring me the wisdom and insight of what I needed to do on a day-to-day basis to achieve my desires. I could think so clearly and everything just started to make sense. I thought, wow, this is so powerful and it started to change my life. I wondered why I had not done this more often in the past. I decided to create the kind of life that would allow me to be empowered all the time. I realised it was as simple as pinpointing the things that drained my energy, like sitting in an office, and eliminating them while at the same time incorporating into my life the things that gave me energy, like walking along the beach.

I used to live in Sydney out in the Western suburbs near Campbelltown. I have got nothing against the Western suburbs of Sydney, but if you know the area you may agree that it is an environment where the energy and the mindset of some of the suburbs are not always conducive to wealth. Unfortunately, in some areas it was more conducive to poverty and still is. So I decided to move suburbs. I moved to a suburb called Balmoral near Mosman, overlooking one of the world's most beautiful harbours and a beautiful harbour beach which, if you know the suburb, you will be aware is much more conducive to wealth. By living near Mosman, I was immediately surrounded by more abundance. **That simple action helped immensely in transforming my mindset to accept more abundance into my life.**

Transforming your mindset will definitely have a huge impact on your life. I know it did on mine. In fact, my income multiplied 15 fold in a period of a little over 12 months. I do not know if I would have had such a dramatic result if I had not moved suburbs. So am I suggesting that you have to move suburbs next week? Maybe not, but you need to identify the things that affect your energy. There were practical things that I did that made a huge difference and if I had not done them, then I would probably still be sitting behind a desk frustrated with my life and not getting the results I wanted.

The first step is to decide what gives you energy and what takes your energy away. Below are some common examples to get you started on your own list:

Drain Energy		**Raise Energy**	
Arguments	Poor Relationships	Having Money	Mentors/Uplifting People
Bad Diet	Stress	Smiling	Loving Relationships
Drugs/Alcohol	Negative Environment	Success	Nature
Negative Emotions	Cluttered Environment	Knowledge/Learning	Meditation/Yoga
Poor Physiology	Poor Health	Overcoming Challenges	Sex
Lack of/too much sleep	Unbalanced Lifestyle	Positive Outlook	Pets
Watching Television	Lack of Money	Lighter Colours	Having Fun/ Laughing
Dysfunctional Relationships	Negative People	Contribution	Oxygen
Boring Job	Interpreting Events as Bad	Music	Excercise/Fitness
Lack of Exercise	Low Standards	Holidays	Recognition/Signifigance

Once you have identified what gives you energy and what takes your energy, you can start to put together some action steps to change your life. This is what I call designing your life at a very basic level, yet often we know it is the simple things we could do that would make a big difference. The question my millionaire mentor always asked me was, "How committed are you?"

What Drains my Energy	**What Raises my Energy**

I will ask you the same question. Are you committed enough to do this exercise right now and redesign your life?

In doing this exercise, you may have noticed that it is not just things that can steal your energy but that some people in your life may drain your energy as well. Once you start changing, you will find as a result that the relationships in your life will also change. The friends you had ten years ago for many people will no doubt have evolved and changed to what they are today. There are possibly many people in your circle of friends now who are in the 96% bracket, but as you evolve you will attract more people from the 4% bracket into your life. In Section 5, I will go into more detail about the impact that the people with whom you associate have on your life.

By committing to raising your life force energy, the people who are drawn into your life in the next ten years will be different to the people currently in your life. By increasing your energy, you are going to stand out and begin to attract leaders into your life. Leaders stand up for what they believe in passionately and are people who usually create successful businesses, make positive contributions to society and make a difference. By associating with leaders, you too will become a leader and in turn will help other people become leaders and so the process continues. You will create a life of contribution and fulfilment.

Now, you know some ways I increased my energy in order to make dramatic changes in my life instantly and attract the wealth I deserve. With all this new found wealth that started flowing into my life as a result, I came across a problem that many people encounter due to their past financial conditioning called self sabotage. You will want to avoid this at all cost, so next you will need to rewire your subconscious for wealth creation, just like I had to.

CHAPTER 6

DEVELOPING THE MINDSET OF A MILLIONAIRE

BY REWIRING YOUR SUBCONSCIOUS FOR WEALTH CREATION

The first thing you need to do in order to rewire your subconscious for wealth creation is to answer a few simple questions about financial pressure. When I refer to financial pressure I am not necessarily talking about being broke and struggling. You can be wealthy and still have financial pressure. There is no right or wrong answer, only answers applicable to you.

1. **When was the last time you felt financial pressure?**

2. **Do you currently feel financial pressure in your life?**

3. **Does having more money really create less financial pressure?**

4. **When have you felt completely free from financial pressure?**

For some people being completely free from financial pressure might have been as far back as when they were at school. It could have been when they got pocket money and had to determine whether to buy a packet of Smarties or put it in their piggy bank, and for others it may have been never!

Apart from happiness, what is it you think that people really want in their life? I dare say the reason you are reading this book is because you want a financial future that you are certain about. You want the certainty to be able to manage money, have plenty of it and never have to worry about not having enough of it. Anyone would want that. Another term for that is security.

I believe that people really want to be certain that in the future they will not have to experience pain, that instead they will have the financial freedom to do whatever they want, whenever they want, wherever they want, with whomever they want, and as much as they want.

I know the quest for financial certainty drove me, because I had so much uncertainty and so much pain in my life and I never wanted to experience that again. So I was driven to become financially successful to avoid that pain. Pain drove me in the beginning more than pleasure. Pain is what drives people the most. If you have made a decision to start changing your life, or changing your financial future, eventually it will lead to more pleasure, but more than likely it is pain that drove you to your initial decision to change. Subconsciously you were probably thinking, "If I do not learn how to master money now, what will it really cost me in the future?"

Another way to begin to rewire your subconscious mind for success is to do, "The Meaning of Money Exercise". This exercise determines exactly what beliefs we have that could be holding us back from our goals around money.

Would you say that people mainly link pleasure or pain to money? From surveys that have been conducted in Australia, university studies have determined that many people actually link more pain than pleasure to money. I know this was definitely a challenge for me. Consciously we may be thinking more money means more pleasure and therefore more happy emotions, but subconsciously what is happening is that most people are linking negative emotions to money.

One of my mentors, Tony Robbins, talks about the fact that humans make decisions based on two primary factors. The first factor is to avoid pain. Is that not true when you think of how many decisions you have made in the past to try and avoid pain. We do not put our hand on a hot stove because at a very young age we learn that equals pain. The second factor is to gain pleasure.

You may say, "Jamie, that is so simplistic!" but when we look at most of our decisions in life you can see that it is true. For example, why do women wear makeup? Some say they wear makeup because it gives them pleasure and they really enjoy it. Others may say, "I do not put it on for pleasure, it is a damn pain! I hate having to do it every morning, but I do it to avoid the pain of what people will say if they see me without it on." (No offence ladies.)

Most of us will do more to avoid pain than we will to gain pleasure. This is important because consciously if we link pleasure to money and get excited and start doing things to be financially successful, we will start to move forward. At the same time, if we are still linking pain to money subconsciously, as soon as we start to see some success, we will end up self-sabotaging it.

This is exactly what happened to me. I would start to move two steps forward and then for some unknown reason I would start being slack, not doing things properly and end up taking three steps back. I could not figure it out.

Many people who become millionaires make it and lose it several times before they figure it out. In other words they will be successful, they will lose it, they will be successful. Usually by the time they make it back again a few times, they will have figured it out and so they remain successful. Once I understood human psychology and knew that subconsciously I was linking painful emotions to money and that my subconscious mind was not wired for success, I could do something about it.

Logically, we know we should save 10% of our income. However, we do not tend to make decisions based on logic, rather we make decisions based on our emotions. Unless we understand what is going on and have this working in our favour, then success can be very elusive. Often, we know what we should do, but we are not doing it.

The following exercise can help you rewire your own mind for financial success. It takes about 20 to 30 minutes and you will need to do it with a friend or your partner. What we want to do is rewire the subconscious mind. I had to rewire my subconscious to link pleasure to making more money. If I could do that, then I would be automatically driven on autopilot to financial success. However, if I did not change, then it would not matter what investment opportunities I came across, I would keep self-sabotaging my success.

How do you know if you are wired like that? If you are like most people you probably will be wired that way because that is how society conditions us. Now you can see the importance of the exercise and it is a simple process to ensure our nervous system is very clear that more wealth will equal more pleasure.

This exercise is designed to go beyond the conscious mind to access the subconscious files we link to money. When you first begin you will more than likely only be answering from your conscious mind, which will give you automatic conscious answers. Eventually, you will exhaust all your conscious answers and begin to call on the files of the subconscious mind. This will be evident from small changes in your physiology. Your eyes will lower and this is a sign you are more in touch with your emotions. Then your brain will begin searching past subconscious files, and past memories will come to consciousness.

An example may be that perhaps as a young kid your parents may have fought over money and you felt stressed about that. Or perhaps, if your father always had to go away for work, this caused you to associate negative emotions with money because he could not be home with your family. As an adult, consciously you can justify it, but subconsciously you may still be upset about it and link the pain to money — when it was actually the lack of money that caused your father to have gone away.

You will be amazed at what may start to come up. Even later, after the exercise is over, maybe even a week from now, your brain will keep coming up with files and you will start to recall memories that you have attached to money. Then you can start to understand what is really going on in your subconscious. It will give you the chance to look at it differently and move on. The benefits of this are enormous because you will then be on autopilot to financial success.

Get your partner to ask you these three questions. As you answer the questions, get your partner to write down your replies. Your partner will need to keep asking each question until your answers have been completely exhausted in each area. Push beyond the automatic answers so that you discover the deeper associations and emotional impacts of money in your life. Ask the question at least 20 times until the answers are completely exhausted, then switch to the second question for 20 times, and then the third question.

1. What is money?

____

____

____

____

____

____

2. What is not having money?

____

____

____

____

____

____

3. What is money, really?

____

____

____

____

____

____

I have included some examples of other people's answers below. Remember though, it is not really the answer we are looking for, it is the memory associated with your answers.

THE MEANING OF MONEY EXERCISE

What is money?	What is not having money?	What is money, really?
Quality	Feelings of scarcity	Amplifier
Gratitude	Being controlled by rules	Energy
Nothing but pieces of paper	Less choice, quality	Turbo charged
Lifestyle	Inability to give	Only what we have decided
Commitment	Arguments	Most powerful influencer of
Ability to give	Hurt	pain/pleasure
Access to resources	Loss of relationship	Choice to live life at highest level
Ability to leverage time	Stupid	Powerful tool for magnifying impact
Entertainment	Not making a difference	A tool that can open doors
Freedom from drudgery	Frustration	Leverage
Gift from God for being a giver	Pain	Opportunity for people
Reflection of value added	Separation	Choice
Reflection of intelligence		
Reflection of intensity of focus		
Commitment		

To condition your nervous system for wealth, use the insights you have gained from completing this exercise to answer the following questions.

1. What are my most limiting beliefs about having absolute financial abundance?

____

____

2. What specific amount of money represents financial abundance to me?

____

3. What will I do today toward developing a financial plan?

____

____

4. What did I learn today that I can use to make progress?

____

____

5. What financial terms and aspects of personal finance do I not currently understand?

____

____

6. Why am I committed to follow through?

____

____

7. Give one or two situations from the past of when you pulled through despite difficulty.

____

____

Once you have completed this exercise you will have commenced the process of rewiring your subconscious association to money. If you would like to learn more about conditioning your subconscious and not only in relation to money but also in other areas of your life, I recommend Anthony Robbins' work on Neuro Linguistic Programming and Neuro Associative Conditioning. He is the world's leader in this field and produces phenomenal results rapidly and consistently. His books titled *Unlimited Power* and *Awaken the Giant Within* are both bestsellers available in most book stores, or to find out about his seminars go to www.21stcenturyacademy.com and go to the link for Tony Robbins.

Now that we have removed the obstacles in the way of our financial freedom, we need to find out exactly what will drive us to do the things necessary to create the life we desire. At the moment you might think that it is the shiny, new red Ferrari that is driving you, pardon the pun! But, if it really was the red Ferrari, I guarantee you would already have one sitting in your driveway. Most people find it is something bigger and more powerful than the fancy cars and the ritzy houses. I will give you a hint, it probably has got something to do with helping your fellow man. In the next chapter let us find out exactly what your primary purpose is.

CHAPTER 7

HOW TO FIND OUT WHAT YOUR PRIMARY PURPOSE IS

Before we move on to financial intelligence and specific wealth creation strategies, do you think it might be important to become clear on what it is that you really want? Some people may already be clear on this, yet many others have no idea what their primary purpose is. This is probably the most important step, because unless you have clarity on what you want, then no amount of strategies will help you get what you want.

In this chapter, we will undertake a process that will help you become clear on what it is you want. What I mean by your primary purpose is what your true purpose or focus for life is. In other words, the essence of who you are and what your life is about.

The following is a broad list of questions that can be helpful for stimulating your thoughts and putting you in the right frame of mind for working on your primary purpose. Take time to think about your answers. Question yourself and then question your answers. There are, of course, no right or wrong answers, just answers that are right for you. Some questions have easy, instant answers, some questions have difficult answers that can take a great deal of thought, and some questions can cause you to rethink your most basic values and attitudes in life. Most importantly, be honest with yourself. In designing one's ideal life, the questions I asked for myself that were very powerful were as follows:

- What do you want your life to look and feel like?
- What do you value most? What is important to you?
- What matters most at this point in life?
- What would you like to be able to say about your life after it is too late to do anything about it?
- Many years from now, at your funeral, what do you hope will be said about you in your eulogy?
- What do you want your life to look and feel like on a day-to-day basis?
- What emotions would you like to feel consistently?
- What would you like people's perceptions of you to be?
- What are your daydreams about? When you were young, what did you want to be when you grew up?

This is one of the first places I would suggest that you start if YOU are not clear on your dream, your purpose. Think back to when you were younger, usually before the age of 14. You probably had different hopes and aspirations for your future and often in that creativity was really the essence of what you could become and what your dreams are. Unfortunately, too many people lose sight of their childhood dreams.

- Do you ever find yourself wishing you were different? What did you wish? Why are you not that way? What gets in your way?
- Of all the things you have done in your life, what has given you the most satisfaction or pleasure?
- If you no longer had to work, how would you spend your time? And with whom?

It is so important to become clear on these questions before you worry about becoming financially free. The challenge for a lot of people is, if you do not know what you are going to do when you are free of the rat race, then your mind has nothing to link pleasure to or move forward to. I know so many people that I have been able to give solutions to in the past, obvious solutions, to enable them to be free of the rat race. For some people, instant financial solutions and for others financial freedom in less than twelve months. Just simple, logical changes. However, I found that some people would not implement those changes, even though they wanted to be financially free! They may have been trapped in a job or business they were not really happy with, however, even though they were not happy, they were not uncomfortable enough to do anything to change the situation. We found their six human wants which I will cover in this book, were being met in their business or job. They were not met at a high level, but just met. For them, to move out of that and become free, they needed something else to move towards that would still meet those six human wants. Unless you figure out what that activity or purpose is for you, then you may never move forward and you will continue to sabotage yourself.

- What is missing from your life? When you find yourself wishing for something, what is it?
- What motivates you to perform above and beyond the call of duty?
- What are your greatest strengths?
- What are your greatest weaknesses?
- What do you want to achieve but find impossible to do? What barriers make it impossible? Are those barriers really insurmountable?

Now that we have set the stage, so to speak, and you are in the right frame of mind, we can continue the process of discovering your primary purpose. There are five steps to the process.

Step 1 — What you do not want in your life

I have found in the past that for most people, it is easier to begin with a list of what they do not want in their life, rather than what they do want because this is the way we have been conditioned. So using the blank spaces below, list everything you can think of that causes you anger, stress, frustration, fear, hatred, embarrassment, dissatisfaction or anything that you do not want in your life. Do not think too much about it, just write as many as you can think of.

Now, go back over your list, thinking carefully about each item. Notice your feelings, your sense of importance about each one. Circle the few items, no more than five or six, that are the most important not to have in your life.

Step 2 — What you do want in your life

Now that you know what you do not want in your life, it is much easier to find out what exactly it is you do want. As before, using the blank spaces below, list everything you can think of that you do want in your life. Look back to what you circled that you did not want. These will tell you about what you really do desire. Your subconscious knows exactly what you really want. Focus on what makes you happy, fulfilled and satisfied, as well as what gets you energised, motivated and purposeful. Avoid the superficial and the material, go for the deeply satisfying, profoundly rewarding life experiences. Again, do not think too much about it, just write as many as you can:

As before, go back over your list, thinking carefully about each item. Again, notice your feelings, your sense of importance about each one. Circle the few items, no more than five or six, that are the most important for you to have in your life. Look over those items and rank them from the most important to the least important.

Step 3 — What are your priorities and what is in your way

Now, what is it that is stopping you having the things you truly want in your life? This step will help determine what you need to overcome. Write down the most important items, the ones you circled previously from the list of what you want in your life. Write them in order of importance. Think carefully about each of them and write down what, if anything, is keeping you from having them. What barriers stand in the way of having these things that are the most important to you. Think especially hard about self-imposed limitations and how these barriers and limitations can be overcome.

Important things I want in life	**Barriers and limitations**
______________________________	______________________________
______________________________	______________________________
______________________________	______________________________
______________________________	______________________________
______________________________	______________________________
______________________________	______________________________
______________________________	______________________________

Step 4 — Write your own eulogy

This step will take you on a journey that will really make things clear on where you want to be at the end of your life. Most people in life have only a vague idea, if any, of where they want to go. There is no real direction in their life. We need to begin with the end in mind, like IBM did when it wanted to become a huge computer corporation. The owners got clear on what they wanted IBM to look like when it was finished. We can do the same thing with our lives. We will take a journey into the future and find out exactly what your life will hold. I learned the concept of beginning with the end in mind for creating businesses from my millionaire mentor and decided to use the concept for my life, not just business. So I began with the end in mind.

I want you to imagine it is a cool, windy day and you are heading off to a church. Unfortunately, you are heading off to a friend's funeral. The funeral is for a distant friend that you have not seen for some time. You pull up outside the church and as you get out of the car, you notice the blustery winds blowing against your clothes.

Slowly, you walk up the steps of the church and notice its big sandstone walls. As you reach the top of the steps you see some other people walking into the church, you follow them inside the large wood panelled doors of the church.

You proceed down the aisle and notice some people sitting in the church that you are familiar with. Some of these people you have not seen for quite some time. But you do not stop to greet them; instead something seems to draw you to continue walking further down the aisle.

As you walk down the aisle you glance to the pews on the right and left, you recognise some more familiar faces. There are some people sitting there you have not seen for many, many years. Some of them are old school friends, some are relations, and there are even some people you would not expect to see there. You are sort of curious, there are so many people here that you know. You think to yourself, "I have not seen some of these people for a long time." You seem to be able to walk effortlessly as you walk further down the aisle to the front of the church.

When you reach the front, you just turn and look around the church. You notice the colour of the internal church walls and the stained-glass windows. Looking towards the front of the church you see how big the church is and how many people are sitting in it.

The soft organ music begins to play. You proceed down the aisle again, getting closer to the front where there are some of your immediate family members sitting. They are obviously upset and you are just glad to notice who is sitting there. They do not seem to recognise you, but maybe they have not noticed you walking down the aisle. You finally get to the front of the church and you see the coffin at the front, it is a large, timber coffin. There is a sombre feeling throughout the church. You are drawn to walk towards the coffin. You walk towards it and notice the casket is open.

As you approach you decide to pay your last respects to your dear friend. You get closer to the coffin and notice someone lying there. You lean over the coffin to pay your deepest respects and notice who is laying in the coffin. All of a sudden, you can not believe what you are seeing, as the person laying in the coffin looks exactly like you! It just does not make sense. For a moment you are startled. You gasp for a breath of air as if you are seeing things. You look again and realise not only does the person look like you, but the feeling starts to sink in that it is you! It is you laying in the coffin, not an old friend!

It suddenly dawns on you that it is actually your funeral. All those people in the church are there to pay their last respects to you. Just as you are trying to come to grips with what is happening, someone stands up at the front of the church and commences delivering a eulogy on your behalf. You notice there are three eulogies to be delivered.

The first is from someone you work with. They start to talk about you to all your family, friends and people that you knew. They talk about what sort of person you were and some of the things you did.

Imagine what they would say about you? How does it make you feel? A second person stands up to deliver your eulogy. This person is one of your close family members, someone who has known you for virtually your entire life. They are someone that loves you dearly. They begin to talk about some funny things from your past. What you were really like as a person, what some of your dreams and ambitions were and the things you accomplished. Imagine what they are saying about you. As they say these things, there is a part of you that wants to say, "You forgot some things! There is more to me. You do not know everything there was to know about me, you only knew some things!" There are some other things you would say if you had the chance. "There is more to my life than just that!" But you realise you can not say anything and the people in the church can not even see you standing there. It is hopeless to try and say anything because no one can hear you.

The last person comes up to deliver your eulogy and speaks to all the people in the church. This is your best friend. Your best friend starts to talk about you, what they thought of you and what sort of person you were. What you did, what you were like, and what your hopes and dreams were. What are they saying about you? What else do they say? Do they cover everything, or maybe even your best friend does not know what some of your dreams were.

When they finish talking it is like you want to jump up and say, "That is not all! There was more to my life than just that!" You just want to express yourself, who you were. But you realise it is hopeless and no one can hear you. People start to exit the church, obviously upset. They can not see you and there is nothing you can do. The reality starts to sink in that your life is over as you know it. There is so much you might want to say and do about the rest of your life but all of a sudden it is too late. You start to realise you had your chance, but that chance is now gone.

With a sense of helplessness you begin to walk down the aisle and out of the church. Feeling heavy and distraught you walk down the steps of the church. As soon as you walk outside you notice different things. You hear the sounds of the birds chirping in the trees and the rustle of the leaves blowing. You breathe in the freshness of the air and begin to see things around you that before you took for granted. You are totally aware of the immense beauty of the outside world.

You begin to walk towards your car thinking, "What if I had just one more chance? I really just want some more time, please." You beg, but no one can hear you. You beg to whoever will listen. You say, "I did not realise! If I knew my time was about to be up, I would have done things differently. I would not have left it until it was too late to experience some of the things I wanted to experience. To express myself, maybe tell some people I love them, while I had the chance."

You realise now that you can not say anything and it is too late, but you do not want to accept that reality. You try begging once again to whoever will listen, your creator, God, whoever. "Please just give me one more chance. Just give me some more time. There are some things I would do if I had some more time in my life."

Think about those things you would do differently. What are some things you would definitely do if you were granted more time? You realise how precious every second of life really is, now that it is gone. What would you be willing to do, just for another hour of life, another day or even an entire week? Imagine a whole week of extra time. What could you do in a whole week if you were granted that time? What if you had an extra month or maybe even a year or two or five? How precious would that be to you? What would you promise in exchange for this extra time? Would you promise to do whatever it takes to not waste another second of your life? Would you promise to never let a day go by without expressing your love to the people you care about? Would you promise to put your passion and belief into everything you do? If only somehow you could be granted that extra time. What would you be willing to do to get that extra time? Just one more chance at life. If you were granted that chance, would you live your life differently?

What are some things in your life you would change? What are some things that would be most important to you that you would focus on? Who are some people you might express some love to and let them know how you really feel while you are alive and while they can hear you? What would you do differently? What are some of the things you would like to change? Would you fulfill your purpose while you had that chance? How would your life be different? As you think about the things you would do differently if only someone would give you one more chance, knowing that your wish may not be granted, you walk to your car despondently.

Now I want you to imagine that your wish, what you are begging for is given to you on the conditions that you agreed on. You agreed to do anything for another second, another hour, another week, another year, maybe another decade or two. You promised you would do all those things for another chance at life. If that were granted to you, would you live up to the conditions that you gave? Would you be absolutely committed to doing whatever it takes to never waste another second of your life again? Would you make it the best life you could possibly make it, so when your time does come again, the day you are laying there in that coffin, you can lay there and the eulogy that will be said about you would be what you want it to be. Instead of someone else talking about your life, imagine it is a recording of yourself played at your funeral of how your life was after you have lived it to the best and fullest it could have possibly been. Imagine how that eulogy would be different. What satisfaction would you have knowing that your life may eventually come to an end, but you gave it everything you could. How would that make you feel? You lived your purpose. You lived with passion, you had courage and you did not dwell on fear, but through creativity you did what it took.

Think about these things for a moment, think about those things you would do differently if you knew you had been granted one more chance at life. Life is the most precious gift we have.

List some of the things you would change in your life and what you would promise, to be granted extra time.

Now that we have taken this journey and you have vowed to live your life to the fullest, it is time to write your own eulogy.

Years and years from now, after a happy and fulfilling life, you are given the opportunity to write the eulogy that will be given at your memorial service. Assuming you have the life you want from this point forward, what will your eulogy say about your life?

Looking back on the life of

____

____

____

____

____

____

____

Now for the final step in discovering your primary purpose:

Step 5 — Put your primary purpose down on paper

Write a very short statement — a phrase, a sentence, no more than a couple of sentences — expressing the essence of what you want your life to be all about. The acid test for your primary purpose statement is your internal barometer. When you write it, you should feel energy, enthusiasm, commitment, a sense of "Yes! This is for me!" If you do not feel this, keep on writing.

As an example, when I did the exercise around eight years ago, my initial statement for my primary purpose was, "My Primary Purpose is to raise the life force energy of every single person I have the privilege to connect with".

It was simple but effective in the beginning. It was enough to get me to think foremost about others and no longer focus just on myself and my problems, which was a selfish way to live.

I have expanded this now to where I have several primary purposes, some which include "creating an ideal 21st century education system for Australia and the world that will positively transform millions of peoples lives, creating a more empowered and prosperous world."

"Building an institute that will help influence, create and implement a more equitable, empowering and compassionate world monetary system that will help eliminate world hunger and poverty, largely created by the current debt-based monetary system which has the majority of the wealth manipulated into the hands of a few."

The essence of my primary purpose is:

____

____

____

____

____

____

____

____

Now that we have discovered what your primary purpose is, it is time to create an action plan to propel you forward to the kind of life you have written about in your eulogy. Your primary purpose is the starting point and guides you to get on track. In the next chapter, we will find out how to design your perfect life.

By becoming clear about my purposes, these two primary purposes drive my entire life and focus, virtually every day.

Already it has resulted in creating a multi million dollar educational organisation in Australia and New Zealand which has impacted over 50,000 people and eventually will be globally impacting millions. It also guided me to start a book on solutions to the world's monetary problems, to help eliminate world poverty and expose one of the world's greatest financial transfers of wealth carried out by the Federal Reserve, centrally controlled banks and the IMF, upon the nations of the world under the guise of globalisation.

My clear purpose has also caused me to begin starting a political movement in Australia known as **"Australians for Australia"** designed to influence Australian government policy to implement changes to improve Australia's chances of excelling as a country in the 21st century. It includes lobbying in regards to high taxation and highly taxed superannuation, inadequate education at schools and universities, and highlighting some of the disastrous effects of "economic rationalisation" to help restore Australia's wealth before we become virtually completely foreign controlled and potentially bankrupt as a nation in the future. This is often as a result of some of the policies of the IMF and World Bank forced upon us. It is designed to one day assist in giving Australia a credible third party alternative to the two major parties who have a monopoly in Australian politics.

It has also led me to educating Australians about financial success and to help change the current financial ploy by large institutions (banks), that own 90% of the financial planning industry. Here, many Australians are led into thinking they are getting unbiased financial advice from their financial planner, when this is often not the case. The financial planners are not trained as money experts and successful investors but often simply commissioned sales people pushing the banks or associated companies' products under the guise of "licensed financial planners".

It also caused me to raise tens of thousands of dollars for charities including Pat Rafter's Cherish the Children Foundation, and to sponsor a whole third world school in Africa, to assist in their education, giving them a better future.

If I had not done the Primary Purpose exercise eight years ago, I would never have been drawn to create a focus on all the above and made such progress in half a decade, let alone a lifetime.

You can see that by having a strong sense of purpose, I am naturally driven more than someone whose purpose or goal is simply to pay off the mortgage.

I am not suggesting you have to want to make a massive difference in the world, however you must develop a strong sense of purpose or vision in your life for "without a vision they will perish", I recall reading in a famous book once.

CHAPTER 8

DESIGNING YOUR LIFE

I have covered how to discover our primary purpose so we now need to create an action plan of goals to ensure we are always moving towards the fulfilment of that primary purpose. It is important to remember though that no individual goal should ever be in conflict with your primary purpose. It is also important to design goals in all areas of your life, which result in a much more balanced life. Sometimes it is difficult to achieve balance in the short term, but long term, if you are not living in balance you will find areas of your life will suffer. The areas I set goals in are: health, family, career/business, financial, intellect, spiritual and social. You can have all the money in the world, but if you have not looked after your health, you are probably not going to enjoy your wealth like you would if you were fit and full of vitality.

Most people set goals that are way too large and become disheartened before they ever come close to reaching them. A goal that works is one that is broken down until it represents a single event. It is the progressive, sequential accumulation of single events that ensure the final desired end result. For example, if your goal is to save $10,000 this year and you are paid fortnightly, you should have 26 single event goals, each written progressively to allow for changed circumstances. Your goals should be what I call SMARTIES! SMARTIES is an acronym for the following:

SPECIFIC

Be absolutely specific when setting your goals, and use only the present tense positive statements. If your goal is to "have specific habits to improve your physical appearance", your goal could be expressed as, "I am so happy I am starting my fitness programme at Noosa Life Gym at 6.30pm to 7.45pm on Monday 16 March, 2004. I will continue this programme Monday through Saturday for the next three months."

MEASURABLE

Your goals need to be measurable, in other words, you need to be able to monitor your progress so you can measure your success. If your goal is to lose weight, obviously monitoring this is an easy thing to do by hopping on the scales once a week, or once a month. If however, it is something like making significant improvements in your career, you may need to ask your boss for regular feedback on your performance to see how much progress you are making with your goal.

ATTAINABLE

You also need to be able to conceive your goal in order to attain it. Unless you can see yourself achieving your goal, it is very unlikely to happen. Napoleon Hill said, "Whatever the mind of man can conceive, he can achieve." This is the secret to success. By using visualisation techniques you can speed up this process.

REALISTIC

Obviously goals need to be within the bounds of logic and circumstance. There is no use setting a goal for example, "to be the No. 1 jockey in the world", if you are six foot four and weigh 250 pounds. Perhaps setting a goal to become the No. 1 basketball player would be more appropriate.

TANGIBLE

Your goal needs to be something that is real or physical, that you can see and touch.

INSPIRATIONAL

If your goals do not inspire you, it is unrealistic to expect that you will be driven to take action to achieve them. Make sure you choose goals that will give you a "buzz", whether it is a sporty red Ferrari or a three-story mansion, or something altruistic like, "saving the whales".

EMOTIONAL

The more emotionally involved you become with your goal the quicker it will manifest into your life. If you want the red Ferrari, go down to the car dealership and sit in one. Smell the leather seats and feel the steering wheel in your hands. Drive one. Get your photo taken with you in the driver's seat. Then every time you look at your goal you will experience the Ferrari rather than just looking at a two dimensional picture.

I have included a short-term and medium-term goal sheet plus a master dream list in this chapter to get you started on writing down some goals. The goal planning sheets are only tools to guide the thinking process. Use additional sheets of paper to map out your plans in detail. Excellence is the result of attention to detail.

During your planning process, as well as writing down your goals, write down every possible benefit you will realise as a result of achieving your goal and its impact on all areas of your life.

Once you have planned and written your goals, I recommend you write them on some small cards and carry them with you so you can read them on a daily basis. Pick half an hour at an exact time each day that you can consistently achieve, to focus on your goal card and mediation to create the necessary operating principles and practices for your life. There was a survey undertaken as to the differences between a millionaire and a billionaire. Strangely enough there was only one definable difference between the two and that was that billionaires reviewed their goals twice a day, while millionaires only reviewed theirs once. Is that not interesting?

HOW TO CREATE A GOAL BOARD AND A VISION POSTER

Another great idea for keeping you tuned into your goals is to create a goal board for yourself. This is one of the processes we do during our three day seminar at *21st Century Academy*. I ask all the participants to bring in a selection of magazines to cover all areas of their life. We then give everyone a sheet of cardboard, glue and scissors and we spend a good amount of time flicking through magazines, choosing the dreams each participant wants to create their perfect lifestyle. If you can get pictures of yourself visiting your dreams, for example a photo in a Ferrari, that is even better. I encourage them to think big, in fact, the bigger the better and I am not talking about just focusing on material aspects of their lives but to think outside the square.

It is a very worthwhile exercise. Many graduates have told me about how they have put their goal boards up on a wall once they arrived back home from the academy, and how so much of what they have put on their vision posters has been very quickly attracted into their lives. I recommend you put your goal board and vision poster in your bedroom so that you will see it just before you drift off to sleep at night and when you awaken first thing in the morning. This will help to embed your dreams and goals into your subconscious.

VISUALISATION

Visualisation is a very powerful tool that can be used to help manifest all that you desire into your life. Visualisations are like a projection or a movie screen in your mind. Fortunately for us, our subconscious can not tell the difference between reality and dreams. Therefore, if you continuously project your goals onto your movie screen in your mind, then your subconscious will automatically create the circumstances necessary for your goal to be achieved. The more detailed and the more often you visualise your goals, the more powerful they will be and the quicker you will manifest them into your life. Remember, we attract into our lives what we continually focus on.

INCANTATIONS

We have discussed the concept of, "motion = emotion", in a previous chapter. Again we can use this to manifest what we want into our lives quickly and easily. Incantations are affirmations with actions. By doing actions to your affirmations, they are set like concrete into our nervous system. By creating actions and movements that relate directly to the words in your incantation, your physiology will instantly be put into a peak state. You may feel a little awkward when you first try this, but after a while when you see how effective it is, it will become like a secret ritual you perform. I use an incantation prior to speaking at my seminars to get me into the best state possible to impact my audience. It goes like this:

"I now command my subconscious mind to direct me in helping as many people as possible today, by giving me the strength, the emotion, the humour, the persuasion, the brevity, whatever it takes to get these people and to show these people to better their lives now".

I say this as many times as possible with hand gestures to get me completely in a state of focus and to have the ability to serve others at the highest level.

The second one I use is:

"God's wealth flows into my life in avalanches of abundance. I give thanks for all my dreams, desires, goals, which are met instantaneously by infinite intelligence and I give thanks for all the good I am now and all of God's riches as I am truly one with God and God is everything".

Because I have consistently conditioned these into my nervous system over many years, I believe it plays a big part in ensuring wealth continuously flows into my life, not just in a financial sense.

Have you ever actually achieved a goal and said, "Is that all there is?" In the next chapter, you will learn that each of us has our own way of getting our needs met. In every situation we make decisions according to our personal criteria of what vehicles meet our needs. To prevent yourself from setting goals that fall short of your expectations you will need to know all about the six human needs.

Short Term Goals

Name ______________________ **Date** ______________

Below write three goals in each of the following areas. Short term goals are things you would like to achieve within one to ninety days.

Health
1. ____________________
2. ____________________
3. ____________________

Family
1. ____________________
2. ____________________
3. ____________________

Career/Business
1. ____________________
2. ____________________
3. ____________________

Financial
1. ____________________
2. ____________________
3. ____________________

Intellect
1. ____________________
2. ____________________
3. ____________________

Spiritual
1. ____________________
2. ____________________
3. ____________________

Social
1. ____________________
2. ____________________
3. ____________________

Other
1. ____________________
2. ____________________
3. ____________________

Medium Term Goals

Name ______________________________ **Date** ______________

Below write three goals in each of the following areas. Medium term goals are things you would like to achieve within twelve months to three years.

Health
1. ______________________________
2. ______________________________
3. ______________________________

Family
1. ______________________________
2. ______________________________
3. ______________________________

Career/Business
1. ______________________________
2. ______________________________
3. ______________________________

Financial
1. ______________________________
2. ______________________________
3. ______________________________

Intellect
1. ______________________________
2. ______________________________
3. ______________________________

Spiritual
1. ______________________________
2. ______________________________
3. ______________________________

Social
1. ______________________________
2. ______________________________
3. ______________________________

Other
1. ______________________________
2. ______________________________
3. ______________________________

Master Dream List

Name **Date**

Write down three things in each category below that you have ever wanted to be, to do, to see or to have. Let your imagination run free, ignore any imagined limitations of money, education or ability. Be completely unrestrained and freewheeling. Add to your master dream list daily, weekly and monthly for the rest of your life.

Health
1. ______
2. ______
3. ______

Family
1. ______
2. ______
3. ______

Career/Business
1. ______
2. ______
3. ______

Financial
1. ______
2. ______
3. ______

Intellect
1. ______
2. ______
3. ______

Spiritual
1. ______
2. ______
3. ______

Social
1. ______
2. ______
3. ______

Other
1. ______
2. ______
3. ______

CHAPTER 9

THE SIX HUMAN NEEDS

The following six human needs are a technology I learned from Tony Robbins and I think is a brilliant way to understand how to be fulfilled in life.

Tony Robbins says, "Everything human beings do, they do for a reason. They are trying to meet one of six basic human needs. While human values may vary, we all have different beliefs, strategies and desires. We all share the same needs. "

I have found that sometimes life is like a balancing act. It is a "seesaw" of making sure your needs are met, without doing it so often and so much that you become habituated or take things for granted.

Have you ever achieved a goal only to say, "Is that all there is?" Have you ever held yourself to a high standard and not been satisfied? Have you ever been in a relationship, really loved someone, but became bored and did something to jeopardise the relationship?

Each of us has our own way of getting our needs met. We could call these vehicles; some are destructive, some neutral, and others are constructive. For example, some people use alcohol, cigarettes or drugs to feel "relaxed" for the moment. Others go shopping, have sex, or read a book. The number of vehicles is almost as unlimited as the number of people who use them. But you must remember that you choose the vehicle, it does not choose you. The secret to meeting your needs is meeting your perceptions or procedures. In other words, you need to adopt a new strategy to get new results.

I learned from Tony that there are two general categories of needs: The first one is, "The Four Fundamental Needs", and the second one is, "The Two Primary and Essential Needs". All must be met for us to experience ultimate fulfilment.

Everyone meets their needs some way. The question is at what level of fulfilment and using what vehicles. Do you meet these needs at a high level, or a low level, or somewhere in between? To have the ultimate life, obviously you need to meet these needs at a high level. That is the key.

Tony has identified the Six Human Needs as:

1. CONNECTION/LOVE

The first of the four basic needs is the need for connection or love. Other ways to meet this need are by bonding, sharing, feeling a part of, being at one with or being intimate with others. Everyone needs to be able to connect with other humans and feel a sense of love. It is important to not only receive love but to also be able to give love.

2. CERTAINTY/COMFORT

The second need is certainty or comfort. This is the ability to produce, eliminate, or avoid stress, or create, increase or intensify pleasure. People want to feel secure in their jobs and relationships. Most people can not wait to get a job because on a cultural level it represents security, which is another word for certainty. However, this could be an illusion. Most people believe that a job will give them certainty. In the past that was possible and it did give some sense of certainty because most people worked for one company all their lives. Today that is not true, this creates a lot of fear and uncertainty for people.

3. UNCERTAINTY/VARIETY

Now at the same time, if you get too much certainty in your life you become bored and your life becomes monotonous. Many people have this challenge so they crave the third need, which is variety or uncertainty in their life. It can also be described as surprise, difference, diversity, challenge or excitement. We have all heard that "variety is the spice of life" have we not? So, when the certainty and comfort becomes boring, we often feel we need to change some things in our life.

4. SIGNIFICANCE

The fourth need is the need for significance, a sense of being needed or having a purpose, uniqueness or the need to feel important. We all have the need for it and we all meet that need in some way.

5. GROWTH

There are also two primary and essential needs. The first one is growth, which is one of the most powerful needs. If you are not growing you are dying. If you help others to be fulfilled, you will be fulfilled.

6. CONTRIBUTION

The second primary need is the need for contribution. Often, we will do more for other people than what we will do for ourselves. To meet this need on a higher level we need to be willing to consistently give to others that which you wish to receive. So to have a rewarding life, we need to go from being "culturally successful", to being fulfilled.

To do that we need to find out how we are currently meeting these needs, and if at the moment we are meeting them in destructive ways, how we can meet them at a higher level. By meeting these needs at a higher level you will find fulfillment on a consistent basis in all areas of your life.

Let us look at what could be destructive ways for meeting these needs. For example, a member of a street gang is meeting their needs for connection by using peer group pressure and their need for significance by having people fear them and their gang.

A person that goes from one job to the next or one relationship to another, is meeting their need for variety and uncertainty in this way. Often, things are going along fine, yet due to their need for uncertainty they sabotage that relationship or job and are forced to move on to something else, which gives them a new "buzz" or a new high. People that gamble are fulfilling their need for variety, as are people that take drugs.

The "tall poppy syndrome" is another way some people meet their need for significance by pulling others down to build themselves up. Robert Kiyosaki talks about how prevalent this syndrome is in Australia and if you can make it here, you can make it anywhere. In the USA people are more enthusiastic and excited about other people's success and they think, "If they can do it, I can do it!"

Let us look at constructive ways of meeting our need for growth. Going to seminars, reading books and listening to tapes are great ways of meeting this need. New relationships can also help you grow. If you are not growing in a relationship, then that relationship will probably not continue for much longer as that need is not being met.

If you want to create tremendous wealth for your future and impact a lot of people it will come from mastering your need for contribution at the highest level. This is the most powerful driver in human beings, unfortunately it is the driver very few people tap into. Anthony Robbins is a prime example of someone who is driven by the need to contribute to others, he links so much pleasure to serving others. He gets so excited and passionate and it has totally transformed his life. As soon as he linked pleasure to that, he could not help but find ways to help more and more people and as a result he has transformed millions of people's lives all around the world. So have a think about what you could contribute. My dream is for you to find ways you can massively serve other people. If you do that, everything you desire will be manifested into your life at a remarkably rapid rate and importantly you will have a fulfilling life by being an outstanding example for others to follow.

Look at the table below for some examples of how you can meet your six basic human needs at different levels. The list contains destructive, neutral and constructive vehicles.

Connection/Love	**Certainty/Comfort**	**Uncertainty/Variety**	**Significance**
Sympathy through sickness or injury	Control	Alcohol	Tearing others down
Crime	Consistency	Drugs	Violence
Smoking	Food	Gambling	Negative identity
Drugs	Learning helplessness	Self sabotage	Disease and disorder
Gangs	Negative identity	New relationships	Material possessions
Attempting to get others to comply with your requests	Completion	New job	Academic degrees
Relationships	Identity	New location	Accomplishments
Spirituality	Faith	Stimulating conversation	Style
Being in natural surroundings	Belief in guidance	Taking on new challenges	Development of new skills and knowledge
Pets	Saving money	Learning	Growing levels of caring or extraordinary compassion
Sex	Debt reduction	Refocussing your goals	Scarcity
Beauty or art	Insurance/hedging	Picking an argument	Saving
Self-sacrifice	Traditions	Investing	Being a leader
Joining a team	Hugs	Extreme sport	Teaching

We have within ourselves the resources to feel completely fulfilled in all six categories, in any situation, regardless of how others respond. To do this, simply ask the question, "What would I need to believe/ appreciate/perceive or do (procedures/vehicles/approach) in order to feel more fulfilled in this category now?"

Now we have identified some negative and positive ways of fulfilling the six basic human needs, take a look at the four classes of human experience in the table below. Obviously it is better to adopt the Class 1 vehicle for meeting your six human needs. Explore the vehicles you may be using now by completing the exercise. I have included a few examples to get you started.

CLASS 1	CLASS 2	CLASS 3	CLASS 4
It feels good	It does not feel good	It feels good	It does not feel good
It is good for you	It is good for you	It is not good for you	It is not good for you
It is good for others	It is good for others	It is not good for others	It is not good for others
It serves the greater good	It serves the greater good	It does not serve the greater good	It does not serve the greater good
What are the Class 1 ways you are currently meeting your needs?	*What are the Class 2 ways you are currently meeting your needs?*	*What are the Class 3 ways you are currently meeting your needs?*	*What are the Class 4 ways you are currently meeting your needs?*
E.g. Saving (certainty/comfort)	*E.g. Starting an exercise program (acceptance/ significance)*	*E.g. Alcohol (variety)*	*E.g. Bad debts (comfort)*
Teaching/Sharing (contribution)	*Working (certainty, contribution, significance)*	*Owning a sports car (significance)*	*Fighting and arguing (variety, significance)*

In this chapter, we have learned what the six human needs are and identified the different vehicles for meeting them. After completing the exercise above, you would have a fair idea of the vehicles you currently use to meet your needs on a consistent basis. These vehicles, up until now have in most cases been chosen by you on a subconscious level and therefore may not always be Class 1 vehicles. What if you could learn how to control what triggers you, and instead of turning to negative vehicles for meeting your needs, you began to consciously choose positive vehicles for your fulfilment? You can do this by learning how to control your emotions through state management and how to put yourself in a peak state.

Lleyton Hewitt with his famous catch phrase, "come on", is an excellent example of someone who can consistently put himself in a peak state. There is no doubt why he became the youngest ranked number 1 tennis player in the world, an inspiration to millions.

The remainder of this book will focus on what it takes to become financially successful in the 21st century, beginning with setting your financial targets.

SECTION THREE

THE SECRETS OF FINANCIAL INTELLIGENCE

CHAPTER 10

Let's Start. Establish Your Financial Goals

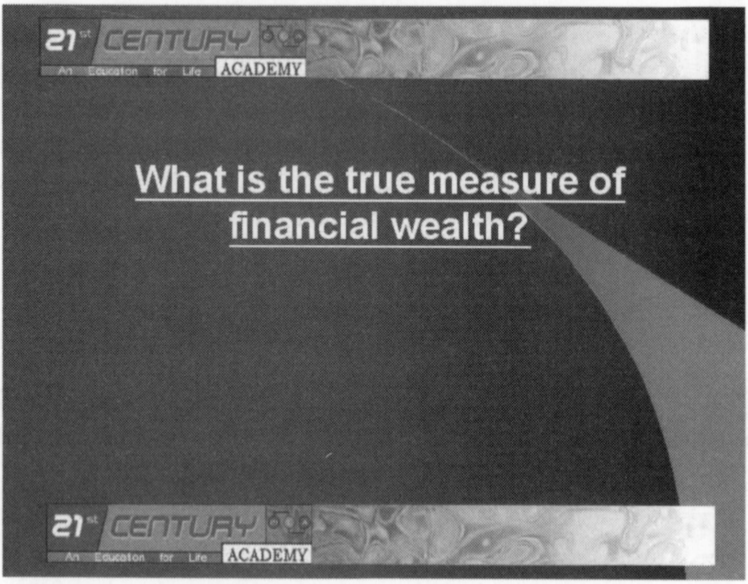
21st CENTURY ACADEMY
An Education for Life
What is the true measure of financial wealth?

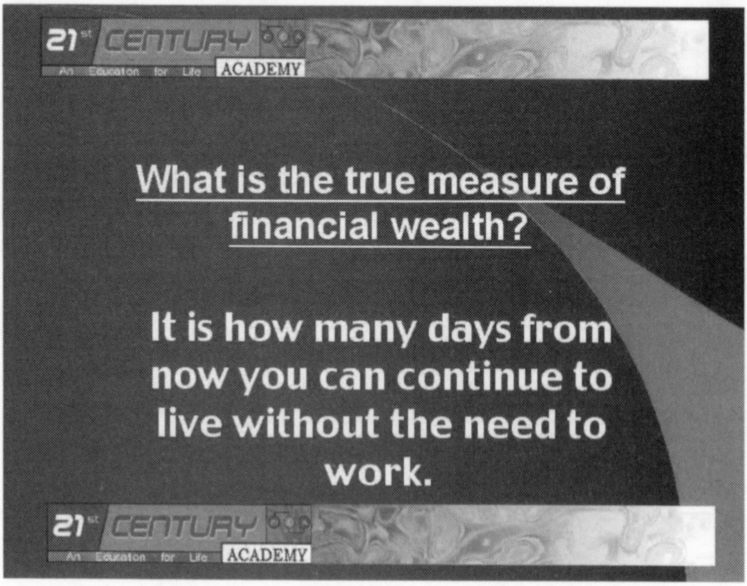
21st CENTURY ACADEMY
An Education for Life
What is the true measure of financial wealth?
It is how many days from now you can continue to live without the need to work.

WHEN ARE YOU FINANCIALLY SECURE, INDEPENDENT OR FREE?

How much will it take for you to be financially free? If you are like most people, you will have very little idea. The following exercise is designed to help you figure out how much it will take.

A How much will it take?

(Simply guess what it will take to be financially secure, independent or free — the first figure that comes to mind, for example, if I won $X million in lotto, I would........)

$ ____

B How long will it take?

(Once again just guess for now as we will figure it out shortly.)

$ ____

MAKING YOUR PERSONAL FINANCIAL DREAMS A REALITY

Everyone has the right to pursue his or her financial dreams. To turn those dreams into a reality, we must identify precisely what they are. The following are five levels of financial well-being that are possible to attain. Use this list to clarify what dreams are most important for you to achieve in your lifetime.

"Remember: Clarity equals Power!"

1 Financial Protection ______________________

2 Financial Security ______________________

3 Financial Independence ______________________

4 Financial Freedom ______________________

5 Absolute Financial Freedom ______________________

Now, let us define each of the goals with precision.

Let us start with defining what you want financially...

Give yourself 3 to 5 minutes to brainstorm what you want in each of these areas.

Goals	Short term 6–36 months	Intermediate 3–10 years	Long term 10+ years
Toys & rewards – things you want to own • House • Car • Art • Yacht • Jewels Things you want to give or experience (for yourself, your family or others) • Travel • Philanthropy • Buy a house for your parents or children Economic goals • Reduction of debt • Cash in hand • Net worth • Annual income from investments • New business profitability			

HOW TO PUT YOUR KIDS THROUGH COLLEGE STARTING WITH A $ 10,000* INVESTMENT

Interest Rate 10%   Tax Rate 28%   Inflation Rate 5%

End of Year	Principal $	Contribution 1997 Dollars $	Interest Earned $	Capital at End of Year $
1	10,000	600	720	11,320
2	11,230	630	815	12,765
3	12,765	662	919	14,346
4	14,346	695	1,033	16,073
5	16,073	729	1,157	19,760
6	17,960	766	1,293	20,019
7	20,019	804	1,441	22,264
8	22,264	844	1,603	24,711
9	24,711	886	1,779	27,377
10	27377	931	1,971	30,279
11	30,279	977	2,180	33,436
12	33,436	1,026	2,407	36,870
13	36,870	1,078	2,655	40,602
14	40,602	1,131	2,923	44,657
15	44,657	1,188	3,215	49,060
16	49,060	1,247	3,532	53,840
17	53,840	1,310	3,876	59,026
18	59,026	1,375	4,250	64,651

Total dollars available: $ 64,651

* Start saving with $10,000 and add an additional $600 per year, or just $50 per month, in 1997 dollars.

If you do not currently have children but plan to in the future, then you could start this plan 2–3 years before the birth of a child by putting aside $300 a month so that when your child is born, you already have the initial $10,000 to start the program.

If you already have children, then you have to start this plan with a larger initial investment of principal. For example, if you have a 6 year-old, you will need $17,960 to start the savings plan.

Education Timer

Your Child's age now	To accumulate these goals by your child's 15th birthday, you must set aside these monthly amounts*						
	$20,000	$40,000	$50,000	$75,000	$100,000	$125,000	$150,000
1	43.01	86.02	107.53	161.29	215.05	268.81	322.58
2	48.18	96.36	120.45	180.68	240.90	301.13	361.35
3	54.16	108.32	135.40	203.10	270.80	338.50	406.20
4	61.11	122.22	152.78	229.16	305.55	381.94	458.33
5	69.28	138.56	173.20	259.80	346.40	433.00	519.60
6	78.95	157.90	197.38	296.06	394.75	493.44	592.13
7	90.56	181.12	226.40	339.60	452.80	566.00	679.20
8	104.67	209.34	261.68	382.51	523.35	654.19	785.03
9	122.12	244.24	305.30	457.95	610.60	763.25	915.90
10	144.19	288.38	360.48	540.71	720.95	901.19	1,081.43
11	172.84	345.68	432.10	648.15	864.20	1,080.25	1,296.30
12	211.36	422.72	528.40	792.60	1,056.80	1,321.00	1,585.20
13	265.70	531.40	664.25	996.38	1,328.50	1,660.63	1,992.75
14	347.73	695.46	869.33	1,303.98	1,738.65	2,173.31	2,607.98
15	485.10	970.22	1,212.75	1,819.13	2,425.50	3,031.88	3,638.25

* Figures in table are based on a fixed 9% interest rate, compounded monthly. The table assumes no fluctuation in value of principal. Figures are not intended to be a projection of any investment results. No adjustment has been made for income taxes.

CUT YOUR MORTGAGE IN HALF!

Home owners, you can literally cut your mortgage term in half simply by making extra principal payments!

The next time you write your monthly mortgage cheque, write a second cheque for the "principal only" portion on next month's payment. This, by the way, is usually the smallest portion of the payment.

For most mortgages, the monthly payment is a constant number; in our example below, it is $1,000. Only a small portion of that $1,000 monthly payment normally goes towards paying off the actual principal of the mortgage itself. Remember, when the principal is paid off, the loan is paid off.

Example of a Typical Mortgage *

Month	Payment	Principal	Interest	Balance
Jan	1,000	40.00	960.00	98,172.85
Feb	1,000	40.39	959.61	98,132.45
Mar	1,000	40.79	959.21	98,091.66
Apr	1,000	41.10	958.81	98,050.47

In the example above, when you make the January payment, you can also write a second cheque for the "principal only" part of the following month's payment, in this case, $40.39 for the February payment. Then, you will not have to pay the interest on $40.39 when making the February payment. The following month, make the March payment for $1,000 and pay the "principal only" portion of the April payment for $41.10.

Continue to do this every month, and you will never have to pay interest on the principal that has been pre-paid. Consistently following this strategy will enable you to pay off a 30-year mortgage in 15 years.

This is a powerful strategy for saving a tremendous amount of money on your interest payments and cutting the term of your mortgage in half.

* If you do not have an amortisation schedule from your lender, get one!

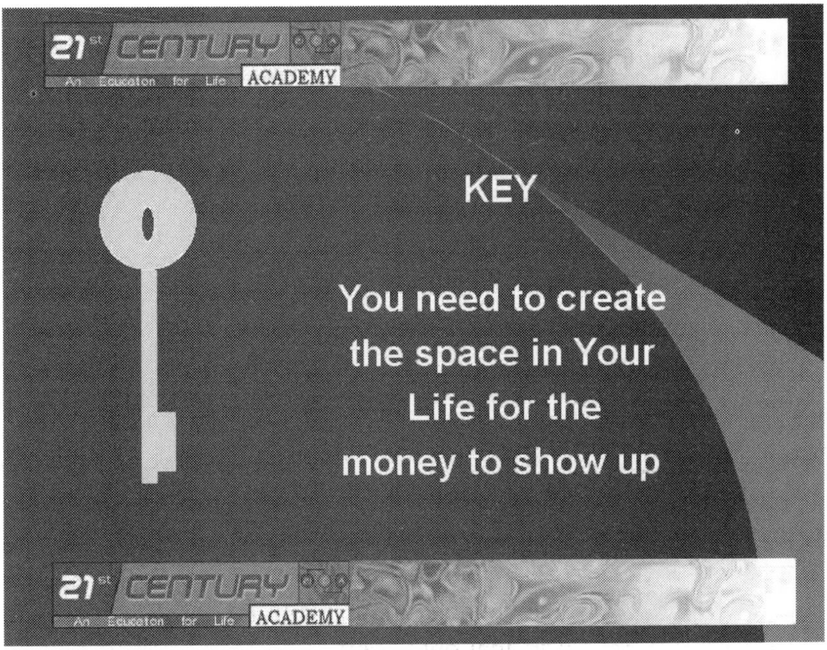
21st CENTURY
An Education for Life ACADEMY
KEY
You need to create the space in Your Life for the money to show up
21st CENTURY
An Education for Life ACADEMY

I. FINANCIAL PROTECTION

The precise amount of money you will require in liquid assets to be financially protected can be established simply by reviewing your current monthly overheads (i.e., the minimums). What does it take for you to keep things together? Listed below are the critical obligations that must be met to ensure that you and your family are financially protected.

Item	Current Cost Per Month
1. **Mortgage payment per month :**	**$** ________
2. Electricity, gas, etc, (average) per month:	+ $________
3. Transportation (average, including car insurance) per month:	+ $________
4. Food (average) per month:	+ $________
5. Insurance (disability, health, etc.) per month:	+ $________
6. Private superannuation plan per month:	+ $________
7. **Total monthly income necessary for protection:**	**+ $**________

MY GOALS

Does not include any credit card or debt repayments. These are the basics required to survive financially, for example, Bill and Mary calculate that they require $2,000 per month and decide to have six months set aside for their financial protection goal. You can choose six months more or less, but six months is the minimum suggested.

____

____

____

____

My financial protection goal is to save enough money to cover ___6___ (no.) months of basic overhead (line 7 x 6 months). TOTAL $ __________

(Bill and Mary chose six months of protection at $2,000 per month, that is, $12,000 required aside to complete their first level in their five step plan.)

II. FINANCIAL SECURITY

The amount of money you will need to achieve financial security is very simple to establish. Remember, this means determining how much you need to be independent of the basic necessities such as food, clothes, and transport, (Financial Protection Figure).

Financial security is achieved when your investments produce an income equal to your Financial Protection Figure, (basic necessities).

(1) Monthly income necessary to achieve Financial Protection = $2,000
x 12 Months = $24,000

MY GOAL

Bill and Mary's is $2,000 per month x 12 months = $24,000 total annual income required.

Your goal would be the monthly figure from the page before x 12 months to achieve the second level called financial security for you.

(1) Annual income needed from investment to create financial security for life = $ ____________________

III. FINANCIAL INDEPENDENCE

The amount of money you will need to achieve financial independence is very simple to establish. Remember, this means determining how much money you need to be independent of work. How much money do you now earn annually? To duplicate your current lifestyle, it is likely you will need to duplicate your present monthly annual income. *

Example:

If you earn $200,000 a year and invest $50,000, then the number you would actually need to be financially independent is $150,000.

Financial independence is achieved when your investments produce an income equal to your "work" income.

(1) Monthly income necessary to support your current lifestyle = $4,000
x 12 Months = $48,000

MY GOAL

Bill and Mary earn $48,000 gross and currently do not save, so the Financial Independence figure is $48,000.

(2) Annual income needed from investment to create financial independence for life for you is:

= $ ____________

* If you are saving or investing a substantial amount of your current income, then the amount of money you need to duplicate your actual current lifestyle not counting investments is less than your current or monthly/annual income. That is, if Bill and Mary are saving say $10,000 out of $48,000 salary, they would only need $38,000 per annum to be financially independent, as this is what they require to meet their current standard of living.

IV. FINANCIAL FREEDOM

This goal is attained when your investments provide enough income for you to live the lifestyle you desire for the rest of your life without ever having to work again. Simply ask yourself, "What annual income would I need to have the lifestyle I want?" The following steps are suggested:

In order to have financial freedom you would have not only your current monthly income, but enough income to also purchase "other things" you would like to have but can not currently afford. Remember that this is not your ultimate dream.

Establish how much these new desires would cost per month and record on line 1.

1. Calculate the additional monthly income needed to meet these desires. (Remember that this is not absolute financial freedom.)

Example:

Item	**Cost**	**Monthly Payment**
Second Home in the country	$350,000	$3,500
35-foot boat	$150,000	$1,500
BMW Z3	$80,000	$1,000
Total additional monthly income needed =		**$6,000**

2. Record on line 2 the total amount of monthly income you need for your current lifestyle, i.e., financial independence (Write in line 1)
3. Add lines 1 and 2 to arrive at your total monthly cost to achieve financial freedom.

Item	Monthly Payment $	Cost $
	Bill and Mary	**You**
1. Total additional monthly income needed:	$6,000	$ ________
2. Monthly amount already needed for financial independence:	+ $4,000	$ ________
3. Total monthly income necessary for financial freedom:	= $10,000	$ ________
	x 12 Months	x 12 Months
	= $120,000	=$ ________

Bill and Mary Line 1 – $6,000
2 – $4,000 ($48,000 pa for financial independence x 12 months)
3 – $10,000

Bill and Mary
= $10,000 per month x 12 = $120,000 $12,000
MY GOAL $ ________

V. ABSOLUTE FINANCIAL FREEDOM

You have achieved absolute financial freedom when your investment income provides you with the certainty that you can do whatever you want, as much as you want, whenever you want, wherever you want, with whomever you want, — without ever working again. Take a moment to establish what you would really need to be absolutely financially free by filling out this worksheet.

1. List all the things you would have if you were absolutely financially free. Specifically, review your financial freedom list.

A) Rewrite the things you would still keep if you were absolutely financially free.
For example, you have a 35-foot boat but now you want a yacht. If you want to keep the boat, then write it down. If not, then write down the cost of the yacht.

B) Now, add to your list all the new things you want that are not on your financial freedom list.

C) Establish how much each of these new desires would cost per month and record on line 1.

Example:

Item	**Cost**	**Monthly Payment**
Keep 2nd home in the country	$ 350,000	$ 3,500
Replace boat with yacht	$ 500,000	$ 5,000
Replace Mercedes with Lamborghini	$ 200,000	$ 2,000
Great Barrier Reef Island	$ 7,000,000	$13,000
New Helicopter	$ 171,595	$ 1,800

Total additional monthly income needed to be absolutely financially free = $25,350

2. Record on line 2 the total amount of monthly income you need for your current lifestyle, i.e., financial independence.

3. Add lines 1 and 2 to arrive at your total monthly cost to achieve absolute financial freedom. Multiply by 12 to find the yearly income you will need.

	Bill and Mary	**You**
1. Total additional monthly income needed:	$25,350	$________
2. Monthly amount already needed for financial independence:	+ $ 4,000	$________
3. Total monthly income necessary for absolute financial freedom:	= $29,350	$________
x 12 Months	=$352,200	$________

MY GOAL

ANNUAL INCOME needed to create financial freedom:	=$352,200	$________

Sample Payment Schedules

30 Year Fixed Mortgage

$	6%	7%	8%	9%	10%	11%	12%
100,000	600	665	734	805	878	952	1.029
250,000	1.499	1.663	1.834	2.012	2.194	2.381	2.572
500,000	2.998	3.327	3.669	4.023	4.3888	4.762	5.143
1,000,000	5.996	6.653	7.338	8.046	8.776	9.523	10.286
3,000,000	17.987	19.959	22.013	24.139	26.327	28.570	30.858

Monthly Car Payments

$	3 Year				4 Year				5 Year				6 Year			
	5%	6%	7%	8%	5%	6%	7%	8%	5%	6%	7%	8%	5%	6%	7%	8%
25000	749	760	772	783	576	587	599	610	472	483	495	507	403	414	426	438
50000	1496	1521	1544	1567	1151	1174	1197	1221	944	967	990	1014	805	829	852	877
75000	2248	2282	2316	2356	1727	1761	1796	1831	1415	1450	1485	1521	1208	1243	1279	1315
100000	2997	3042	3088	3134	2303	2349	2395	2441	1887	1933	1980	2028	1610	1657	1705	1753

Boat Loan Monthly

$	7 Year				10 Year				15 Year			
35' Boat	8%	9%	10%	11%	8%	9%	10%	11%	8%	9%	10%	11%
150000	2338	2413	2490	2568	1820	1900	1982	2066	1433	1521	1612	1705

1.

Which of your dreams is really important for you to turn into reality?

____

2.

By what age must you accomplish it? ______________

____

(This timeline may change when you discover what it will take to achieve it.)

3.

Write down the amount you guessed you would need to be financially secure. $______________

(Check back to the beginning of this exercise.)

4.

Write down the amount that is actually needed to be financially secure. Is this figure higher or lower than the one you wrote?

$ ______________

(Majority of people realise it is lower.)

5.

Where are you today? ______________

The Wealthy Are Scarce

Adjusted Gross income	Percentage of households
$0–$24,999	58.9% (about 2 in 3)

*59% of the US population makes less than $25,000 a year.

*Nearly 80% of the Australian population makes less than $52,000 per year.

$25,000–$ 49,999	27.1% (1 in 4)

*86% of the US population makes less than $50,000 a year.

$50,000–$99,999	11.7% (1 in 10)

*The top 12% of the nation makes $50,000–$100,000 a year.
This represents the top 1% for women.

$100,000–$ 199,999	1.6% (1 in 50)

*Only 1% of the nation makes $100,000+.

$200,000–$499,999	0.5% (1 in 200)

*This represents one half of 1% of the population.

$500,000–$999,999	0.1% (1 in 1,000)

*This represents one tenth of 1% of the population.

$1,000,000+	0.05% (1 in 2,000)

*This represents one twentieth of 1% of the population.

YOUR PERSONAL FINANCIAL DREAMS REALISED

Your Master Goals!

1. Financial Protection

You have accumulated enough liquid assets to cover your basic overhead for a minimum of six months. You have begun a superfund and now have disability insurance.

My goal is to accumulate enough money to cover six months of my economic needs of: $___________

Bill and Mary's was $12,000

2. Financial Security

You have accumulated a critical mass of capital, invested in a secure environment at a 10% rate of return that will cover the cost of your monthly mortgage payment, food, utilities, insurance and transportation.

The annual income I need to accumulate in order to be Financially Secure is: $___________

Bill and Mary's was $24,000

3. Financial Independence

You have accumulated a critical mass of capital, invested in a secure environment at a 10% return to provide enough income to maintain your current lifestyle adjusted for inflation without ever having to work again for the rest of your life. You work only because you choose to.

The annual income I need to accumulate to be Financially Independent is: $___________

Bill and Mary's was $48,000

4. Financial Freedom

Your investments now provide sufficient income that you can live the lifestyle you desire for the rest of your life without ever having to work again. You work only because you choose to!

The annual income I need to accumulate in order to be Financially Free is: $__________

Bill and Mary's was $120,000

5. Absolute Financial Freedom

Your investments provide a sufficient annual income that you are now certain you can do whatever you want, whenever you want, with whomever you want, as much as you want in a way that empowers you and others forever! You work only because you choose to!

The annual income I need to accumulate to be Absolutely Financially Free is: $__________

Bill and Mary's was $352,200

Wealth Bucket

Bill and Mary's example:

	Investment required Income per annum
5. Absolute Financial Freedom	$352,200
4. Financial Freedom	$120,000
3. Financial Independance	$48,000
2. Financial Security	$24,000

If you want a more conservative plan, say 5% return, then you would use $24,000 x 20 = $480,000, ie. (5 ÷ 100 = 20).

We are going to assume you are able to achieve a 10% rate of return on your investments; $24,000 x 10 = $240,000. This means Bill and Mary would require $240,000 to generate $24,000 per year without working to achieve financial security.

Wealth Bucket

Assuming 10% Rate of Return	Investment required Income per annum	Your Figures
5. Absolute Financial Freedom	$3.52 million	$_________
4. Financial Freedom	$1.2 million	$_________
3. Financial Independance	$480,000	$_________
2. Financial Security	$240,000	$_________
1. Financial Security Protection Lump Sum Figure	$12,000	$_________

Assuming 5% Rate of Return	Investment required Income per annum	Your Figures
5. Absolute Financial Freedom	$7.04 million	$_________
4. Financial Freedom	$2.4 million	$_________
3. Financial Independance	$960,000	$_________
2. Financial Security	$480,000	$_________
1. Financial Security Protection Lump Sum Figure	$12,000	$_________

To create an effective financial plan, you must determine how much "critical mass" you need in order to achieve your desired annual lifetime income.

"Critical Mass"	Annual Income at 10%	Monthly income at 10%
125,000	12,500	1,042
250,000	25,000	2,083
375,000	37,500	3,125
500,000	50,000	4,167
625,000	62,500	5,208
750,000	75,000	6,250
875,000	87,500	7,292
1,000,000	100,000	8,333
1,125,000	112,500	9,375
1,250,000	125,000	10,417
1,500,000	150,000	12,500
1,750,000	175,000	14,583
2,000,000	200,000	16,667
2,500,000	250,000	20,833
3,000,000	300,000	25,000
3,500,000	350,000	29,167
4,000,000	400,000	33,333
5,000,000	500,000	41,667
6,000,000	600,000	50,000
7,000,000	700,000	58,333
8,000,000	800,000	66,667
10,000,000	1,000,000	83,333
12,500,000	1,250,000	104,167
20,000,000	2,000,000	166,667
25,000,000	2,500,000	208,333
50,000,000	5,000,000	416,667
100,000,000	10,000,000	833,333

HOW YOU CAN PAY FOR YOUR CHILD'S EDUCATION AND MORE

$50 PER MONTH

$50 per month (beginning at your child's birth) **earning 15% annually** will be worth...

$55,212 by the time your child turns 19.

If **no more contributions** are made and the money continues **growing at 15%** (taxes excluded), it will be worth...

$4.8 million by age 50
$19.6 million by age 60
$79.1 million by age 70

$100 PER MONTH

$100 per month (beginning at your child's birth) **earning 15% annually** will be worth...

$110,424 by the time your child turns 19.

If **no more contributions** are made and the **money continues growing at 15%** (taxes excluded), it will be worth...

$9.6 million by age 50
$39.2 million by age 60
$158.2 million by age 70.

$50 per month is just $11.70 per week and only $1.70 per day!
$100 per month is just $23.30 per week and only $3.33 per day

HOW MUCH MONEY GOES THROUGH YOUR HANDS UNNOTICED EACH WEEK?

How Your Money Grows Annually

15% ANNUAL RETURN

$ per month	1 Year $	5 Years $	10 Years $	20 Years $	30 Years $	40 Years $	50 Years $
50	651	4,484	13,933	75,798	350,491	1,571,188	6,985,901
75	977	6,726	20,899	113,697	525,737	2,356,782	10,478,852
100	1,302	8,968	27,866	151,596	700,982	3,142,376	13,971,803
150	1,953	13,452	41,799	227,393	1,051,473	4,713,563	20,957,704
200	2,604	17,936	55,731	303,191	1,401,964	6,284,751	27,943,606
250	3,255	22,420	69,664	378,989	1,752,455	7,855,939	34,929,507
300	3,906	26,904	83,597	454,787	2,102,946	9,427,127	41,915,408
350	4,557	31,389	97,530	530,584	2,453,437	10,998,314	48,901,310
400	5,208	35,873	111,463	606,382	2,803,928	12,569,502	55,887,211
450	5,860	40,357	125,396	682,180	3,154,419	14,140,690	62,873,112
500	6,511	44,841	139,329	757,978	3,504,910	15,711,878	69,859,014
750	9,766	67,261	208,993	1,136,966	5,257,365	23,567,817	104,788,521
1,000	13,021	89,682	278,657	1,515,955	7,009,821	31,423,755	$139,718,028

20% ANNUAL RETURN

$ per month	1 Year $	5 Years $	10 Years $	20 Years $	30 Years $	40 Years $	50 Years $
50	669	5,173	19,118	158,074	1,168,040	8,508,731	61,862,747
75	1,004	7,759	28,677	237,112	1,752,060	12,763,097	92,794,121
100	1,228	10,345	38,236	316,148	2,336,080	17,017,463	123,725,495
150	2,007	15,518	57,355	474,222	3,504,120	25,526,194	185,588,242
200	2,677	20,691	76,473	632,296	4,672,160	34,034,926	247,450,990
250	3,346	25,864	95,591	790,370	5,840,200	42,543,657	309,313,737
300	4,015	31,036	114,709	948,444	7,008,241	51,052,388	371,176,485
350	4,684	36,209	133,827	1,106,518	8,176,281	59,561,120	433,039,232
400	5,353	41,382	152,945	1,264,592	9,344,321	68,069,851	494,901,980
450	6,022	46,554	172,064	1,422,666	10,512,361	76,578,582	556,764,727
500	6,691	51,727	191,182	1,580,740	11,680,401	85,087,314	618,627,475
750	10,037	77,591	286,773	2,371,110	17,520,601	127,630,971	927,941,212
1,000	13,383	103,454	382,364	3,161,479	23,360,802	170,174,628	1,237,254,950

25% ANNUAL RETURN

$ per month	1 Year $	5 Years $	10 Years $	20 Years $	30 Years $	40 Years $	50 Years $
50	698	5,992	26,640	342,955	4,098,736	48,693,244	578,189,014
75	1,032	8,988	39,960	514,432	6,248,104	73,039,866	867,283,522
100	1,376	11,984	53,280	685,909	8,197,472	97,386,488	1,156,378,029
150	2,063	17,977	79,921	1,028,864	12,296,207	146,079,731	1,734,567,043
200	2,751	23,969	106,561	1,371,819	16,394,943	194,772,975	2,312,756,058
250	3,439	29,961	133,201	1,714,774	20,493,679	243,466,219	2,890,945,072
300	4,127	35,953	159,841	2,057,728	24,592,415	292,159,463	3,469,134,087
350	4,815	41,946	186,482	2,400,683	28,691,150	340,852,707	4,047,323,101
400	5,502	47,938	213,122	2,743,638	32,789,886	389,545,995	4,625,512,116
450	6,190	53,930	239,762	3,086,592	36,888,622	438,239,194	5,203,701,130
500	6,878	59,922	266,402	3,429,547	40,987,358	486,932,438	5,781,890,145
750	10,317	89,883	399,603	5,144,321	61,481,036	730,398,657	8,672,835,217
1,000	13,756	119,844	532,805	6,859,094	81,974,715	973,864,876	11,563,780,289

How Your Money Grows Annually

15% ANNUAL RETURN

$ per month	1 Year $	5 Years $	10 Years $	20 Years $	30 Years $	40 Years $	50 Years $
1,500	19,532	134,522	417,986	2,273,932	10,514,731	47,105,533	209,577,042
2,000	26,042	179,363	557,315	3,031,909	14,019,641	62,807,511	279,436,055
2,500	32,553	224,204	696,643	3,789,886	17,524,552	78,509,389	349,295,069
5,000	65,106	448,408	1,393,286	7,579,772	35,049,103	157,018,777	698,590,139
10,000	130,211	896,816	2,786,573	15,159,544	70,098,206	314,037,555	1,397,180,277
20,000	260,422	1,793,632	5,573,146	30,319,099	140,196,412	628,075,105	2,794,360,554

20% ANNUAL RETURN

$ per month	1 Year $	5 Years $	10 Years $	20 Years $	30 Years $	40 Years $	50 Years $
1,500	20,074	155,181	573,545	4,742,219	35,041,203	255,261,941	1,855,882,425
2,000	26,766	206,908	764,727	6,322,959	46,721,604	340,349,255	2,474,509,900
2,500	33,457	258,635	955,909	7,903,698	58,402,004	425,436,569	3,093,137,374
5,000	66,914	517,271	1,911,818	15,807,397	116,804,009	850,873,138	6,186,274,749
10,000	133,829	1,043,542	3,823,636	31,614,794	233,608,018	1,701,746,275	12,372,549,498
20,000	267,657	2,069,084	7,647,271	63,229,587	467,216,035	3,403,492,551	24,745,098,995

25% ANNUAL RETURN

$ per month	1 Year $	5 Years $	10 Years $	20 Years $	30 Years $	40 Years $	50 Years $
1,500	20,634	179,767	799,207	10,288,643	122,962,072	1,460,797,314	17,345,670,434
2,000	27,512	239,689	1,065,609	13,718,190	163,949,430	1,947,729,751	23,127,560,579
2,500	34,390	299,611	1,332,012	17,147,738	204,936,787	2,434,662,189	28,909,450,723
5,000	68,779	599,222	2,664,023	34,295,478	409,873,575	4,869,324,379	57,818,901,446
10,000	137,558	1,198,444	5,328,047	68,590,952	819,747,149	9,738,648,757	115,637,802,893
20,000	275,117	2,396,888	10,656,093	137,181,905	1,639,494,299	19,477,297,514	231,275,605,785

Remember! No Investment is without risk! We do not guarantee any specific results or returns.

THE EFFECTS OF COMPOUND INTEREST

This table shows the incredible power of compound interest over time. It also shows the dramatic effect of letting interest compound WITHOUT TAXES BEING TAKEN OUT. All the example investors enjoy the advantage of tax-deferred compounding, but the table also shows how much difference it makes to start your tax-deferred investing early in life.

	INVESTOR A		INVESTOR B		INVESTOR C		INVESTOR D		INVESTOR E	
Age	Contribution	Year-End Value	Contribution	Year-End Value	Contribution	Year-End Value	Contribution	Year-End Value	Contribution	Year-End Value
8	0	0	0	0	0	0	500	550	500	550
9	0	0	0	0	0	0	750	1,430	750	1,430
10	0	0	0	0	0	0	1,000	2,673	1,000	2,673
11	0	0	0	0	0	0	1,250	4,315	1,250	4,315
12	0	0	0	0	0	0	1,500	6,397	1,500	6,397
13	0	0	0	0	0	0	1,750	8,962	1,750	8,962
14	0	0	0	0	2,000	2,200	0	9,858	2,000	12,058
15	0	0	0	0	2,000	4,620	0	10,843	2,000	15,463
16	0	0	0	0	2,000	7,282	0	11,928	2,000	19,210
17	0	0	0	0	2,000	10,210	0	13,121	2,000	23,331
18	0	0	0	0	2,000	13,431	0	14,433	2,000	27,864
19	0	0	2,000	2,200	0	14,774	0	15,876	2,000	32,850
20	0	0	2,000	4,620	0	16,252	0	17,463	2,000	38,335
21	0	0	2,000	7,282	0	17,877	0	19,210	2,000	44,369
22	0	0	2,000	10,210	0	19,665	0	21,131	2,000	51,006
23	0	0	2,000	13,431	0	21,631	0	23,244	2,000	58,306
24	0	0	2,000	16,974	0	23,794	0	25,568	2,000	66,337
25	0	0	2,000	20,872	0	26,174	0	28,125	2,000	75,170
26	2,000	2,200	0	22,959	0	28,791	0	30,938	2,000	84,888
27	2,000	4,620	0	25,255	0	31,670	0	34,031	2,000	95,576
28	2,000	7,282	0	27,780	0	34,837	0	37,434	2,000	107,334
29	2,000	10,210	0	30,558	0	38,321	0	41,178	2,000	120,267
30	2,000	13,431	0	33,614	0	42,153	0	45,296	2,000	134,494
31	2,000	16,794	0	36,976	0	46,368	0	49,825	2,000	150,143
32	2,000	20,872	0	40,673	0	51,005	0	54,808	2,000	167,358
33	2,000	25,159	0	44,741	0	56,106	0	60,289	2,000	186,294
34	2,000	29,875	0	49,215	0	61,716	0	66,317	2,000	207,123
35	2,000	35,062	0	54,136	0	67,888	0	72,949	2,000	230,035
36	2,000	40,769	0	59,550	0	74,676	0	80,244	2,000	255,239
37	2,000	47,045	0	65,505	0	82,144	0	88,269	2,000	282,963
38	2,000	53,950	0	72,055	0	90,359	0	97,095	2,000	313,459
39	2,000	61,545	0	79,261	0	99,394	0	106,805	2,000	347,005
40	2,000	69,899	0	87,187	0	109,334	0	117,485	2,000	383,905
41	2,000	79,089	0	95,905	0	120,267	0	129,234	2,000	424,496
42	2,000	89,198	0	105,496	0	132,294	0	142,157	2,000	469,145
43	2,000	100,318	0	116,045	0	145,523	0	156,373	2,000	518,260
44	2,000	112,550	0	127,650	0	160,076	0	172,010	2,000	572,286
45	2,000	126,005	0	140,415	0	176,083	0	189,211	2,000	631,714
46	2,000	140,805	0	154,456	0	193,692	0	208,133	2,000	697,086
47	2,000	157,086	0	169,902	0	213,061	0	228,946	2,000	768,995
48	2,000	174,995	0	186,892	0	234,367	0	251,840	2,000	848,094
49	2,000	194,694	0	205,581	0	257,803	0	277,024	2,000	935,103
50	2,000	216,364	0	226,140	0	283,584	0	304,727	2,000	1,030,814
51	2,000	240,200	0	248,754	0	311,942	0	335,200	2,000	1,136,095
52	2,000	266,420	0	273,629	0	343,136	0	368,719	2,000	1,251,905
53	2,000	295,262	0	300,992	0	377,450	0	405,591	2,000	1,379,295
54	2,000	326,988	0	331,091	0	415,195	0	446,151	2,000	1,519,425
55	2,000	361,887	0	364,200	0	456,715	0	490,766	2,000	1,673,567
56	2,000	400,276	0	400,620	0	502,386	0	539,842	2,000	1,843,124
57	2,000	442,503	0	440,682	0	552,625	0	593,826	2,000	2,029,636
58	2,000	488,953	0	484,750	0	607,887	0	653,209	2,000	2,234,800
59	2,000	540,049	0	533,225	0	668,676	0	718,530	2,000	2,460,480
60	2,000	596,254	0	586,548	0	735,543	0	790,383	2,000	2,708,728
61	2,000	658,079	0	645,203	0	809,098	0	869,421	2,000	2,981,800
62	2,000	726,087	0	709,723	0	890,007	0	956,363	2,000	3,282,180
63	2,000	800,896	0	780,695	0	979,008	0	1,052,000	2,000	3,612,598
64	2,000	883,185	0	858,765	0	1,076,909	0	1,157,200	2,000	3,976,058
65	2,000	973,704	0	944,641	0	1,184,600	0	1,272,920	2,000	4,375,864
Less Total Invested:		(80,000)		(14,000)		(10,000)		(6,750)		(110,750)
Equals Net Earnings:		893,704		930,641		1,174,600		1,266,170		4,265,114
Money Grew:		11-Fold		66-Fold		117-Fold		118-Fold		38-Fold

HOT DOG PARABLE

There once was a man who lived by the side of the road and sold hot dogs. In fact, he sold very good hot dogs.

He put up highway signs telling people how good his hot dogs tasted. He stood by the side of the road and called out, "Buy a hot dog, mister?"

And people bought his hot dogs. They bought so many hot dogs, the man increased his meat and bun orders.

He bought a bigger stove so he could meet his customers' demands. And finally, he brought his son home from college to help out in the family business.

But something happened. His son said, "Father, do you not watch television, or read the newspapers? Do you not know we are heading for a recession? The European situation is unstable, and the domestic economy is getting worse."

And the father thought, "My son is a smart boy. He has been to college. He ought to know what he is talking about."

So the man cut down his meat and bun orders, took down his highway signs, and no longer stood by the side of the road to sell his hot dogs.

His sales fell almost overnight. "You are right son," said the father. "We certainly are in a serious recession."

The Benefit of Cutting Expenses

This can save you years of critical mass accumulation! (@ 8% return)

Amount of Expenses Cut from Monthly Budget $	=	A Savings of Critical Mass $
100		15,000
200		30,000
300		45,000
400		60,000
500		75,000
600		90,000
700		105,000
800		120,000
900		135,000
1,000		150,000
1,100		165,000
1,200		180,000
1,300		195,000
1,400		210,000
1,500		225,000
1,600		240,000
1,700		255,000
1,800		270,000
1,900		285,000
2,000		300,000
2,500		375,000
3,000		450,000
3,500		525,000
4,000		600,000
4,500		675,000
5,000		750,000
5,500		825,000
6,000		900,000
6,500		975,000
7,000		1,050,000

A GRAIN OF RICE

The daughter of the Chinese Emperor was ill, and he promised riches beyond compare to whoever could cure her. A young peasant named Pong Lo entered the palace. With his wit and bravery he restored the Princess's health, and won her heart. As his reward, Pong Lo asked for her hand in marriage. The Emperor refused and asked the peasant to think of anything else he would like.

After several moments of thought, Pong Lo said, "I would like a grain of rice".

"A grain of rice! That is nonsense! Ask me for fine silks, the grandest room in the palace, a stable full of wild stallions — they shall be yours!"

"A grain of rice will do," said Pong Lo. "But if His Majesty insists, he may double the amount every day for a hundred days."

So on the first day a grain of rice was delivered to Pong Lo. On the second day, two grains of rice were delivered. On the third day Pong Lo received four grains, and on the fourth day, eight grains.

On the fifth day – 16 grains
On the sixth day – 32 grains
On the seventh day – 64 grains
On the eighth day – 128 grains

By the twelfth day the grains of rice numbered 2,048. By the twentieth day, 524,288 grains were delivered. And by the thirtieth day 536,870,912 grains — requiring 40 servants to carry them — were brought to Pong Lo.

In desperation the Emperor did the only honourable thing he could do and consented to the marriage. Out of consideration for the Emperor's feelings, no rice was served at the wedding banquet.

CHAPTER 11

DEBT REDUCTION AND CASHFLOW MANAGEMENT

DEBT REDUCTION STRATEGY

Bad debt is often like a ball and chain around your ankle which can drag you down. This chapter is designed to solve the debt problem. Remember, there is a difference between good debt and bad debt.

Bad debt is something that you borrow to purchase, that goes down in value and generally is not tax deductible, that is a car, holiday and clothes.

A good debt is something you borrow for that goes up in value and ideally is a tax deductible debt, that is a quality property or share portfolio.

This chapter is designed to eliminate bad debt, especially if it is out of control.

If you are in an uncontrollable amount of debt, you can use the following strategy. These days though it may be better to use debt agreement companies to arrange your affairs.

The following is a sample letter you could use as a guide in drafting your own letter.

Dear ______________________

As you know, I am in debt to you for $_________, and I intend to pay you in full, plus interest. In order to achieve this goal, I have been devising a plan during the past few days to put myself in a stable financial position. To this end, I have opened a "Debt Clearance Account" and twenty percent of my income is going directly into that account. That will enable me to have sufficient resources to live on, without worry or stress, and it will prevent me from falling further into debt.

Each week (or month) you will receive a cheque for $_______ from my "DCA", until my account with you is clear. I am aware that this is not the figure I had previously agreed to pay you, but I am sure you will be understanding and appreciate what I am doing.

If you have any questions, please feel free to contact me. I am quite excited about my new plans, and if you would like to have me review them with you so that you might help others who are in your debt, I would be pleased to do so.

Thank you in advance for your kind co-operation.

Have a wonderful day!

Sincerely

John Doe

Understand that your letter to your creditor is a statement of fact and not a request — it is you who are in charge of your finances, not your creditors!

Be sure to have your letters neatly typed and enclose your first new payment with your covering letter. Realise there is an "outside chance" that some unreasonable person will not want to co-operate with you. They might even go so far as to phone you, and attempt to intimidate you, with threats of taking you to court, etc. But please hold your ground because there is no court in the country that would not congratulate you, when you explained your entire plan for Financial Independence. Moreover, you will find that 95% of the people whom you write to will be most co-operative.

Now give yourself a good "pat on the back" because as of this moment, you are well on your way to starting a completely new way of life!

This graph can come in handy as a guide to eliminate debts.

Debt-Elimination Time Calculator

Total Monthly Payment Amount Over Time

Total Debt Amount ($)	1 Yr	2 Yrs	3 Yrs	4 Yrs	5 Yrs	6 Yrs	7 Yrs
1,000.00	88	46	32	25	21	19	17
3,000.00	264	138	97	76	64	56	50
5,000.00	440	231	161	127	106	93	83
7,000.00	615	323	226	178	149	130	116
10,000.00	879	461	323	254	212	185	166
15,000.00	1,319	692	484	380	319	278	249
20,000.00	1,758	923	645	507	425	371	332
30,000.00	2,637	1,384	968	761	637	556	498
40,000.00	3,517	1,846	1,291	1,015	850	741	664
50,000.00	4,395	2,307	1,603	1,268	1,062	926	830
75,000.00	6,591	3,461	2,470	1,902	1,594	1,389	1,245
100,000.00	8,792	4,614	3,267	2,536	2,125	1,853	1,660
125,000.00	10,989	5,768	4,023	3,170	2,656	2,316	2,075
150,000.00	13,187	6,922	4,830	3,804	3,187	2,779	2,490
200,000.00	17,583	9,229	6,453	5,073	4,249	3,705	3,320
250,000.00	21,979	11,536	8,067	6,341	5,312	4,631	4,150
300,000.00	26,375	13,843	9,680	7,609	6,374	5,558	4,980

Wealth-Building/Retirement Calculator

Monthly Investment Amount ($)	After 5 Yrs	Monthly Income	After 10 Yrs	Monthly Income	After 15 Yrs	Monthly Income
500.00	39,041	312	103,276	826	208,962	1,672
1,000.00	78,082	625	206,552	1,652	417,924	3,343
2,000.00	156,165	1,249	413,104	3,305	835,849	6,687
3,000.00	234,247	1,874	619,656	4,957	1,253,772	10,303
5,000.00	390,412	3,123	1,032,760	8,262	2,089,621	16,717
7,500.00	585,618	4,685	1,549,140	12,393	3,134,431	25,075

Example: If you invest $7,500 each month for 15 years, you will have $3,134,431 in total principal and you will be able to retire at an income of $25,075 per month for the rest of your life without putting another cent in. Based on an average 10% Return on Investment.

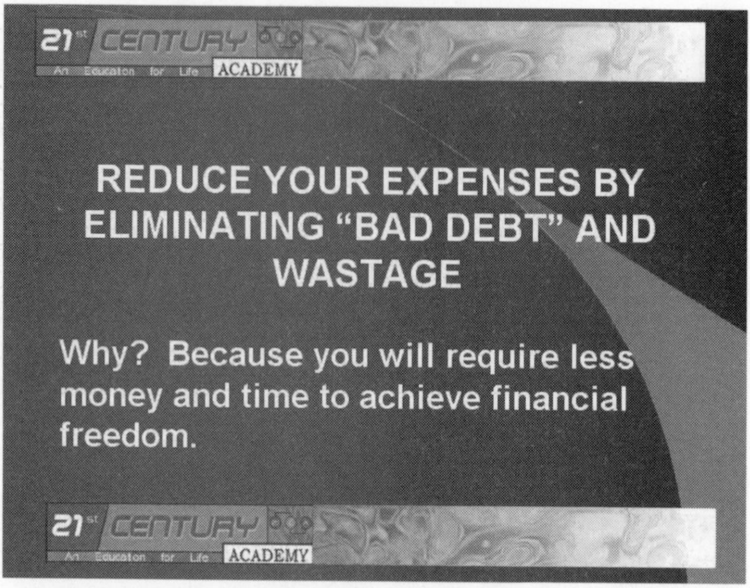
REDUCE YOUR EXPENSES BY ELIMINATING "BAD DEBT" AND WASTAGE
Why? Because you will require less money and time to achieve financial freedom.

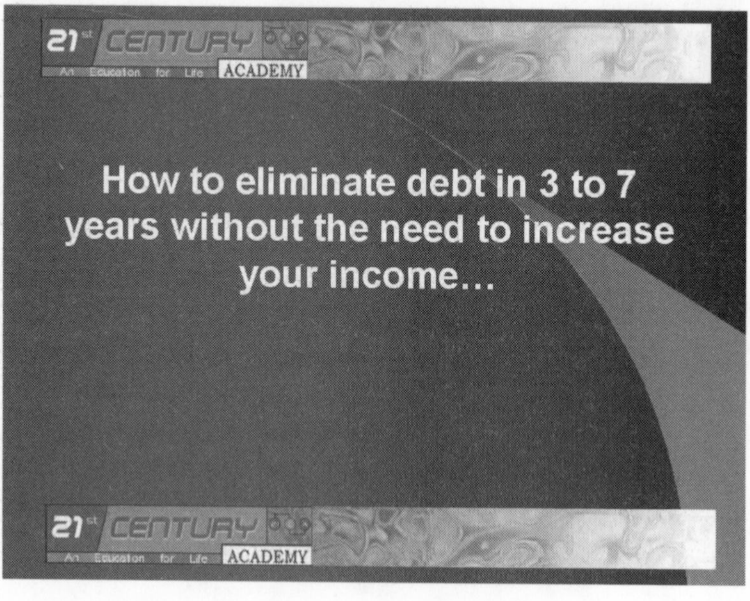
How to eliminate debt in 3 to 7 years without the need to increase your income…

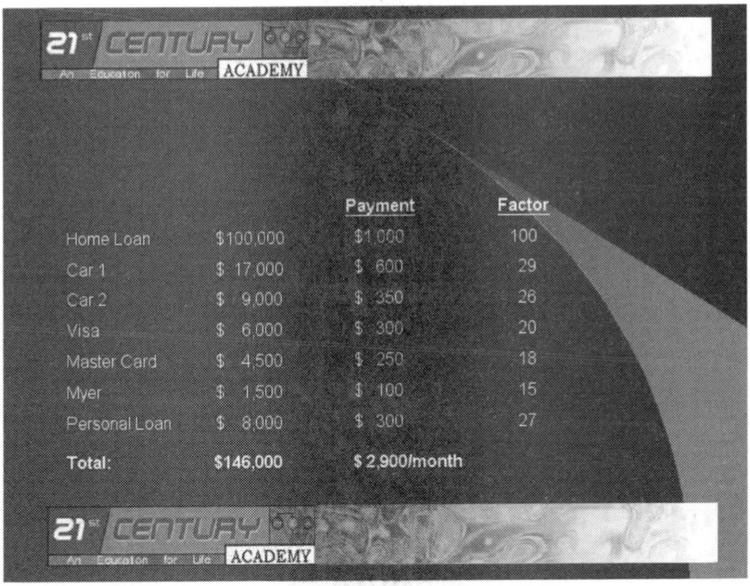
Payment
Factor
Home Loan $100,000 $1,000 100
Car 1 $ 17,000 $ 600 29
Car 2 $ 9,000 $ 350 26
Visa $ 6,000 $ 300 20
Master Card $ 4,500 $ 250 18
Myer $ 1,500 $ 100 15
Personal Loan $ 8,000 $ 300 27
Total: $146,000 $ 2,900/month

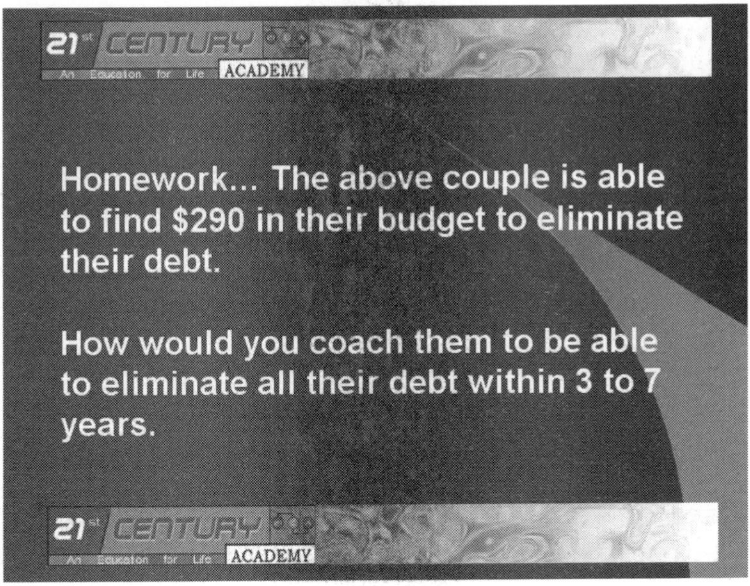
Homework... The above couple is able to find $290 in their budget to eliminate their debt.
How would you coach them to be able to eliminate all their debt within 3 to 7 years.

Firstly, you need to consider the 'factor' column. This column represents how many payments are remaining, that is a Personal Loan of $8,000 at $300 per month will take about 27 payments. We are going to look at the lowest factor, which is the Myer Card of $1,500 at $100 payment with a factor of 15 as it is the lowest. We want to pay this off first as it is the quickest to pay off. Therefore, we take the $290 spare we have and add it to the $100 per month payment already being paid towards the Myer card, which equals a total of $390. Divide this into the $1,500 balance on the Myer card balance which equals approximately 4 more monthly payments and the $1,500 is completely paid off.

Then we go to the next lowest factor, that is Mastercard $4,500 with a $250 payment. We now add the $390 we were paying off the Myer card as it is now spare. We can now pay $250 + $390 = $640 per month of the $4,500 on Myer card = 7 months. 4 months + 7 months = 11 months since we started the debt elimination strategy and already Bill and Mary can see significant progress.

Now we look at the next lowest factor which is Visa at $6,000 at $300 per month and we repeat the cycle. $300 plus $640, now spare = $940 total into $6,000 balance on Visa = 6 months approximately to pay off. 6 + 11 = 17 months for Visa, Mastercard and Myer card to be all paid off.

The next lowest factor is Car 2 with a balance of $9,000 at $350 per month. $350 and $940 spare = $1,290 total into $9,000 = approximately 7 months. 7 months plus 17 months = 24 months or 2 years into the debt elimination plan.

In reality, it would be sooner as the $9,000 would already have reduced to less due to payments made in the first 17 months, therefore our plan is conservative.

The next lowest factor is the Personal Loan of $8,000 at $300 per month. $300 + $1,290 is now spare = $1,590 total into $8,000 = 5 months approximately. 5 months + 24 months = 29 months in total so far.

The next lowest factor is Car 1 of $17,000 + $600 per month. $600 + $1,590 is now spare = $2,190 per month into $17,000 = 8 months approximately. 8 months + 29 months = 37 months so far.

The last one is the Home loan of $100,000 at $1,000 per month. $1,000 per month + $2,190 now spare = $3,190 into $100,000 is 31 months approximately. 31 Months + 37 months = 68 months or 5 to 6 years.

This strategy is often far more effective than consolidation of loans as many people consolidate, but they run up their credit cards again which defeats the purpose as they get in more debt. Remember, getting into debt is a habit. It is the habit that has to change and consolidation loans do not guarantee a habit change.

There are numerous ways to eliminate this debt in 3 to 7 years. I have covered just one way which is effective.

YOUR WEALTH CREATION SYSTEM

Wealth creation is probably the most important aspect of financial planning. It is through this strategy that we can become financially independent, yet it is an area in which very few people are skilled or familiar with.

The foundation of our system is strategic spending. Most of us know how much we earn each year, but have no idea what we spend the money on. Like every successful business, we need to constantly monitor income and expenditure while also ensuring that we are making a profit, in other words, saving some money.

We have created a strategic spending system which has worked successfully for our clients for many years now. The idea of strategic spending is to divide your hard earned income up into small, easily controlled bundles. The first bundle taken out should be savings — a minimum 10% of your gross pay, which is transferred monthly into your Cash Management Trust Account. If you leave savings to what is left over, you will always find that there is nothing left.

The second bundle is your Cash Account/s. This is your daily living expenses for which you normally pay cash, a bit like your pocket money. These are all non deductible items. This account/s is simply accessed by a 24 hour access keycard.

The third bundle is your Operations Account. This is for those larger amounts which are usually paid monthly, quarterly or yearly by cheque. This account should not be linked to the Cash Account/s (that is, you can not access it with your Cash Account keycard). We keep the bundles separate. It is wise to use this account in conjunction with a credit card for those occasions when your monthly expenses are higher than the budgeted amount. The card acts as a "smoother" as next month will be a surplus that can be paid back into the credit card.

In addition to your savings which go into your Cash Management Trust Account, you should also put in enough funds to cover all your tax deductible expenses. This will save time and effort for your accountant when preparing tax returns.

The system is linked by the use of the Transfer Account, into which your pay is banked. From there, periodic payments are set up to transfer funds to all the accounts on the 15th of each month. You should maintain a small float in the Cash Account and Operations Account. The main aim is to accumulate as much as possible in the Cash Management Trust Account and to use these funds wisely to create wealth.

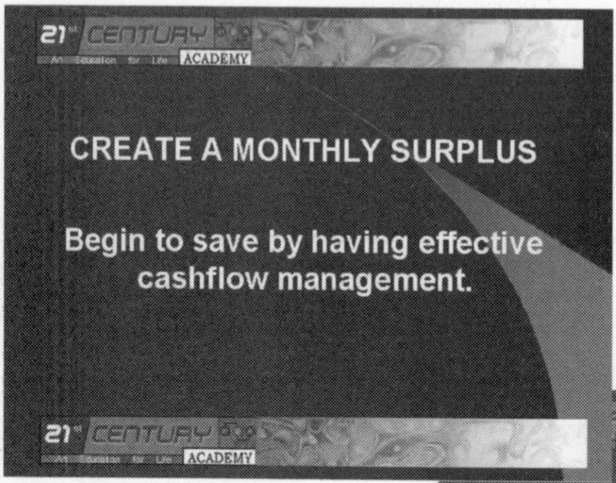

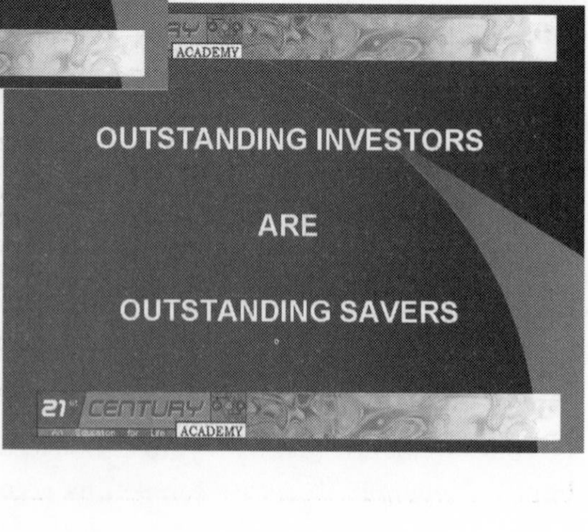

Client ______________________ **Date** ______________

Business Name ______________________

INVESTMENT PORTFOLIO

Tax Deductable Items
- Accounting fees
- Financial Success Fees
- Negative Gearing
- Disability Insurance

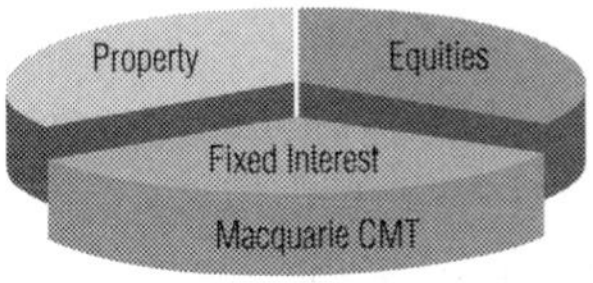

Unearned Income
- Tax Refunds
- Interest/Dividends
- Trust Income
- Social Security
- Rent
- Other

10% Saving at CMT

Bank ________
BSB ________
ACCT ________
Name ________

TRANSFER ACCOUNT
Net Income per Month $________

Earned Income
- Wages
- Commission
- Bonuses
- Tips/Gratuities
- Other

Bank ________
BSB ________
ACCT ________
Name ________
No 1

Bank ________
BSB ________
ACCT ________
Name ________
No 2

Key Cards

Not Linked

No 3
Bank ________
BSB ________
ACCT ________
Name ________

Cheque Account

Cash Accounts No 1 and No 2

Monthly Living Expenses	Client 1	Client 2
Food	____	____
Beverages	____	____
Dining Out	____	____
Clothes	____	____
Hair/Personal Care	____	____
Gifts	____	____
Fares	____	____
Other	____	____
Total A	$____	$____

Operations Account No 3

Housing		Transport		Miscellaneous	
Rent/Morgage	____	Car Payments	____	Installments	____
Maintenance	____	Insurance	____	Credit Cards	____
Rates	____	Petrol	____	Education	____
Insurance	____	Maintenance	____	Medical	____
Electricity	____	Registration	____	Dental	____
Telephone	____	Other	____	Contributions	____
Gas	____	Insurance	____	Holidays	____
		Life	____	Other	____
		Health	____	Other	____

Total B $ ______________

Total A & B $ ______________

To give you an idea of how you currently manage money, tick which box applies to you from each column.

The Poor Money Manager

- ❑ spends all their pay immediately
- ❑ must have it now, no matter how it hurts or how much credit they must use
- ❑ has no goals or plans other than to be rich and famous – 'one day'
- ❑ follows the crowd and their friends
- ❑ mixes with people who have similar money problems
- ❑ believes they don't need advice
- ❑ has no interest in gaining financial knowledge
- ❑ spends on items which lose value, eg. cars, stereos, etc

_________ **Total**

The Good Money Manager

- ❑ saves minimum of 10% out of every pay
- ❑ minimises borrowing for items which depreciate in value
- ❑ has definate goals, eg. 6–12 months, 5, 10 and 20 years
- ❑ has a plan that they actually implement
- ❑ mixes with people who are successful money managers
- ❑ knows that strategic spending is a must
- ❑ seeks professional advice and has a wealth coach
- ❑ is keen to learn new things and ideas about managing money
- ❑ invests in items which gain in value by quality

_________ **Total**

CHAPTER 12

8 STEPS TO START YOU ON THE PATH TO BECOMING A MILLIONAIRE

To begin this exercise, let us use Bill and Mary as our example. Let us assume Bill and Mary are an average couple. Collectively they earn $48,000 gross per year, both are working full time. Bill and Mary are typical Australians in the sense that they have a very poor savings record, they tend to spend more money than they earn and they are heading nowhere fast financially. However, what we want to see with the right coaching, commitment and action is how Bill and Mary could, in a very short period of time, replace the income they earn by working with money coming in while they sleep. In other words, with money coming in from their investments they could be setting themselves up financially and eliminating any bad debts without a large amount of hard work, just by commitment, focus, working smart and knowing the right strategies to use.

First of all what we are going to look at is where can an average couple look at investing.

1. THE BANK

First of all they could put their money in the bank, in other words cash. All that the majority of people know about investing is putting their money in the bank because you know "which bank" came around to your school when you were at a young age to teach you to put money in the bank. Obviously, saving is a good habit but just putting money in the bank usually only makes the banks richer. If you put your money in the bank at the moment, the cash interest rates may be 2%, 3%, 4%, 5% or even 6% if you are very lucky, so it is going to take a lot of money to become wealthy. That is why many people think they need to win lotto because if they have a million dollars from lotto and they got 5% or 6% on it, then they get their $50,000–$60,000 per year to replace their income.

Other than that, where can people put their money?

THE SHARE MARKET

We can look at putting money into the share market, however the share market for many people would be considered highly risky. Therefore, a lot of people do not put their money directly in the share market. Instead, they often seek the advice of a financial planner and because financial planners tend to earn large commissions on selling managed funds and super funds, they tend to get people to put their money into a managed fund. Hence, people let someone else invest their money, which sounds smart in many ways. They do not have to worry about it but the obvious question if you want to be financially independent, is who is going to look after your money better, you or someone else. Many of these financial planners are not wealthy individuals themselves. They are right down the pay ladder, even in the banking structure, and they are often just selling products with little or no training in financial success. Many are not successful investors so it is sort of like the blind leading the blind. I did not become wealthy as a self-made millionaire by going and sitting down in front of a financial planner. Actually, I would not have become a millionaire by following their advice. Why would I do that if they are not successful investors themselves? The obvious question my millionaire mentor told me to always ask of a financial planner is, if they could help me to become financially independent and live my ideal lifestyle, then why are they not doing it themselves. Mmm, something to think about, he told me. It was a very valuable lesson.

What you want to look for in learning financial success is to learn from people who have produced results, not people who just have a licence to advise on money, because anyone can get a licence to advise on money without the need to even be an investor themselves. With the Paul Clitheroe types, they always promote seeing a financial planner because they have their own agenda to grow their own financial planning businesses. The question always remains, are they really money experts or simply glorified financial planners selling commissioned products? I think the only way to determine that is to see the results of the people that you are taking notice of. As my millionaire mentor always said, the truth is in the results and unfortunately the majority of financial planners are not millionaires, let alone financially independent or even affluent. (The few that are, have generally become millionaires by growing their financial planning businesses and selling them for a small fortune, as they are highly profitable from all the commissions they earn. This is regardless of whether their clients make money or not. For instance, Paul Clitheroe made over $20 million from the sale of his share of his financial planning business). If you find one that is, listen to them, otherwise do not blindly take advice from them or anyone. This is why financial educators that are actually wealthy from investing are in such high demand as they can teach from real life experience, and their courses are swamped by people wanting to learn how to do it themselves as opposed to relying on financial planners for risky commission driven advice. I decided to educate myself so I knew how to become wealthy myself, so that I was not at the mercy of taking other peoples advice, as they often have their own agenda behind the advice. I have never seen a financial planner in order to become a millionaire, and never will need to, to remain a millionaire. Actually, I am yet to meet a single person that has become wealthy as a result of a licenced financial planner. I, and all my millionaire friends (many who did it in our 20s and 30s), achieved millionaire status by investing into seminars to learn of sucessful investors and entrepreneurs, and/or working with wealthy mentors. We did not hesitate in investing thousands into courses to become wealthy as compared to a university degree or the alternative of not knowing how to do it, this was by far the cheapest option. I suggest being wary of some financial planners as many are not wealthy investors themselves and even journalists that write money type books or magazines that are not investors, as often all they can teach is theory. If you are like me and are prepared to invest into your education, then select seminars and homestudy courses presented by people you feel you can learn from and simlpy ensure their courses offer a 100% money back guarantee. That way, if it is not as good as promised, or just not suitable for you, then you can get your money back. In other words risk free education. You are welcome to email, customerservice@21stcenturyacademy for courses in the wealth education industry that are worthwhile attending.

PROPERTY

Another place where people can invest their money is in property. Property is very popular, mainly because everyone lives in a property either as a tenant or at some stage buys a house. When the $14,000 grant was made available in 2001, many people bought their first property instead of renting as a result. Once again, many people that start investing in property fail to buy more than one or two investment properties. They usually use the typical negative gearing scenario where they buy some properties but because they do not like any debt whatsoever, they work even harder now to pay off the properties and hopefully retire off the rent. But what they do not realise when they pay off the property is that even though they are becoming wealthier they have to work harder to do it, and it is a fifteen to twenty year plan before they can retire and then live off the rent. They then have to share that rent with "guess who?", the tax man as it is classified as income. So they are going to have to work hard over a very long period of time in order to gain enough properties to be able to live off the rent. That is not what we call working smart, it is certainly called working hard. It is possible but there is a faster, easier way. We will be looking at strategies that are much faster and much more effective than that and allow you to retire in a much shorter period of time. Rather than a 15 to 20 year plan, we are going to look at a 3 to 10 year plan and less for some people. The same thing we will look at in chapter 13 is how you can do that in a much shorter period of time and often with much less risk. Sounds exciting and it is. Remember what my millionaire mentor always told me. Life is too important to simply work for money. You want to enjoy life more by having money work for you.

The only other area people can really invest in, other than collectables, antiques, etc., is in businesses.

BUSINESSES

I just want to make a point about this and highlight why I think many people go into business and what some of the downsides are. Michael

Gerber is an entrepreneur guru so to speak and the author of the book titled *The E-Myth*. He often talks about how 80% of businesses fail in the first five years. He said, "If you have been in business for more than five years, do not get too excited as the next five years after that 80% of those will also fail. So, if the first five years in business does not wipe you out the next five years most certainly will. Most people become sick of working for their idiot bosses, as they call them, so they decide to start their own business and they end up becoming the idiot boss. Instead of working five days per week for a guaranteed pay cheque they now get to work six to seven days per week and often for no pay cheque". For those who have been in business you may be able to relate to these sad statistics.

As a successful coach and 21st century educator, I have been working with tens of thousands of Australians, helping many people become millionaires. This has allowed thousands of people to retire in a reasonably short period of time, creating the lifestyle they desired. Originally, they thought it was going to take them twenty to thirty years, yet many have been able to achieve it in a matter of a few years. One thing I have noticed though is a big mistake many Australians have made. What they will do is borrow money out of their house in a line of credit and use that to start a traditional business. Often that traditional business fails and as a result they lose the business, plus possibly the house as well and it ends in a total financial disaster. I have seen this happen so many times and I consider that a big no, no. One of the things I am going to suggest if we are going to take money out of property, is we do not want to put it into a business unless we can afford to lose it. I consider a business to be what we call a high risk investment. Now, I am not saying do not go into business. Starting a business from scratch, and low investment type businesses like network marketing businesses which many people get involved in these days and which are set up with low cost, are certainly not the high risk factor. But to buy a coffee shop for say $100,000 like my mother did, is a high risk investment. It is taking money out of a more secure investment like property and borrowing against that to put into a business which is considered a high risk and often it also means you have to work hard for it as well.

TRUE DEFINITION OF A BUSINESS

A true business is a profitable enterprise that will work ideally without you. Think about that, a profitable enterprise that will work ideally without you. Most people do not really have a business, they just have another job that creates a lot more stress. The idea of a real business, and Robert Kiyosaki talks about it in the "Cashflow Quadrant", which I highly recommend, is becoming a business owner where you have an organisation or business that will work without you having to be there. In other words, if you wanted to go away for six months you could and it would still bring in a passive income. That is money while you sleep if you are interested. Most people do not know how to set up businesses like that. To know how to do that, you have to understand a thing called systems. I highly recommend Michael Gerber's book, *The E-myth* or *The E-myth Revisited*, if you want to study how to develop systems in your business. My last point is, to borrow against a business is very difficult. The bank will always want security on your house or property and that gives you a very good idea of how banks are not silly in that regard, they know where the security is, and that is putting all your financial future at risk.

Two strategies we are going to look at that generally have less risk than traditional business, I believe are companies and property. They can create capital growth and also provide cashflow to live on and both can create substantial cashflow in the short term as well, you just need to know what most people don't.

Before we do that what we need to look at is how to get started. Now, I am going to assume for Bill and Mary, the reason many people do not even get started in becoming wealthy is that they think they need a lot of money. I am here to eliminate that myth. Here is what I am going to suggest. If I was to coach Bill and Mary the way my millionaire mentor coached me, I would ask them if they could initially come up with $10,000 to $15,000 to start an investment plan that could see them set up financially in the next 3 to 10 years. Now, Bill and Mary might say yes, or like a lot of people they might say no, I do not have $10,000 or $15,000. I would then say as a friend and coach if I was assisting them, "allow me to help come up with some ways to get $10,000 to $15,000. All I need to decide is whether you are absolutely committed". If they are absolutely committed I can assist them to become wealthy, if they are not committed no one can help them, not even Warren Buffet or Robert Kiyosaki. No one can help anyone become wealthy unless they are committed themselves. So let us make the assumption Bill and Mary are committed, want to become financially free and want to set themselves up for a nice lifestyle. Let us look at eight ways to get started with $10,000 to $15,000 to start investing, so one day they will be making money while they sleep to replace their current income. If I can do it, and if I can help Bill and Mary too, then just maybe you can do it as well.

STEP 1 — SAVINGS

The number one way I would suggest, is saving money. In other words, "all great investors are great savers". If you are not saving money now then you are never going to become wealthy until you start.

When I first started off, I was trying to convince my millionaire mentor to give me some coaching on how to become wealthy and one of the first questions I remember him asking me was how much money I was saving. I said, "Well, actually nothing to be honest". He quickly responded, "Then do not waste my time. I thought you told me you were committed to becoming wealthy and now you are telling me you are not saving any money. You are either committed or you are not," he said.

I said, "Yes, I am committed. I really want to become wealthy". He replied, "Go away and prove it then and start saving and show me proof that you are committed."

He went on to say, "A lot of people can talk the talk but very few people can walk the walk." I was in a state of shock for a moment. I thought, you rich people are rude and arrogant. Although at the time I thought he was being rude and arrogant, I later realised he was just being very firm. He was also proving a point and being truthful with me. In other words, if you can not save money you can not become wealthy. A lot of people say, "Well it is okay for you Jamie, you are wealthy, you can save money." But it does not matter how much you earn, you can save money. You must make a way to make yourself start saving. You must pay yourself first, it is the golden rule to wealth and you must look at ways to start saving money immediately. Even if it is only a small amount, it is a subconscious shift that is required. Predominantly in Australia we are one of the worst saving nations on the entire planet, which is a real shame.

Following is a newspaper article outlining this.

Australian savings at an all-time low

Australians and New Zealanders are dismal savers when compared with people in 19 other OECD countries, according to the Association of Superannuation Funds of Australia (ASFA).

Our household savings have fallen from 11 per cent of income in the late 1970s to 7.3 per cent in the 1980s down to a current low of 4.3 per cent, says ASFA's chief executive, Philippa Smith.

"With increasingly long and hopefully active lives to look forward to, it is shortsighted to focus only on the mortgage, school fees or car repayments," she says. "Most individuals, when asked specifically, estimate they will need 60 per cent of their pre-retirement income to live comfortably in retirement. To achieve this target an individual would have to save 15 per cent of wages for 40 years."

But the fault does not lie with the saving public alone. Smith says Australia is the only country that taxes super at every stage of its life cycle — contributions, earnings, benefits and now the surcharge. Most European countries adopt an approach that means benefits are taxed only when paid out on retirement.

"Most academics and commentators agree that taxing super once at the benefits stage would be simpler and fairer," she says.

STEP 2 — SELL SOMETHING

The second thing to look at is; could you sell something? I do not mean run out and join Tupperware and have a Tupperware party, (nothing against Tupperware, great products). What I am suggesting is that you could have a garage sale. Are there some things you no longer need or are willing to sacrifice in the short term to set yourself up financially? If you have a spare fridge, spare piece of furniture, spare boat, spare bike, spare car that you could sacrifice and convert to cash, maybe even a spare spouse or spare kid you could sell for cash, (just joking). But anything you could convert to cash to come up with a few thousand dollars is great.

My sister and brother-in-law did this and it was quite effective. They trade the options market and live a simple life in Glen Innes where we all grew up. My brother-in-law started to replace his income and was trading full time, which they were very excited about. They decided to use this strategy to have a garage sale to sell off some of their things they did not really need so they would have more money to put into the market. That way they could obviously make more returns on their investments. They ran the garage sale, as a result generated a couple of thousand dollars from what they sold and that became extra money to invest in the market. It was interesting though how some people can see things differently and the rumours that were going around that small country town at the time. People were saying, "They must be going broke because they need to have a garage sale to sell everything to live. We knew he would have been better off keeping his safe secure job."

We all thought it was quite humorous because the reality was quite different. They were committed to financial success and they were sacrificing some things in the process of becoming wealthier. Despite the perception of some people who thought they had been doing something on the market and must have lost a lot of money. They had actually learnt how to replace their income by working from home trading the market.

My millionaire mentor taught me, "Jamie if you are going to become wealthy, what other people think is none of your business. If you are concerned about what other people think, then forget about becoming wealthy. You will not do it because you will be held back by other people's limitations and fears. You just have to ignore that and focus on what you are doing as you know the truth of why you are doing what is required."

STEP 3 — TAX

The third step is tax minimisation. Certainly many people are paying a large amount of tax, especially people who fit into the middle class categories in Australia. You could use some of that tax money for investing, either in negative gearing into shares or property where your tax money will pay for many of your investments. There are other ways, you could set yourself up as a consultant or contractor to your company, rather than an employee. Rather than earn a salary you can contract or consult to your employer where you get paid the gross amount and you have to pay your own taxes later, often at a lower rate. There is an 80/20 rule with it though where you have to have at least 20% of your income generated from another source. The rule is constantly changing, but there are often ways to achieve that. You may want to discuss it with your employer as many industries actually encourage it now. It is also known as outsourcing, a new buzz word in the 21st century.

Also, if you have an investment property, you may not be aware that you can have your tax benefits contributed weekly, rather than wait for a refund cheque at the end of the year, immediately improving your cashflow and take home pay. The form used to be called a 221D form. See your accountant for details.

STEP 4 — INCOME

The fourth step is to increase your income. If you can increase your income by an extra 10%, that is an extra 10% you could put aside for savings and investing. To increase your income is not that difficult. I will not go into too much detail now but I will give you a hint. If you want to increase your income, the areas you want to look at are how can you add more value. To create wealth, my millionaire mentor always said, "Jamie you must add more value. One way you can do that is to develop your skills". The four skills of a 21st century education are:

1. **the ability to think creatively and solve problems;**
2. **the ability to communicate more effectively;**
3. **the ability to market an idea or concept to bring it to reality;**
4. **the ability to negotiate.**

If you go to work on those four skills, I guarantee your income will go up substantially because they are all skills involved in being able to add more value and increase your income. The reason most people do not generate a lot of income is that they just show up at work. They are often sending personal emails while they work, they steal the paper clips and pens every day and they are not proactive in making a profit for the company for which they work. They are often only interested in getting their pay cheque, that is it.

My millionaire mentor said, "Jamie, to become wealthy what you must focus on is how to help the company you work for make more money. If you can help them make more money, you can negotiate a share in those extra profits. One way you can help a company make more money is obviously look at how to help eliminate expenses. You can look around at the company you work for as I guarantee there are thousands of dollars being wasted. If you can figure out a way to cut that wastage, you can negotiate with your boss or your managers and say, "If I can help this company save $20,000 per year will you sign this piece of paper agreeing to give me a bonus?" You could say, "You do not have to use these ideas but if I present you with the ideas and you adopt and use them to save the company money, say $20,000 as an example, will you allow me to share in a percentage of that?" Maybe 5%, 10%, 20% whatever you can negotiate and get them to sign it off up front. If you know how to negotiate then they will often agree to it. It is a win win situation, they do not have to adopt the strategy but if they do and it helps them save money, say $20,000, out of that you might get 10%, $2,000 extra bonus for one simple idea. I did a lot of these things in the beginning and it is amazing how effectively they can work as companies waste a lot of money.

My millionaire mentor went on to say that the other area you can help the company increase its profits is to just be more committed. How many employers would love their employees to come to them Monday morning and say, "I have just been thinking over the weekend how I can help the company make more profit. I just wanted to let you know I am absolutely committed to helping you do that, I have some ideas I would like to share. If there is anything you can suggest I do to make this company more profitable, I am very open to that because I want to be more valuable and the only way I can do that is to help the company do better". It is a win win scenario and you can put proposals to accomplish that. It may take some time but it is worth it. In some companies, though you may find it is not like that, as some managers may not accept your proposals. What you will find in some companies is that people have managers who if they found out that you put in a proposal where you could make more money than them, your potential success causes their ego to get in the way and they will try to sabotage your success. You need to be aware of that if this occurs. You may need to go to another person in the company or another company altogether, which leads me to the next strategy.

WHAT ARE YOU WORTH

My millionaire mentor taught me, "Another way you can quickly increase your income is to find out what you are worth". Let us say you work for one company. Can you go out and look for more job options with other companies? To be in a stronger position to negotiate what you want to have is at least three or more alternatives where you could work. If you had three or four companies that would be interested in your services you would have to go out and investigate, and find out what you would be worth. Then, you can go back and negotiate with your current employer — "I am considering leaving, I believe I am worth this amount of money and this is what I am prepared to do to add the value that makes me worth that amount of money. This is the money that I would like to be compensated for doing that. I would like you to consider that. It is okay if you are not prepared to agree with my proposal because I am quite happy to leave as other companies are willing to reward me to the level that I believe I am worth." Now as long as you are committed to adding value and you communicate that effectively, then what you will find (I have had many graduates from my seminars do this) is the company suddenly realises the value you add and how hard it is to replace you. (Remember, your boss is never usually going to walk up to you and say I am going to give you a pay rise today. You normally have to ask for it — but to get something you must first give, so you must put a plan to them that is going to provide evidence as to why they should pay you more). It is not until you are willing to leave that they realise how valuable you are and they are willing to pay you more. This has happened so many times so if you apply this strategy, you could be pleasantly surprised.

I had a friend that works for one of our companies. She used to work in a large bank and when she made the choice that she was willing to leave and had arranged to go on contract to one of our companies to provide services, her company immediately increased her salary by close to $10,000 if she stayed. She did not even ask for it. If she wanted to she could have stayed with the bank and picked up an extra $10,000 just by one simple negotiating method because she was adding value, she was valuable, and she was willing to walk away. To be a strong negotiator you must put yourself into a position where you are willing to walk away. Sometimes they might not give it to you but if you know you can go to another company and generate extra income, obviously you are in a much better position to negotiate.

Five Forms of Income Game

What forms of income do you currently have?

______________________ $ __________
______________________ $ __________
______________________ $ __________
______________________ $ __________
______________________ $ __________
______________________ $ __________

____

What extra forms of income can you think of?

______________________ $ __________
______________________ $ __________
______________________ $ __________
______________________ $ __________
______________________ $ __________

Which of these forms of income could you most easily obtain?

______________________ $ __________
______________________ $ __________
______________________ $ __________
______________________ $ __________
______________________ $ __________

List possible forms of income:

1. ______________________
2. ______________________
3. ______________________

4.____
5.____
6.____
7.____
8.____
9.____

STEP 5 — OPM

The fifth step we are going to look at is called OPM. **OPM stands for Other People's Money.** To become wealthy you may need to consider using other people's money and that is something we will look at later on.

Let me give you an example. Let us say for example you wanted $15,000 to invest and you did not have it right now. Could you go out and get a personal loan? If you have a job I dare say you would be able to get a personal loan or be able to borrow that money from someone. Let us say you were able to borrow $15,000 if this was appropriate for you. Let us compare that to Bill and Mary who did not do that. For Bill and Mary to save $15,000 may take them, if they are saving $100 per week, three years of consistent effort. If they are like most Australians, guess what they mostly will do after they start saving, they will then spend it on a holiday, another car or something insignificant.

So it takes a lot of hard work and discipline to save that up. But what if they were committed to investing and willing to borrow $15,000? Now, if they borrow on a personal loan that would probably only cost them around $75 per week to pay off. If they are already committed to saving $100 per week, that $100 per week they are saving could now cover the cost of that loan and it would not put any extra stress on them financially but what it gives them is $15,000 immediately to use for investing.

There are some financial strategies we will look at in a moment where $15,000 invested (for instance in the market with a low to medium risk strategy, if they were to do it according to the way I teach people) could generate anywhere from $300 up to as much, in some cases, as $1,000 many months of the year in additional cash flow. That is with less risk than most people are taking right now.

$15,000 can generate $300 to $1,000 per month in some fast track strategies with less risk than buying a car.

So you might say, "Jamie, can we move right on to that topic and show me how to do that." Well, if you stay tuned we will go through that in some detail in the next few chapters. The point is to illustrate that using other people's money, borrowing money, etc., if it is done smartly and wisely, can increase potential returns — however it can also produce a negative return if done incorrectly. Most will say, "I am not going to do that, it is too risky to invest in the market", but how many people will go out and borrow $15,000 or more for a car? And what do we know about a car, a car is a classic poor investment. As soon as we drive it out of the showroom door we lose 20%. Within 5 to 10 years what is our $15,000 car worth? Could be down to say $5,000 or less, therefore, we have lost a considerable amount of money. Plus does this car, every time you drive into a service station, put money into your pocket? Obviously not, it takes money out of your pocket. Cars cost money monthly and they lose value. They are a guaranteed loss, but how many Australians have at least one or two cars? Many people, and they consider that smart. I realise a car is considered a necessity in Australia but really it is a luxury people get before they can really afford it. It is a complete waste of money for most people, yet the same Australians could go and borrow $15,000 to invest. Even if it was invested in the worst companies available on the market, they would still not perform as badly as a car over the next 5 to 10 years. We have got to look at our mindset. What is risky here? The biggest risk you will take with money is not investing and not saving, that is the greatest risk. When you are investing I agree you can lose. At times you will, but that amount can be manageable. You can learn to deal with that and you will be way ahead of someone who did not decide to invest.

Remember that I am not advising you what to do with these strategies. They are suggestions to consider. You need to adjust them to your personal situation and also consider whether you are willing to develop your mindset to have these ideas work for you. Otherwise, if you are not willing to, then the Money Magazine type advice is about the best you will get where you hope to retire in 100 years from now. Now there is nothing wrong with that advice. It is just slow and boring and is often offered by financial planners who made their wealth through selling advice and earning their commissions, or journalists who are yet to produce real life results. Always seek financial mentors who have real life results for further help, or attend seminars or home study courses taught by self-made millionaires to continually educate yourself.

STEP 6 — USING EQUITY

The sixth step is what we call using equity. In other words many people have equity in their homes, equity being a portion of their house that they actually own. Much of that equity could be put to good use, because it is just sitting there. The challenge with many people is that they become asset rich and cashflow poor because predominantly we have been taught to get a good education, work hard all our lives, pay off the house and retire to the good life.

For many couples, as they get older, by the time they pay off their house, they may be fortunate to find if it is in a good suburb it could be worth half a million to a million dollars. But the challenge is the house is really big and the kids have left home. They no longer need a big house but they still have to continue to work because all their money is tied up in their house. It is not producing any cashflow.

So I suggest using some of that equity to invest in investments that are going to generate some cashflow. Some people might say, "I do not want to do that, it is too risky." Often, what I say is what my millionaire mentor taught me, which is that life is a risky business. **There is not one of us who is going to get out of it alive.** When you think about it, life is a risky business, we must take risks. The greatest risk in life is to do nothing at all.

My millionaire mentor used to share with me the story of an 86 year old lady who was on her death bed. In her dying moments she said to some of her closest family and friends, "You know the only thing I regret as I look back on my life and it is now virtually over, is why I did not take more risks. What was I so scared of?" You see the challenge for many people is that day is going to come and they will regret it. The question is, in investing are the risks you can take less risky than not investing. I just want to help you understand and illustrate this important point. Most people are currently taking far greater risks than what is necessary, yet could take less risk to become incredibly wealthy in a very short period of time. I am going to suggest possibly considering using some of your equity but do not use it to put into a high-risk business. We will take that equity and put it into either another property with a good strategy or the market with a good strategy where you can insure your position, etc. (I will explain insuring later.) Other people might say, "Well Jamie, that is fine if you have equity, but what if I do not have any equity?"

Remember, there is always a solution if you are absolutely committed. Also remember these are only suggestions. You do not have to do anything. It is just a matter of choices. You could try to avoid all risks in life and do nothing, however, you will just risk wasting your entire life, my millionaire mentor told me. Now that is a risk I was not prepared to take!

I decided to start investing as it carried the least risk.

STEP 7 — PARENTS EQUITY

Step 7, in these 8 steps to kick starting your investments is about using your parents' equity. If you do not have any equity maybe your parents or your grandparents do. Most people wait until their parents die to inherit the house. It is sad and I do not like to mention it to many people, but how many fights are there after someone dies over their money and their parent's assets? It is sad and it is a selfish part of human nature. What I am going to suggest is, why wait until your parents die to inherit their wealth? Do the exact opposite, the law of opposites. Why wait? Why not ask to draw down your inheritance early. A reporter who once came to one of my seminars reported later that I was suggesting a ruthless strategy because I said this. The reporter was also broke, had a poor mindset around money and did not like people getting too excited about freedom, which the hundreds of people there were. The sad part is that he was not open to learning. To him nothing worked. He said, "This sounds really ruthless, I can not believe you are even suggesting it." Let me ask you this question which I posed to the audience and reporter. Do most parents want to see their sons and daughters do well in life? Yes or No? I would say yes. Not all of them — you might say, "Jamie you do not know my parents." But let us assume most of them do. One way they think they are helping their sons or daughters is to first of all help them to get their first investment, which is usually a car. We know a car is a classic investment, so they use the family assets to buy cars, etc., and become guarantor for them, which is not really helping them to become wealthy. What if you approached your parents and said, "Look I want to buy my first investment property and get into some real investing. I have done my homework, I have looked into the potential downsides, the upsides and how to manage the risk and I want to borrow some of your equity to get started. If you do, these are my guarantees. I am willing to guarantee I will pay it back in time, if I am even one day late paying back the money I owe I agree to pay an additional $500 in late fees (sounds like the banks), plus you can have the rights to take over my investment property if I am late more than three times". If you look at the investment property, it is virtually guaranteed to go up in value. The average Australian residential investment property doubles every 7 to 10 years. Now that does not mean every investment property is going to double every 7 to 10 years, some will double in less. I have had properties that have doubled in a little over two years. That is unusual, I know. One of them was worth a million dollars when I bought it. Some properties do not double in twenty years and in some places properties will never double. But a good property is virtually guaranteed to eventually go up, just as likely as the sun is to rise tomorrow. Whereas investing in a car or something like that, it is virtually guaranteed to go down, just as likely as the sun will go down tomorrow. Do you follow what I mean? There is always risk, we just have to compare one risk to the other to be able to make a financially intelligent decision. So maybe you can consider using your parent's equity. Remember, you do not have to. It is just an option. If you do not have parents or grandparents perhaps use some friend's equity. There is that much equity sitting around in this country not being utilised. The amazing thing about using equity out of a property is that the property can still go up in value, even if you take some of the equity out of the property and invest it somewhere else. So the property can still go up in value and if the equity you have drawn out of the property is invested somewhere else where it can also go up in value, you have your money working for you twice. Now that is magic.

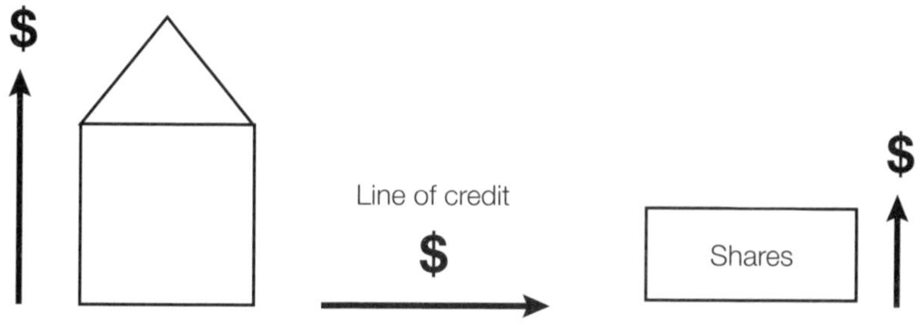

STEP 8 — SUPERANNUATION

The eighth step is superannuation. Our group of companies helps many people I coach access their super by setting up self managed super funds where they can actively invest and manage their own super. I think if the Australian government was more creative and wanted to help increase savings in this country they would really look at changing superannuation. We are the only country in the world that gets taxed at all three levels. When our money goes in, we get taxed at fifteen percent. When the money is sitting there, we are getting taxed and when it comes out we get taxed. It is absolutely insane, they seem to want to prevent people from becoming wealthy. A smart government would completely revolutionise superannuation and make it more beneficial.

For instance, what I would suggest is instead of the employer having to pay the super, the employees, like in countries like Singapore, have to equally match the employers contribution. Right now the employer has to put into super about nine percent. Rather than slugging the employer another nine percent to increase it, why not create some incentive for the employees to match that nine percent? In other words, say if employees put in at least the equivalent to what the employer put into the super fund, they would get a tax incentive so the funds go into their super tax-free. If they change the rules of super then people can actively use it.

I think the reason a lot of people are not excited about super is that they do not count it as real money as they generally can not touch it until age 65. So what if we encouraged more people to invest in super by providing further tax benefits but allowed a portion of that super to be accessible if they made additional profits. Say if you could generate profits above five or six percent, and you are allowed to actually pull some of it out before retirement age. In other words, like the politicians, they do not have to wait till retirement age to access their super. You may note that many of the laws of this country are set up to benefit those in power and the masses suffer as a result.

If you could access some of your super well before retirement age, would you be more motivated to consider putting more money into super? The obvious answer is yes. The government could create a massive increase in savings across the entire nation and that extra wealth in the country could be used to invest in Australian businesses. Rather than having to beg for multinationals to invest here, with most of our profits going back overseas tax free, Australians could create more jobs and create a wealthier Australia. We could actually be buying out companies overseas such as Singapore companies. (Countries like Singapore, which used to be third world countries, that are tiny dots in size compared to Australia, are able to come and buy out our companies because they are much better savers and investors and therefore in a much stronger position than Australia).

Instead of being bought out and at the mercy of the world markets and detriment of globalisation, Australia could become even wealthier as a nation.

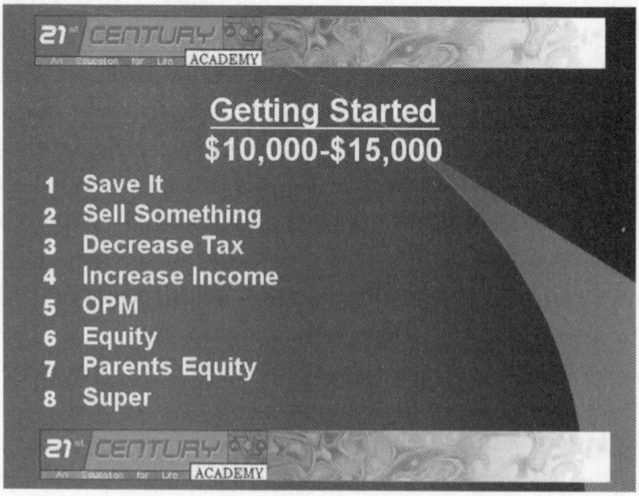
21st CENTURY
ACADEMY
Getting Started
$10,000-$15,000
1 Save It
2 Sell Something
3 Decrease Tax
4 Increase Income
5 OPM
6 Equity
7 Parents Equity
8 Super
21st CENTURY
ACADEMY

So with superannuation — there are still ways despite the government's restrictions that you can actually use your super to be actively investing and that is something you may want to consider looking into more.

NEXT STEP

HOW TO MAKE MONEY OUT OF THIN AIR

Now we have looked at eight ways to come up with money to get started. There are many other ways out there but let us now look at how we make some money out of thin air.

The first step we need to look at is adding value, which I mentioned before, and if we can add value to anything, in other words add value to the businesses that we work in, we can generate more wealth. If we add value to a property, we are going to create more wealth.

So let us first have a look at how we can make some money out of thin air to increase the amount of money we have to invest. Let us imagine that you have a house or your parents have a house. One of the first things you can do is look at utilising equity. You could go and arrange a line of credit on this property. A line of credit is a facility where you can draw out some money from the property.

So let us use Bill and Mary for an example. Bill and Mary have a property that is worth $150,000. The bank happens to own $100,000 of that, that means Bill and Mary's equity would be $50,000. $50,000 being their portion of the house that they actually own. Bill and Mary could use a line of credit to use some of their equity for investing. Say they needed $10,000–$15,000, Bill and Mary might be thinking, "Well Jamie, I do not have $10,000 or $15,000". But I would say, "You have equity in this property. That $50,000 is yours just sitting there. You could potentially be using that for investing." To work out how much that could be, the maximum the banks will let you draw out of a property is generally up to 80%.

So let us look at $150,000 as the value of the property, 80% of that is approximately $120,000 but then you have to take off what you already owe to the bank. In this case, you have to take off $100,000 because that is what Bill and Mary owe to the bank. They have already borrowed that amount so they can not re-borrow what they have already borrowed. So $120,000 less $100,000 would equal approximately $20,000. Bill and Mary, depending upon their ability to get the finance, would be able to potentially draw out in a line of credit as much as $20,000. When using a line of credit I always suggest leaving some there as a buffer in case of emergencies, but they could draw some of that out and use it for investing immediately. Let us say they took out $15,000. I will show you shortly an example, of how they can turn that into monthly extra cashflow that would be coming in without them needing to work. And that is when it gets really exciting. It is not something that takes years to set up, it is something that could be occurring for them within a month. That is why people get excited with these strategies once they understand what is possible. Especially if you have the right mindset, and someone shares with you the fast track strategies to implement in simple terms.

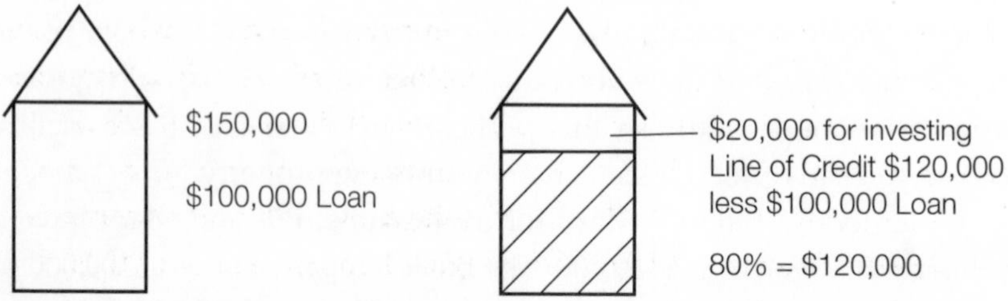

The next step for Bill and Mary to help them create more money for investing is to utilise the $150,000 house. They could potentially get that re-valued. Properties in most capital cities around Australia and also in many cities in New Zealand tend to rise in value.

So we could ask Bill and Mary when they last had their house re-valued. If they are like most Australians, probably several years. I would get them to call their bank immediately and ask to get a valuation done on their property. It is going to cost them around $300–$400, sometimes the bank will pay for it, but it could be worthwhile. They could get their house re-valued and the bank valuation might say that the house is actually worth $160,000 now, not

$150,000 because properties have risen in the area. Therefore, they now would have more money they could draw out in a line of credit than what they had previously.

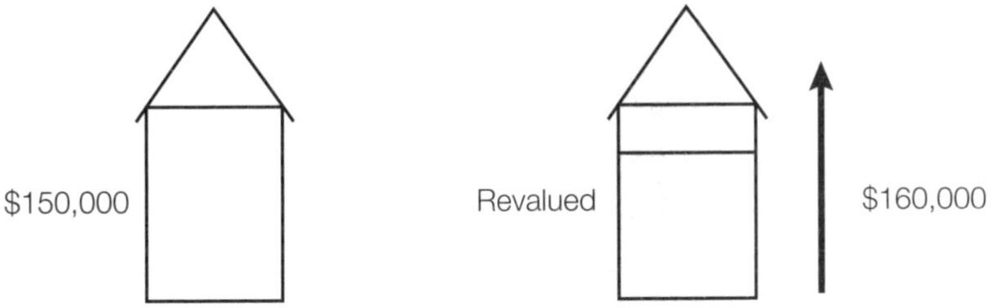

RENOVATIONS

What if they do some quick renovations to the house that are inexpensive but would add significant value to the house before they get the valuation done. Let us consider this for a moment. What they would want to do is add value to this property to make it worth more.

They could "Backyard Blitz" it, in other words if you watch those popular TV shows like *Backyard Blitz*, *Ground Force*, or *The Block*, it is amazing how they can transform and landscape a back yard in a matter of a weekend. Admittedly, they have quite a few hands to help but they completely transform the properties. What I am thinking in the back of my mind is that these people are so fortunate and they get so excited about a beautiful back yard. Really, the *Backyard Blitz* team has added in many cases $20,000, $30,000, $40,000, $50,000 value to the property because they have a beautiful garden and landscape and a new valuation would often reflect that the houses are worth a lot more as a result.

The first obvious step is what sort of landscaping we can do to fix up the garden but keeping this inexpensive. We do not want to spend too much money. The less we can spend, the better. Could they maybe repaint the outside and inside of the house and make it tidier? Could they possibly redo the kitchen and bathroom, the two most important areas of the house, and they can be done quite inexpensively if one is creative. Could they maybe re-carpet or have polished floorboards? Simple things they could do to add value, to make that house look better.

By doing that, let us say they were to invest maybe $20,000 into improving that property. Then they were able to get a revaluation on the house as it looks much more desirable. It is now better than other houses in the street, etc., and it could be revalued at say $200,000. I used that as a real life example. In some cases, it may not go up by that much and in some cases it will go up by more but let us assume $200,000. They spent $20,000 doing it up and it is now worth $200,000. The increase in value is some $50,000, less the $20,000 they have spent to fix it up. **They have created an extra $30,000 in value out of thin air. That is money out of thin air.** Let me ask you a question, how long has it taken you to save your last $30,000?

You can start to see by thinking smart and outside the box in a very short period of time you can create significant extra money out of thin air by just taking some action. A problem people might suggest is what if they do not have $20,000 to fix up the house? The reality is for as little as $3,000 to $4,000 or $5,000 you could add tremendous value to properties. I often say this strategy is so damn good it even works in Adelaide and people often laugh at that. Not to pick on people in Adelaide but often people say, "It is okay if people live in Sydney and Melbourne, what if I live in a city like Adelaide?" It still works, you can add value to anything.

I have a story of a young girl in Adelaide. She told me she took this strategy I shared with her and all she did was spend $1,000 on her property and was able to get an increase in value by $20,000. In other words, it cost $1,000 outlay and to increase of $20,000, that is a net $19,000 gain she made out of one idea after she attended our 3-hour seminar I conducted in Adelaide. She was very happy with just that one idea. She was able then to start investing that money into other things. So you can see how she could get massive momentum in an investment strategy very quickly. It almost sounds too good to be true.

Here are a few rules of what not to do, to ensure it becomes true for you. This strategy is very difficult to not be successful at, yet many Australians figure out a way for it not to work. One of the big mistakes with people doing renovations to improve the cosmetic appearance of the house is they want to do major renovations, they want to put in a big pool, build a three car garage and spend an absolute fortune. They might spend $50,000 and the house might only go up by $20,000. That is how not to make it work. You want to spend as little as possible, least outlay for the greatest potential gain and in certain areas you are going to get a great increase in value, other areas only a small increase.

Bill and Mary now have more money and are more excited to now invest into other potential investments to make money while they sleep.

We are now going to look at some other strategies. Let us take a look at the market. I love the market today but initially I did not. I used to think it was too risky and too time consuming until my millionaire mentor helped me understand certain strategies. When I adopted them, I had such success with them that I became a raving fan of the market. I still am to this day and I have helped many people generate substantial amounts of money from it. It is exciting because it can generate a cashflow quickly if it is done properly and you can minimise your risk as well. A lot of people do not understand this. Even though I did not start investing in the market initially to create my wealth, it is still a good place for many to start, even if they have never invested before.

CREATING CASHFLOW THROUGH RENTING

One of the most exciting strategies is how you go about renting. A lot of people say, "Jamie is this a misprint 'renting'. I know you can rent out property but how do you rent companies?" It is actually true, you can rent out companies. "Renting" is a word that I created as a communicator and educator to educate Australians on how to go about carrying out the strategy in a very simple format. There are more technical words that people generally use to describe this strategy, as I will explain later, but generally the challenge for a lot of people to be successful in the market is learning the language. The words are coded and it sounds complicated but it really isn't. Another thing I am going to talk about is how you can insure your position. Most people have no idea that they can insure their position through this strategy, and we will come back to that in a moment.

I want to look at how I help Bill and Mary, as a friend and coach, to come up with some ideas to generate an extra $1,000 a week. That is, money coming in while they sleep in the shortest time possible without them needing to work to earn that income, and by managing risk and utilising their money more effectively. The reason they are after $1,000 a week is because that is approximately what they jointly earn right now. That amount would replace their income and give them some major choices in their life. In other words, they could cut back to part time work if they wanted to. They could go on more holidays, only work six months of the year, maybe even consider not working at all. Maybe moving to another career that they enjoy because they want to, not just because they have to for the money. It would completely transform their lives just by implementing a few strategies.

You may be interested in doing the same.

I will go through half a dozen fast track strategies, going into the last couple in detail, in particular renting. I have no doubt that if you are like tens of thousands of people who have attended my seminars, you will get very excited about some of these strategies because they are real. They can be done quickly and I am going to give you the fundamental understanding of how you would go about doing these things if it is applicable to your current situation or your future situation.

CHAPTER 13

Instant Cashflow Strategies

My name is Leigh Barker. I am a qualified accountant, a qualified company secretary, an authorised representative of an Australian Financial Services Licence holder and a private investor. In this chapter, I will provide factual information dealing with strategies that have been devised and used by many successful investors, including Jamie McIntyre. I will also use certain expressions that have been coined by Jamie, namely "channelling", "insuring" and "renting shares".

The following information is provided as an information service only and does not constitute financial product advice and should not be relied upon as financial product advice. None of the information takes into account the reader's personal objectives, financial situation or needs. The reader must determine whether the information is appropriate for their particular circumstances. For financial product advice that takes into account the reader's particular objectives, financial situation or needs, seek independent financial advice from an Australian Financial Services Licensee before making a financial decision.

As a private investor, I have been fortunate enough to apply many investment concepts and principles, some of which are discussed in this book. More importantly it has always made good business sense to seek the guidance of an authorised and recognised specialist to assist with the implementation of investment strategies.

For some time I have personally worked with Jamie at both a business level and a private level. I have spoken at, and provided factual information within the scope of my authorisation at many of Jamie's seminars in both Australia and New Zealand.

My goal is not all that different to that of Jamie's. While I have the capacity to provide factual information within the scope of my authorisations, be that as a public accountant or an authorised representative of an Australian Financial Services Licence holder, I elect not to provide such advice. My goal is to provide you with information that is objectively ascertainable and factual in nature about strategies that have been adopted by others.

INTRODUCTION

Selecting the right share for investment is no different in principle to identifying the right company to purchase as a business investment or a property purchase as part of a property investment portfolio. An astute investor will treat share investing as a business.

For the purposes of this chapter we assume that our investor has decided to purchase an imaginary share that trades on the Australian Market.

The first objective of our investor clients is to obtain some information about their potential investment. Investors are not always aware that a lot of factual information is published about a share, which can be accessed through many media outlets such as the newspaper, the Internet and many other sources. This information is generally free. Given the availability of such information, there maybe little benefit in spending say $10,000 on a software package if you are attempting to keep your concepts and strategies simple like Jamie.

On a daily basis, most major daily newspapers publish share market tables that provide a daily summary of trading of many stocks. These market share tables are prepared for the general public and contain a lot of useful information such as how a share has traded over the last 12 months and the last day. Other useful information includes the last sale price of a share, and whether or not the share has increased or decreased in value the previous day.

So let us look at the process of researching our imaginary share. The daily newspaper informs our investor how a share has traded in the last 12 months. Research on our imaginary share will identify that the share has traded to a high of say $26 and it has been down to a low of say $16. If an investor was unaware of this information and a recommendation was made to purchase this imaginary share at $19, on what basis would an investor make a decision to purchase? Surprisingly, many clients have purchased shares by applying the guess or hot tip technique. Astute investors understand that guessing about your financial future or taking someone's hot tip is not a sound basis for making a business decision. Many of the world's astute investors would never adopt the guess or hot tip philosophy. Our investor client has now identified that in the last 12 months our imaginary share has peaked at $26, bottomed at $16 and is currently trading at $19. Having done so, further research should be undertaken to identify what factual information has been published to assist in making a business decision.

Websites that provide free research information include but are not limited to

www.asx.com.au
www.comsec.com.au
www.macquarie.com.au
www.stanford.com.au

The next objective is to determine at what price to buy the share and whether the share is good value.

To assist with this decision, there are two forms of analysis that are available to investors. One is called **technical analysis** and the other is **fundamental analysis**. While Jamie tends to use a little bit of both, his primary reason for succeeding at investing in the market comes from his ability to make and keep concepts very simple. Most of our clients now use one or more of the many expressions coined by Jamie to explain their investment objectives in a very simple and uncomplicated format. Simplicity in understanding and communicating a strategy has been advantageous to most clients. Many people make life difficult and complicated, therefore if something seems too simple, human reaction is to be negative to the concept. A mistake many people make is to believe that in order to be wealthy and successful, you must operate from within a complicated environment. An important ingredient that both Jamie and many other clients appreciate is that in order to implement an investment strategy you require focus and commitment, while simultaneously allowing the process to be simple and uncomplicated. Human nature is to complicate simple concepts and strategies.

Two things that an investor must understand that drive the market are the emotions of humanity — **basically fear and greed**. For the market to rise, the emotion of greed will in most cases drive the market up. The emotion that tends to drive the market down more rapidly is that of fear. We have all witnessed the panic and fear following September 11. Unless you follow the market closely you may not be aware that when common sense prevailed, the market picked up and regained lost ground. It is interesting to note that since World War II there have been around 26 crises that have caused the market to drop suddenly. On each of those occasions, the market has rebounded to a higher level than its previous high.

FORMS OF ANALYSIS

The first strategy that a potential investor may consider is commonly termed technical analysis. Here you examine patterns of share price changes, rates of share price changes and changes in the volume of shares traded in the hope of being able to predict and profit from future trends. Investors may also consider fundamental analysis. Here an investor can review such factors as sales, profits and assets of the business, which are "fundamental" to the company in question. It is always handy to know if the company in question is making a profit and is relatively large and stable. Some investor clients prefer to trade in large stable companies that usually make a profit, as they believe this strategy significantly reduces their risk.

Investors generally review the low and high prices for the previous twelve months to gain an indication of whether they are paying too much for a particular share or are purchasing the share for a much better value and price. Some investors believe that this form of analysis will eliminate some but not all of their investment risk. If necessary, the more careful investor can paper trade a share to build confidence. For those who are unaware of the concept of paper trading, this is a process in which you make investment decisions without committing real money. The investor will approach a paper trade just as they would a real trade, taking into account everything an investor would consider if they were making a real investment, and recording their investment decisions on paper. By looking at how a theoretical investment performs an investor can evaluate how well their investment approach is working, without the pressures of possible financial loss. Once the confidence level is satisfied, a paper trader will become a live trader. In this transition from paper trading to live trading most of our clients have sought guidance from an authorised and licensed full service broker who can assist with the provision of advice associated with both technical and fundamental analysis for a particular share.

CHANNELLING

The second strategy for an investor client is a concept that Jamie coined "channelling". For the technically minded, this strategy is referring to the price range of a share, that is, the range between the highest price and the lowest price reached by a share during any specific day, week or year.

By following the charts of many companies, one can visually identify that the price range of a share will move in patterns. For instance, our imaginary share traded as low as $16 before trading as high as $26 within a single price range cycle. In a subsequent price range cycle, our imaginary share ran back down to say $16, then returned to $19, then back down to $16, back up to $19. Investors begin to recognise that our imaginary share is following a pattern. In this example, our imaginary share is channelling sideways. In some instances shares will channel upwards and in other instances shares will channel downwards. Astute investors who follow the market become aware of those shares forming a pattern. Armed with this information, next time that share is around $16 an investor may consider purchasing the share having the benefit of

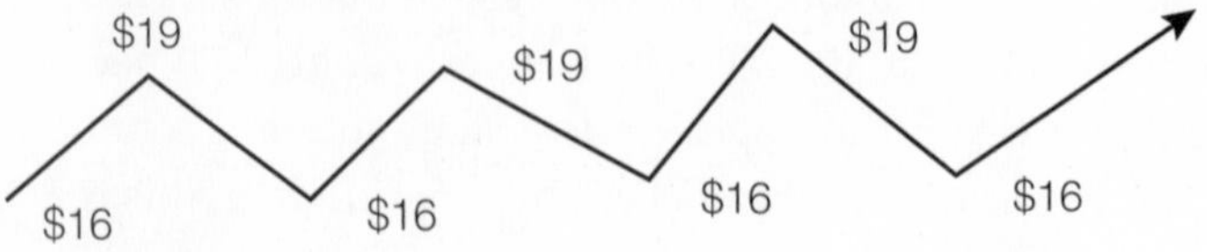

understanding the price range over an historical period, be that a week, a month, a year or longer.

Assuming that the share price returns to $19, the investor must decide if the share is to be retained or sold. Common sense dictates that the share should be sold making the investor a potential profit of 20%. If this were the decision, the investor may instruct his brokers to repurchase the share when the share price is trading at the low end of its price range.

Assuming that our imaginary share has channelled up and down four times in a year, and assuming that the investor is making 20% profit every time the share is bought and sold, after the fourth time, the potential profit would equate to a profit of 80% per annum. Thus by adopting a channelling strategy, the investor can theoretically increase investment returns dramatically. The concept of channelling has been adopted by many investors who can identify those companies who channel up and down within a relatively consistent price range.

While the strategy of channelling is relatively simple and uncomplicated, many investors fail to follow the fundamentals of this concept. Investors fail to check the price movements of a share and to identify if the share price has moved up or down. Not adhering to the fundamentals often leads to investors purchasing a share at the top end of the price range, which in the case of our imaginary share is $26.

Observing the financially educated client investing in an opposite manner to that of the unsophisticated investor is an education in itself. In its simplest format investing in the opposite manner is generally the process of selling a share at a price and accepting the profits of the trade. For example, when our imaginary share is trading at $19, the financially educated investor may elect to sell whereas the unsophisticated investor may hold onto the share. Doing the opposite to other investors may require the financially educated investor to make decisions that are contrary or opposite to the opinions of some financial advisors or professional share traders.

Greed may stop many investors from selling our imaginary share at $19 and fear would stop most investors from buying our imaginary share at $16. Remember, fear and greed may be your greatest enemies and that is why a large proportion of this book is devoted to developing the right mindset of the investor. While many clients simply wish to understand and immediately implement an investment strategy, in the early stages, it may be more advantageous to adopt, develop and work on a mindset. Astute investors understand that if the mindset is not addressed then emotions will interfere with common sense investment decisions.

LEVERAGE

The third strategy for an investor client is a concept termed leverage. Leverage is another word for gearing, which in its simplest format is the process of increasing the funds available for investment through borrowing.

Leverage has the potential to increase returns as the more money that is invested in the market, the greater the potential return from dividends and other distributions inclusive of capital growth in a share. With more funds to invest, an investor has an opportunity to spread the potential investment risk across a wider range of shares and industry sectors.

Assuming that an investor has $20,000 to invest in the stock market and that these funds were used to purchase 1,000 of our imaginary shares when the market value is $16 per share. With leverage, in other words using other people's money, an investor can effectively double the number of shares purchased in our imaginary share to 2,000 shares with a market value of $32,000. The investor now has 2,000 of our imaginary share working for a return instead of just 1,000.

With a suitable deposit, which in our example is $20,000, an investor may borrow an additional $20,000 as leverage. Some providers of margin lending services will have a loan limit that starts from $20,000 while others may have other loan limits.

While increasing leverage can increase potential returns, it can also increase potential losses to the investor if they fail to manage investments correctly. Most importantly an investor requires the right securities and investment structure for their personal situation. In putting together a margin-lending portfolio, the financially educated investor will control the balance between risk and reward. For these reasons, seek advice from a competent Australian Financial Services Licence holder before considering leveraged products, as a competent Australian Financial Services Licence holder will advise which strategy is appropriate for your personal circumstances.

INSURING

The fourth strategy for an investor client is a concept that Jamie has coined "insuring". For the technically minded, insuring is described as purchasing a Put Option over the stock that you want to insure. A Put Option is simply the right to sell a share at a specified price before the expiry date of the option.

Most investors are unaware of their ability to protect the value of their investment in the event of the stock market correction or a major crash. Protecting the value of an investment is a key element of investing in shares. Insurance allows investors to hedge against a possible fall in the value of shares in their portfolio. After taking out some insurance, the sale price of our imaginary share is locked in for the term of the insurance no matter how low our imaginary share price may fall. Without using insurance, in a market downturn the options available are to watch the share fall in value, or to sell the share. For this reason alone the many investors will insure the underlying share in the event that the share price falls.

If an investor is not familiar with the jargon and terminology of the investment industry then the concept of insurance may be confusing. For those seeking a basic understanding of this terminology, insurance is where the investor takes out a put option and a put option is what gives the owner of our imaginary share the right to **sell** the underlying share for a pre-determined value. An investor therefore may use insurance when he believes that a share price will fall or is concerned that it may fall and the investor wants to benefit from or be protected against the fall. There is a cost to the owner of the shares when taking out insurance.

In order to understand the maths of this process, let us assume that an investor purchased 1000 shares in our imaginary stock at $19 and wants to protect this investment should the share price fall below a predetermined level, which we will assume is $16. An investor who has taken out this form of insurance will have the comfort that should the share price fall below $16, the investor will have the ability to sell the imaginary share at $16 no matter what level the share has fallen to providing that this decision is made within the time period of the insurance.

While the cost of insurance will vary, assume that an insurance premium costs 20 cents per share or $200 for 1000 shares.

Investor clients take comfort from this process as they are addressing the balance between risk and reward.

THE WAY DOWN STRATEGY

The fifth strategy for an investor client is a concept Jamie has coined "the way down strategy". For those who prefer technical terminology, this concept refers to buying put options without owning the actual share.

The purpose of this investment strategy is to speculate that the share price will fall. Investor clients see this concept as a way of making money without owning the share. The investor client understands that when the price of a share falls, the value of the put increases. Therefore, the investor client will purchase a put with the intention of selling the put at a higher price.

Investors who understand the way down strategy recognise that there are not many steps associated with this concept. As with the principles associated with Insuring, investors purchase insurance without owning the actual share. By way of example, assume the investor has purchased insurance for $0.30 per share to insure the price of our imaginary share at $16. As the market falls, the value of the right to sell the shares increases. This can be measured by deducting the new market price of say $13 from the price of the original cover, $16, the difference is $3.

For an outlay of $0.30, our client can potentially increase its investment return by selling this insurance at a substantial profit. Conversely, if the market does not fall, the cost of this investment concept to the investor is $0.30.

The way down strategy is a difficult concept to incorporate in a business forecast, as there are many variables.

THE WAY UP AND THE WAY DOWN STRATEGY

The sixth strategy for an investor client is a concept Jamie has coined "the way up and down strategy". This concept is similar to the "Way down strategy". The main difference is that the investor has a view that the share price will move upwards and therefore a call option is purchased.

If an investor is not familiar with the jargon and terminology of the investment industry the way up and down strategy may be confusing. For those seeking a basic understanding of this terminology, a call option gives the investor the right to **buy** the underlying share for a pre-determined value. Investors therefore use insurance when they believe that a share price will rise and the investor wants to benefit from the movement.

The purpose of this investment strategy is to speculate that the share price will rise. Investor clients who apply this strategy have the opportunity to earn income when the share price rises (on the way up) and when the share price falls (on the way down) without owning the underlying stock.

RENTING FOR CASHFLOW

Another strategy for an investor client is a concept that Jamie coined "renting shares". The term share renting is used as an introductory explanation so that those who are neither technically minded nor familiar with industry jargon can come to grips with the basic concepts of an investment strategy known by the market as covered calls or buy/write.

The term share renting is used by investors who understand that a regular cash flow can be received from options premiums issued against a stock that an investor owns. The owner of the imaginary share as identified early on in this chapter, can offer their imaginary share as security in order for the share renting transaction to take place. Investor clients are aware that from the perspective of risk, in the event of the exercise price being reached, the investor may be forced to sell the imaginary share at a pre-determined price.

Since Jamie coined the term "share renting", my accounting practice has engaged many clients who openly use this expression as method to communicate their investment decisions in very simple terms. Associates of my accounting practice that include mortgage brokers, financial planners, solicitors and share traders have also adopted this terminology in communications with their investor clients.

My accounting practice has identified that investor clients who share rent, manage this investment concept, as they would with any other form of business be that property or any other form of commercial enterprise. As with any form of business, the mindset of the business owner is a key factor to the success of any commercial venture therefore understanding such matters as risk and reward, return on investment, the ability to liquidate assets and income potential are business essentials that those who elect to be financially educated will benefit from over time.

Many of the investor clients of my accounting practice advise that they have generated a part time or full time income from this one investment concept. It was enlightening to identify and understand the returns that some clients were receiving through the share renting process. It was also encouraging to engage investor clients who adopted the practice of making sensible investment decisions as opposed to risky decisions based on hot tips and guess work.

Investor clients enter into these investment strategies with the right mindset and understanding to make this work. Many clients have expressed an opinion that to implement a business strategy such as investing without having the right mindset will not generate the result that they need.

One of the keys to mindset is in keeping the process extremely simple and uncomplicated. This has been one of the cornerstones that has made Jamie so successful over many years. It is not necessary at all to use software, or to spend more than a couple of hour's per month researching and reviewing an investment business, sometimes less. Jamie has been in the business of applying his business skills in this area for long enough to prove to himself that he is comfortable with his preferred investment strategy. Jamie has applied his preferred investment strategy through the good and bad times (generally referred to as investment cycles). Jamie as with other investor clients adopt this concept for the purpose of generating a regular cash flow from investments in the market.

While some investor clients purchase shares for capital growth, others purchase shares for income generation. Other investor clients purchase property for capital growth and build a share portfolio that can provide a predictable cash flow from share renting.

Investor clients make comparisons between competing investment concepts. Investors generally have limited financial resources and unlimited investment opportunities. Therefore, comparing the risk and reward of a traditional business to that of a business that is involved in share renting is common practice.

For a **traditional business**, a business owner will review many of the following concepts when putting together a business plan before making an investment decision.

INVESTMENT — This is the asset that is purchased for the purpose of producing income for the business owner.

RISK MANAGEMENT — To borrow for a traditional business, there is a risk management factor to consider. Here we look at the various risk factors of an investment with the aim of minimising them. Risk can take many forms, for example, valuation risk. Thus, if borrowing to invest, a lending institution would require security over the business assets and potentially over other personal assets.

INCOME POTENTIAL — In the first phase of operating a traditional business, most small business owners do not draw a wage as profits are reinvested back into the business. Income levels are low.

HANDS ON — Operating a traditional small business requires a hands on approach. In most instances, the business will not run without the business owner being present.

LIFESTYLE — Owning and operating a small business may require a commitment of 5 to 7 days per week. Lifestyle will be a casualty of extensive working hours.

STRESS LEVELS — Most owners of a small business experience high stress levels as the business goes through its start up then future business cycles.

STAFF — A traditional business will require staff to service the needs of the business. The business owner is therefore required to manage the staff which in itself is a significant business challenge.

LOCATION — A traditional business will operate from a fixed location. The business owner is tied to a particular area, which will affect lifestyle.

RETURN ON INVESTMENT — This financial indicator is a measure of the amount of money received annually for an investment. A traditional business receives a low return through the early stages.

ABILITY TO LIQUIDATE — If a traditional business is to provide security in the form of property, liquidating business assets may take some time for the business owner.

For a business owner involved with share renting, there is the need to review all the same concepts as a traditional business owner when putting together a business plan before making an investment decision.

INVESTMENT — This is the asset that is purchased for the purpose of producing income for the business owner. The value of the investment may be no different to that of a traditional business owner.

Alternatively, the value of the investment may be significantly lower as the cost of entry into a share renting business is generally around $20,000.

RISK MANAGEMENT — Every business decision has risk and share renting is no exception to this rule. In this form of investment an investor monitors and controls risk factors with the aim of minimising the volatility of investment returns.

In its simplest format, risk is the variability of investment returns. Risk can take many forms, valuation risk, currency risk, exchange risk, market risk, political risk and volatility. The risk adverse investor will settle for a relatively low risk portfolio where the returns are predictable. A risk taker investor will require a relatively high return in order to compensate for the risk and uncertainty with an investment result. Investors who share rent review the concept of risk prior to making an investment decision. Investors who are financially educated make an informed decision as to the required amount of investment return knowing the risk associated with their decision. Investor clients have taken out **insurance** to further minimise the risk associated with their investment in the belief that if there were to be another crash in the market, they would protect their downside and potentially profit from such an event. Most investor clients of my accounting practice consider themselves to be low risk investors.

INCOME POTENTIAL — Is a function of the risk being taken when making an investment decision. The higher the risk, the higher the return which will be less predictable. The lower the risk, the lower the return which will be more predictable.

HANDS ON — Share renting may take considerably less time to manage than a traditional business. Every investor will be different. Jamie devotes no more than 30 to 60 minutes a month to managing his investments. This is a highly effective use of time.

LIFESTYLE — Compared to a traditional business where the owner may be required a commitment of 5 to 7 days per week, lifestyle can be materially different for those investors who derive part or all of their income from share renting concepts. Opportunities exist to develop other forms of income from regular employment or other forms of business.

STRESS LEVELS — As with any form of business, there is the possibility of experiencing stress through share renting. Investors who adopt this concept without the assistance of an accredited licensed share trader face higher stress levels than those who engage the services of an accredited licensed share trader. The difficulty here is identifying a licensed and accredited broker that understands and can manage efficiently the concept of share renting.

STAFF — Generally NIL.

LOCATION — While a traditional business will operate from a fixed location, there is no fixed location required to manage the share-renting concept. Communications around the world are at a generally high standard. Jamie manages his business activities using the Internet and SMS services.

RETURN ON INVESTMENT — This financial indicator is a measure of the amount of money received annually for an investment. As indicated, risk management will be a significant factor in determining the size of any investment return.

ABILITY TO LIQUIDATE — the ability of an investment to be easily converted into cash with little or no loss in capital and with minimal delay is a measure of liquidity. To close up shop quickly and efficiently is important. Winding up the affairs of a traditional business including the sale of assets, the settlement of liabilities and the payment of cash to shareholders can be a time consuming, laborious and stressful task. In some instances a traditional business may have little to no resale value.

Investors who adopt the share-renting concept initially purchase shares as a way of getting started. Shares are purchases in the market through an accredited and licensed share trader. Not all shares can be rented. To determine which shares can be rented visit the ASX website www.asx.com.au. Investor clients of the accounting practice initially paper trade as paper trading provides the opportunity to practice, and learn, without the danger of real losses. Paper traders experiment with different trading approaches, and test and refine trading strategies in practice before applying them in the market. Paper traders observe how premiums move.

In preparing a financial statement for an investor client an understanding of the basic fundamentals of the share renting process is required. Assuming that our investor has purchased 1000 shares in our imaginary stock at $16 after researching the price range movement of our imaginary share as outlined in the section headed "channelling". The cash outlay will be $16,000.

Our investor client will offer these shares to the market where an alternative investor will offer our investor a rental income (more commonly known as a premium) for the opportunity to purchase our imaginary share should its share price reach the exercise price. Assume that the alternative investor is prepared to pay our investor $0.44 cents for share renting. Our investor will receive a rental income of $440 regardless of the actual share price movement over the period of the option. If the strike price is achieved, the alternative investor has the right to purchase our imaginary share any time prior to the expiry of the option.

The alternative investor is of the belief that our imaginary share will increase in value above the strike price, therefore renting our imaginary share is a cost effective method of purchasing a share at a discount. These types of investment decisions are generally made at the beginning of a calendar month.

Assuming the price of our imaginary share increases to $17 or higher, the alternative investor will most likely purchase our investors imaginary shares. Our investor must sell all shares if exercised. To sell our imaginary share at $17 will generate additional profits for our investor of $1 per imaginary share or $1000 for the 1000 imaginary shares. Our investor has now made $440 for renting the shares plus an additional $1000 which equals $1440 gross less brokerage fees.

Assuming the price of our imaginary share goes down to $15.50 or lower, our investor clients have a theoretical paper loss of $0.50 cents per share after having received from our alternative investor $0.44 cents for share renting. The net effect is a reduction in share price of $0.06 cents per share. At the end of each financial year the actual price of each share is obtained to account for any price movement in the books of our investor clients.

Taking out insurance to protect against a fall in the share price is an investment strategy that is to be recognised when accounting for some investment transactions. Put options allow investor clients to protect the value of particular share or portfolio against falls. By buying a put option, they lock in a selling price for the underlying shares for the life of the option. Investor clients purchase a put option as a form of insurance however unlike an insurance policy the term of the protection can be for relatively short periods. Any time our investor clients no longer consider it necessary to protect the value of a share the option can be sold. An investor can mix and match strategies such as renting shares in conjunction with taking out insurance.

SELLING INSURANCE

While some of our investor clients earn income against shares held, other investor clients earn income against shares they are looking to buy. Therefore, in the same way investors that sell call options are paid a premium for undertaking to sell shares, selling put options also generates premiums. In the case of selling a put option the obligation is to potentially buy shares if the share falls below a predetermined price. In this instance our investor clients are selling put options as a way of being paid to buy shares at a lower price than they are currently worth where they have sold a put option with a lower strike price than the current trading price.

For this investment strategy, assume our imaginary share is trading at $16 and that our investor sells a put option for our imaginary share with a promise to the market that our investor will purchase the imaginary share at $15.50. An alternative investor requiring insurance will pay a premium to insure their holdings of our imaginary share should the market price fall below $15.50. Assuming the cost of insurance is $0.40 per share, our investor will receive this premium in return for the promise to the market to purchase each imaginary share at the predetermined strike price. If the put option is not exercised, then we account for the insurance as income. If the put option is exercised, we account for the insurance as a reduction in the capital value of the imaginary share, i.e. the imaginary share is recorded as being purchased for $15.10.

Investor clients who implement this concept recognise that they must have the capacity to purchase the imaginary share if required under the terms and conditions of the put option.

SUMMARY

In summary, we see our investor clients becoming more and more involved with Exchange Traded Options. At one stage our accounting practice viewed this style of investment as one to be used by speculators. Today, Exchange Traded Options are just as likely to be used by our investor clients who are long-term investors managing risk, investors buying shares on margin or in a Self Managed Super Fund (SMSF).

Options are being used in a variety of ways by our investor clients to profit from a rise or fall in prices. The most basic strategies adopted by our investor clients are put and call options as a low cost means of getting exposure. Options are being used to offer protection from a decline in market price or as a hedge against rising prices. They have enabled investors to buy shares at a lower price, sell shares at a higher price, or create additional income. The versatility of options has made the concepts as described in this chapter very popular with our investor clients looking to build and protect long-term wealth.

SUMMARY OF INSTANT CASHFLOW STRATEGIES

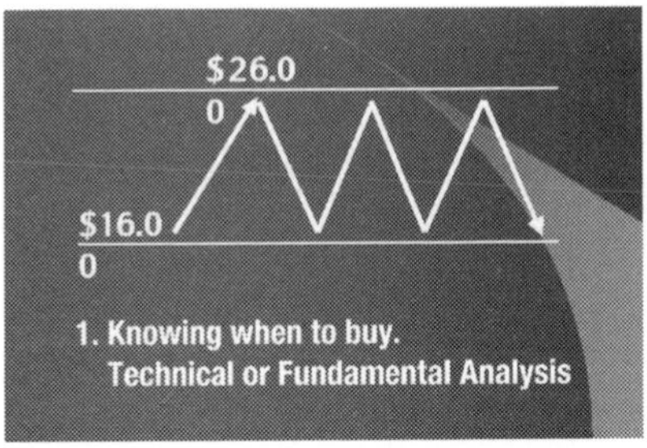
$26.00
$16.00
1. Knowing when to buy.
Technical or Fundamental Analysis

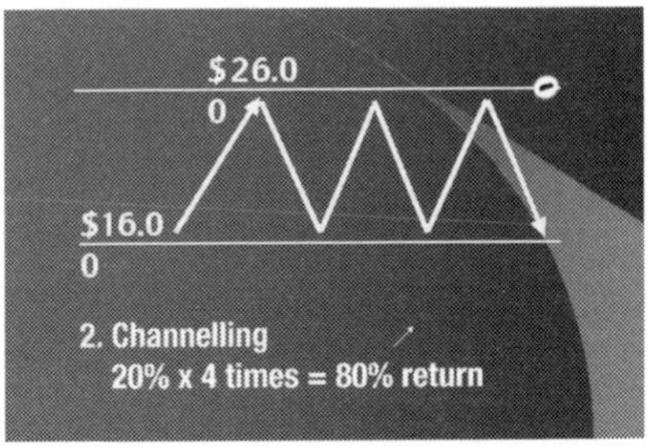
$26.00
$16.00
2. Channelling
20% x 4 times = 80% return

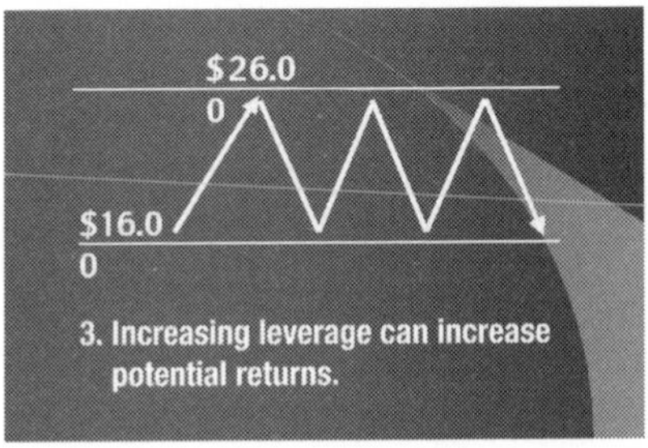
$26.00
$16.00
3. Increasing leverage can increase
potential returns.

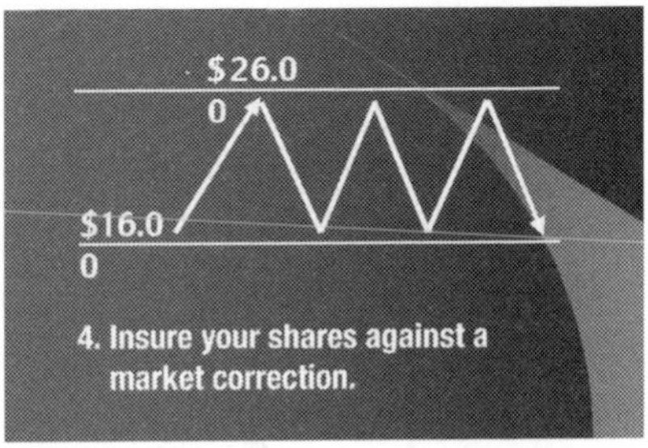
$26.00
$16.00
4. Insure your shares against a
market correction.

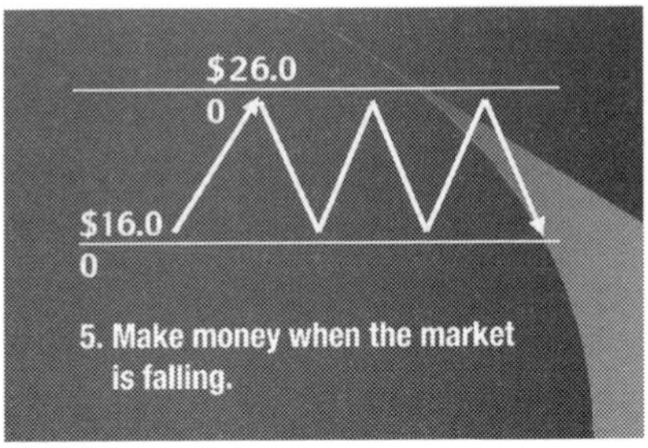
$26.00
$16.00
5. Make money when the market
is falling.

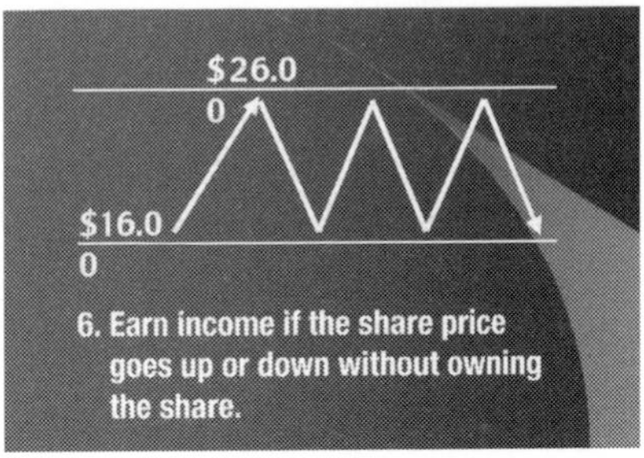
$26.00
$16.00
6. Earn income if the share price
goes up or down without owning
the share.

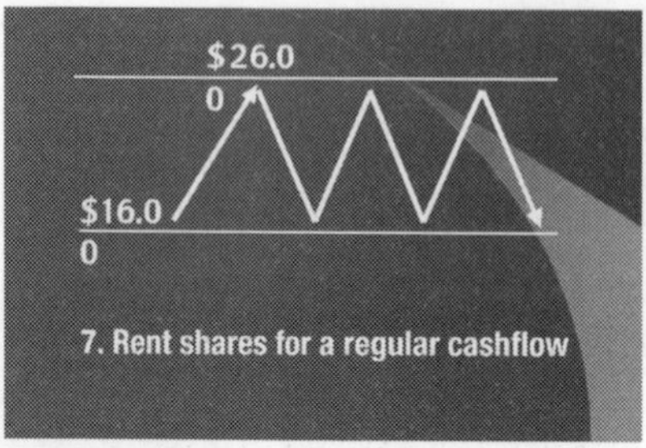
$26.0
0
$16.0
0
7. Rent shares for a regular cashflow

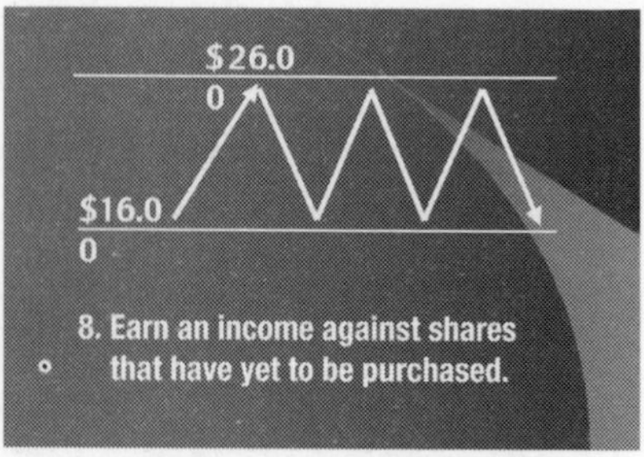
$26.0
0
$16.0
0
8. Earn an income against shares
that have yet to be purchased.

CHAPTER 14

PROPERTY STRATEGIES

FAST TRACK PROPERTY STRATEGIES

- How to find Motivated Sellers
- How to Buy at Wholesale
- How to Obtain 100% Finance
- How to Buy Property No Money Down
- How to get Finance for Property even on a Small Income

WHY INVEST IN REAL ESTATE?

One reason is because many people have made money out of real estate and I expect many more to make even more money in the years to come. It is an easily accessible market that has many favourable advantages. If you are using real estate, make sure that you do your homework properly. Like any investment area — there are sensible and risky ways of investing in real estate and depending on your experience, determination and skill, you can just as easily lose money as make money.

MILLIONAIRES FROM REAL ESTATE

Intelligent use of real estate can enable ordinary Australians to become millionaires in about 10 years or less. Despite the "concept" of property belonging to the "rich", most Australian property investors earn below the average wage, (which has recently increased to $42,000 approximately). So property is clearly not just for the super wealthy — it is for anyone who wishes to increase his or her net worth in a steady, appreciating environment.

Bear in mind that if you wish to be one of the "wealthy" people in the future you should probably be using property to your advantage. Statistics show us that home ownership is decreasing in Australia. As property prices keep rising, less and less people are able to afford their "dream home". It is expected that by the year 2010 only 49% of Australians will own their own home. This is down from 73% in 1980. So there is a definite trend of many people sidestepping real estate. This means that these people are going to be "renters" for their entire lives.

Personally, I like to buy property no money down because I do not like to tie up cash in property if I can avoid it. I learned how to buy property virtually no money down. Recently, for instance, I bought four properties in Brisbane. $1,200,000 worth of property which I bought at around $80,000 below the bank valuation, and my only cash outlay was no more than $2,400. That means that $80,000 is profit straight away and I do not have to pay for those properties for over a year. In a year those properties could be worth $1.3 or $1.4 million with an outlay of virtually nothing. In the meantime, the cash I saved outlaying is tied up making returns from renting strategies rather than putting 10% deposit in a trust account earning zero. You can see how investing is not a bad hobby, especially when you get to a point where you do not need the money. It is fun and you can do a lot of things with it.

A lot of statisticians say that on average across the board, property has doubled on average every 7 to 10 years in the last 146 years in Australia. Not all property though. Some people have properties that double in 5 years, or 20 years — it obviously depends on the location and quality of property and price you pay for it.

For instance, Bill and Mary are earning $50,000 a year and they want to replace their income. I am going to suggest that just by buying two investment properties, they could achieve this. Let us look at how they can buy two investment properties for them to retire. $50,000 a year is approximately $35,000 per year after tax. So would you be committed to buying 2 properties in the next decade if you could retire from them?

In year 1 of the plan, we are going to buy one property. The properties I tend to buy are often around $300,000, which we will use for this strategy. The second year we do not buy any property and the third year we buy our second property. You do not have to buy 100 properties and become a property guru to make this work. In ten years time, these properties could be worth $600,000. That is ten years after you buy them, especially if you are buying them with good criteria and they are good quality properties. (Always make your plans conservative as it could take 10 years or longer.) I generally buy properties in capital cities because these properties will continue to grow. I have some properties outside capital cities that have made phenomenal returns but I prefer capital cities. You have to work out your own criteria. The strategy is not going to work in a small country town because the property will not double in 10 years or even 100 years and could go the other way. Imagine Broken Hill — property does not double every 10 years in Broken Hill. You can buy a property for as little as $1,300, people just leave town and they are left sitting there.

If the property doubles in 10 years (ideally 7 but 10 to be conservative), this is $300,000 in extra money we have made over 10 years per property, i.e., $300,000 each, now worth $600,000. You have bought this property probably on a 10% deposit, unless you have learned how to buy virtually no money down, borrowed the difference and it is now worth $600,000. You have earned $300,000 from capital growth. Bill and Mary need $35,000 a year net to replace their current incomes. They are probably thinking if they buy the property, they have to work harder. If they buy and sell to make a profit, they generally have to pay capital gains tax. In this strategy, we are going to buy a good property and keep it ideally forever. It is worth 600,000. They need $35,000 net cash to replace their income. Where can they get that from?

What about a line of credit?

A line of credit allows us to draw equity/cash out of property by setting up a bank account from which to draw this down. They can draw out $35,000 in the first year. Is there any law saying they can not spend that money? The banks do not care where they spend it as long as they meet their commitments. In Year 2, they can do the same thing and draw out $35,000, and take another $35,000 in year 3. Are they spending money they worked hard for or are they spending money they made out of thin air while they slept? They do not want to take any more money out of that property even though they could. Remember, they have waited 10 years before they have started to draw this down.

In years 4, 5 and 6 they could take say $35,000 out of the second property. It is just sitting there so why not use it? If they do not use it, when they die someone else gets it, so they might as well use the money they have made.

Six years after the first property is worth more than $600,000, being in a capital city, good growth area, it may be worth $900,000 to $1 million, i.e., if it has doubled in 10 years to $600,000, 6 years later it could be $900,000 plus. We will use that as an example. That gives them another $300,000 sitting there available to use. They have not finished using the first $300,000 and now they have another $300,000 and the property keeps going up in value whether they like it or not.

Now if they are not careful, they could get into a cycle of making more money than they can spend, which will mean they have more than they need for retirement. Do they have to pay income tax on the $35,000 per year they draw out? The answer is no because it is not income. They are spending thin air so there is not a thin air tax yet! That money is legally tax free. The ATO will let you do that because it is borrowings, plus if you do not invest and buy properties to house Australians the government has to.

If you recall, super duper extra good debt is something you borrowed for that goes up in value that you do not have to necessarily pay back. Do you have to pay back this debt or do you simply have to meet the interest payments? The answer is you never actually have to pay this debt back unless you choose. That is what insurance companies are for. They take your money to insure your debt. When you die, your debt and life insurance will pay out the properties. If you want to pay this debt, you can, as critics may say this is a debt ridden strategy. However, let us consider what a real debt ridden strategy is. Most people work hard to try to pay their property off. Is that really smart? No, because they have been taught to work hard for money and they have to get out of this way of thinking. The banks do not work hard for money. Have you noticed that the banks own most buildings in the cities, and do you think they are working hard to pay those off? They know they are increasing in value. Do you think they are not pulling that money out and using it? They are using it all the time.

McDonalds makes more money from its real estate than it does from its hamburgers because they use that equity. A lot of wealthy people understand this and that is why they are wealthy, (i.e., Gerry Harvey of *Harvey Norman* fame makes a lot of his wealth from the property that he develops for his franchised *Harvey Norman* stores).

If we wanted to pay off the debt with this strategy and live off the rent, we could now sell the second property and use this money to pay off the first property and wipe out our debt without having to work hard to pay the debt. This is another example of working smart versus working hard. A different way of looking at money.

10 YEAR PLAN

Year	**Property Value**
1.	Buy $300,000
2.	Nil
3.	Buy second $300,000

Property Value in 10 years time

		Extra Equity	
Property 1	$600,000	$300,000	
		Year 1	Draw out $35,000 in line of credit TAX FREE to replace Bill and Mary's income $50,000 salary less tax, gross $35,000 net
		Year 2	Draw out $35,000
		Year 3	Draw out $35,000

Property 2 $600,000 – $300,000 Equity

Year 4	Draw out $35,000 line of credit from Property 2
Year 5	Draw out $35,000
Year 6	Draw out $35,000
Year 7	Property 1 is now worth $900K plus approx. equals another $300,000 in additional equity. Draw out $35,000
Year 8	Draw out $35,000
Year 9	Draw out $35,000
Year 10	Property 2 is now worth $900K plus approximately equals $300,000 in additional equity. Cycle continues.

NB Year 1 commences ten years from purchase of first property in this example, however they could start drawing down equity sooner if needed.

I have illustrated this as a concept only. Obviously in reality there are obstacles that may have to be overcome, such as qualifying for finance, getting good valuations and being comfortable spending equity (thin air) rather than just leaving it to go to waste and dying with it unspent. Or what if the property market goes flat (then you may have to adjust

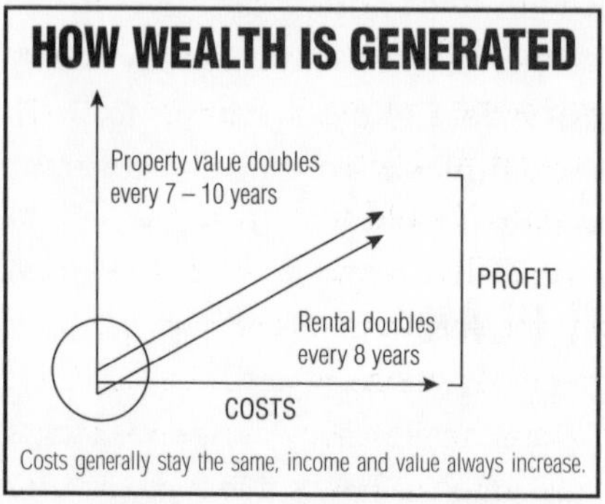

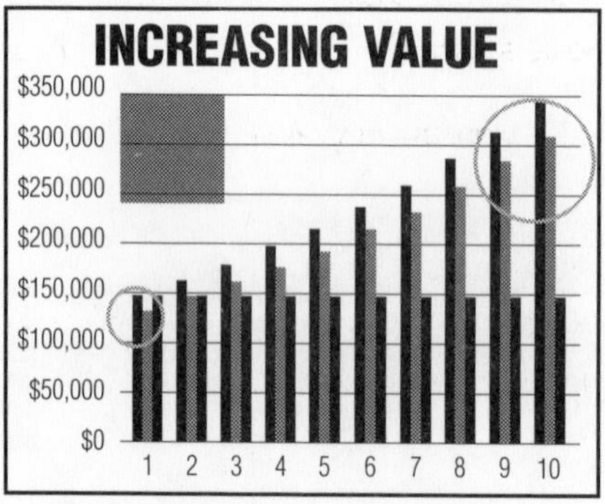

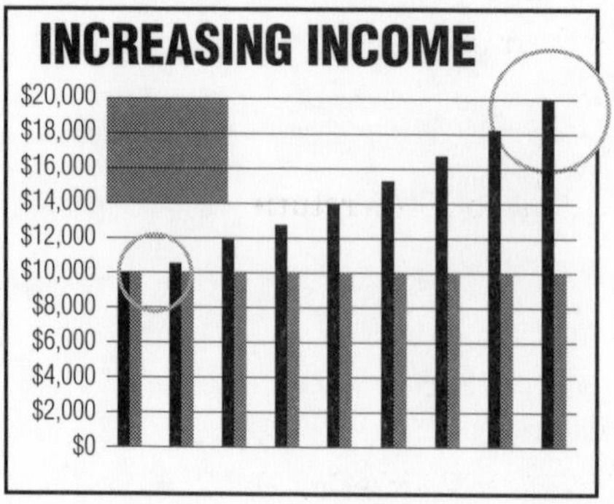

If property income is $10,000 and expenses are $10,000 this is geared neutrally.

your plan to a 15 year plan rather than 10 years, or 5 years as it has been in the last 5 years)? Is this still better though than no plan or the pension plan? I'd say most definately.

However, if you get the concept you are 80% there.

One question I asked my millionaire mentor when I first learned how he did this was, "How do I pay the interest bill in the line of credits, as it will be increasing the more I draw on the $35,000 year after year". He told me that I need to be creative and overcome any challenges that I may encounter. For instance, he said rents tend to double every 7 to 9 years. That is additional income that can be used. Could you draw some extra equity to cover some of the interest shortfall if need be? Could you still qualify for tax deductions to help fund the shortfall? Could you generate some income from the renting strategy, for instance, to cover some of the interest bill without the need to work to ensure you enjoy your retirement?

The answer was obviously yes, as long as I was willing to think outside the box and compare it to my other alternatives of working hard and not really enjoying the fruits of one's wealth.

Fast Track Property Strategies to make you money while you sleep.

WHAT IF YOU COULD...

- Buy property virtually no money down
- Avoid being ripped off by paying way too much for Gold Coast style properties
- Ensure property goes up in value
- Have tenants who:
  a) will pay rent on time all the time
  b) treat the property as if it is their own
  c) be willing to pay more rent
  d) sign 3–5 year leases
- Get returns in property equivalent to 100% return in companies
- Legally minimise tax
- Find motivated sellers
- Massively reduce stamp duty
- Learn more about secrets of successful property investors

Property vs Companies

Example:

Property	Versus
Purchase $1 million property portfolio Generally a 10% deposit, i.e. $100,000 would be required.	$100k deposit company portfolio
90% loan as possible to gain greater leverage with property than shares	To equal the return of our property portfolio would require a 100% gain on our company
Assuming 10% Capital Growth in 1 year then $1.1 million would be new value of property portfolio	Assuming same 10% capital growth as property
= $100,000 equity gain on $100,000 outlay (10% deposit)	= $10,000
= 100% net ROI (return on investment)	= 10% ROI only

Property in this example is 10 times more profitable when measured as return on outlay. This is due to it being common to borrow 80% – 90% or even 100% on property, where it is not common to do so with companies due to the high risk. Few financial planners are honest enough to highlight this mainly due to them earning commissions on selling managed funds which are invested predominately in the market. I personally invest in both property and companies, however, I realise it is easier and takes less time, involvement and less skill to get up to 10% pa gain on a quality investment property portfolio versus needing a 100% gain in companies to achieve the same ROI. It is true you can margin loan up to 70% on companies, however, this carries substantial risk in comparison to borrowing for property.

PROPERTY ORGANISING PRINCIPLES

I have enclosed my key organising principles I have generally used to build a large property portfolio. I was able to build over a $10 million property portfolio in little over 24 months using many of these principles, including many of them no money down.

Treat it as a Business. Therefore, a business must:

1) Add Value
2) Make a Profit

A successful business must treat its clients like VIPs.
The clients therefore in residential property are your tenants.
A successful business must have a Unique selling proposition (USP).
If you own 1 out of 50 similar properties in a CBD appartment, is your business unique.

YES/NO I would suggest, no.

Commercial property is treated as a business.
What if we adopted commercial property principles to residential property? Increase rent and automatically increase value of property, i.e.:

- Easier to buy no money down
- Tax benefits and 221D form to assist in your cashflow.

ADDING VALUE

1) Add value to property including your own house
List five things you can do to add value to a property

	Original value	New Value	Extra equity
	$300k	$350k	= $50K
1 ____			e.g. Renovate bathroom and kitchen
2 ____			Paint it
3 ____			New carpet, floorboards
4 ____			Landscape gardens, (Backyard Blitz)
5 ____			Clean up & tidy

Re-value house. Best to use a new bank to re-value and re-finance. Why?

They will value on similar properties in area compared to existing bank, who will value upwards of original purchase price which is likely to be a lower valuation.

2) Add value to the tenant:
Think what they would want. List five ways to attract a better quality, higher paying and longer staying tenant for your property. I have included some examples which can work effectively in different circumstances.

1 ______________________	e.g. Include pool or garden maintenance, furniture package
2 ______________________	A furniture package, they get to own if they agree to a longer lease, pay higher rent & always pay
3 ______________________	If rent paid on time, give the tenant a share in percentage of capital growth, if they sign
4 ______________________	A 5 yr lease & agree to the above. For university students you could include a free car subject to costs. Charge higher rent, use higher rent to cover cost of car payments.
5 ______________________	

By adding value you can

1) Charge more rent as property is more desirable;
   Increase capital value ($$), the higher the rent the higher the property value.
   Increase access to cash (as you can draw more out in a line of credit).
   Speed up your retirement plan as you can do it sooner.
2) Also if a tenant will sign a 3 – 5 year lease;
   It increases capital valuation instantly as property is worth more.
   Increase cash (line of credit) that you can draw out which you could use to buy furniture etc. (or use 12 monthly interest free offers for furniture which will entice a better quality, longer stay tenant in many cases).

EXAMPLE OF NO MONEY DOWN / 100% FINANCE

1. Purchase property worth $300,000.
2. You negotiate 10% discount = $270,000. Target developers or vendors who are prepared to consider offering discounts. You do not need to be ruthless. That is just a story critics use to discredit many successful

investors. To get a discount — you do not have to take advantage of desperate vendors to get discounts. Always look for a win win opportunity, as many people are happy to sell at a discount and glad if you are willing to buy at an agreeable price.

3. A $27,000 deposit — use deposit bond.
4. Exchange contracts at point A.
5. Have time to increase savings, gain extra equity from other properties and get better finance.
6. Prior to settlement re-valued at say $330,000, i.e., 10% increase.
7. 90% (LVR loan $297,000) which is over 100% finance. 80% (LVR loan $264,000) nearly 100%. Delayed settlement 12 months later. Get bank to finance based on contract price or revaluation, whichever is the higher.

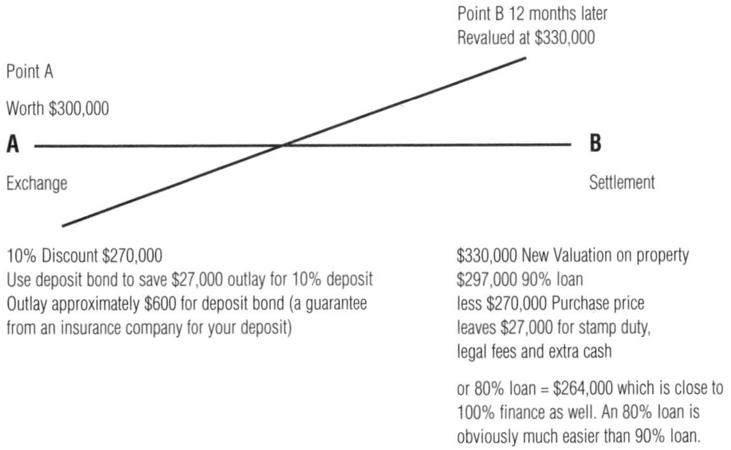
Point B 12 months later
Revalued at $330,000
Point A
Worth $300,000
A
B
Exchange
Settlement
10% Discount $270,000
Use deposit bond to save $27,000 outlay for 10% deposit
Outlay approximately $600 for deposit bond (a guarantee
from an insurance company for your deposit)
$330,000 New Valuation on property
$297,000 90% loan
less $270,000 Purchase price
leaves $27,000 for stamp duty,
legal fees and extra cash
or 80% loan = $264,000 which is close to
100% finance as well. An 80% loan is
obviously much easier than 90% loan.

I recently purchased several properties valued at $330,000, negotiated a $22,000 discount per property as a group of us bought the whole development.

Purchase price $308,000 with six months delayed settlement. Revalued at $355K, put one unit on market at $375K allowing option to sell it prior to settlement if desired at a $80,000 profit (on zero outlay as I used a deposit bond to save a 10% deposit). However, generally my preferred strategy is to hold properties and never sell unless I need some quick cash. Six months delayed settlement allows time to arrange tenants and improve my financial position to obtain better finance, i.e., higher LVR 90% instead of 80%. These days 100% investment loans are quite common as well. Plus my associates often pay one of my companies a sourcing fee for helping put the deal together. For instance, would you pay $2,000 in fees if a friend or associated arranged a property at a $22,000 to $35,000 discount that increases by a further $25,000 within six months and is likely to double in value within 7 to 10 years. This is one way to earn additional income. You could find property yourself and earn a fee by bringing them to offer property investors or just benefit from discounts due to buying in bulk.

If you can gain just a 1% discount on a $300,000 property it equals $3,000. Is it worth asking for a discount 5% = $15,000. Critics will say:

1. If you can buy a property at a discount, it was not really worth that in the first place. My comment would be how many critics become self made millionaires? Not many! Discounts are available if you target the right people and negotiate well, and create win win relationships and do not take advantage of people.

2. What if the property drops in value? The solution is to use criteria to select carefully. Either way, if you negotiated a discount you automatically reduce your risk as you buy below value and quality property rarely drops in value, unless of course you buy overpriced Gold Coast property, which has occurred to a lot of interstate investors.

Instead of getting a $300,000 property at a 10% discount, property sharks (marketeers) often add 20% and more to the value and sell properties to gullible interstate investors (punters) at say $360,000 collecting the $60,000 extra as profit. The investor then finds out several years later that their property is worth less than they paid for it.

Warning: If you go to wealth seminars, make sure all they are selling are education courses and they offer a 100% money back guarantee. Be wary of property seminars selling negative geared property and always get an independent valuation if you wish to proceed. Hopefully increased regulations will reduce some property marketeers from selling overpriced properties to consumers. However, regulation will not protect everyone. Only self education will, which is a good reason to educate yourself by reading books and attending educational only seminars or home study courses.

Following is an article highlighting Gold Coast rip offs. I have included a 21 Point Criteria Checklist I use to build a property portfolio fast.

INVESTOR

Housing investment self-regulator's watchdog chases its tail

Buyers lose out

By JOHN SYNNOTT

PROPERTY ONE

N	$ 139500	11/09/95	KIDSON, STEPHEN	7 ILLANONG STREET CHEVRON ISLAND 4
E	$ 84000	17/08/98	CJR LIFESTYLE PTY LTD.	7 ILLANONG STREET CHEVRON ISLAND 4

PROPERTY TWO

G	$ 132500	26/04/95	LIM, HUEY	7 ILLANONG STREET CHEVRON ISLAND 4
H	$ 71000	12/03/98	ASIA PACIFIC MANAGEMENT C	7 ILLANONG STREET CHEVRON ISLAND 4

REALTY REALITY: How the prices at one Gold Coast addresses have fluctuated in just three years.

A COMPLAINTS hotline, set up by Queensland investment property marketers to identify high pressure operators, is now ringing in the office of the Epic Group, one of the largest marketers.

Epic is run by the president of the Australian Federation of Property Developers and Marketers, Chris Bilborough.

Mr Bilborough promised a code of ethics, self-regulation and a constitution when the federation was formed in November by 10 marketing companies amid revelations by *The Sun-Herald* of battlers losing out in negative gearing property investment deals.

The constitution and code of practice were still being drawn up, the federation's spokeswoman said.

Mr Bilborough's company was criticised by solicitor Kelvin Legg, who rang *The Sun-Herald* to tell of a trip to Queensland to view properties being sold as part of a negative gearing investment package by National Asset Planning Corporation (NAPC), now called Epic.

When Mr Legg and his wife did not sign up during the trip, saying they were "uncertain" about the whole deal, they were taken back to Coolangatta airport five hours before their return flight.

Checking later, he found that NAPC had the same director as Investland, the company supposed to give purchasers independent financial advice.

The federation spokeswoman on the lapsed hotline said she doubted there was any conflict but would take up the issue with Mr Bilborough. He did not return the call.

In another development, extracts from the Gold Coast City Council reveal recent auction sales of investment units have shown 40 per cent losses on prices originally charged by some marketers above the local going rates.

One buyer, Yeok Chan, discovered this when his $130,000 Gold Coast Paradise Views unit on Chevron Island, bought in 1995 for $130,500, was sold last month for $75,000 by L J Hooker. Now marketers are facing a crackdown on several fronts.

Queensland Fair Trading Minister Judy Spence is drafting laws to crack down on the hard-sell marketers who convince naive NSW investors to buy overpriced units and houses on the Gold Coast and Brisbane using optimistic return-on-investment figures.

The marketers can add up to 25 per cent of the purchase price, compared with 5pc by real estate agents. There are plans for a NSW-style cooling off period for real estate deals in Queensland.

"I am shocked at the activities of some solicitors and the way banks are lending money in the full knowledge that clients are buying properties at inflated prices," Ms Spence said

Because many Sydney investors use their home as security, there is little risk for the banks if the investment property is sold at a loss.

Financial advisers and lawyers who are tied to the marketers and used to provide independent advice are also under the microscope.

Kerry Davis, managing director of L J Hooker at Surfers Paradise, said they were great sales machines but the problem was that they were selling properties in some cases for $30,000 to $100,000 more than market price.

"They charge up to $5,000 for a financial plan we do in the office for free," he said.

"I started complaining about them in 1993 and they were selling 50 properties a month, now they are doing 500."

Some marketers have come out and attacked others, with a new Sydney company, BestInvest advertising that "investors are paying up to $50,000 more than market value for property pushed on to them by hard sell marketers".

BestInvest is offering a referral service to "property investment companies that have a proven record of integrity and provide a full management service package".

The five-star checklist includes a guarantee to select locations with well researched growth projections for 10 years, priced in line with the local market, independently valued with rental guarantee for the life of the property and a repairs and maintenance warranty.

Timely warning saves targeted investors

AN official warning about the dangers of being "cold called" by shonky overseas promoters has saved Australian investors hundreds of thousands of dollars.

The Australian Securities and Investments Commission issued the warning about telephone "cold calling" in *The Sun-Herald* last month

"In the two weeks following the warning, we received more calls from the public than we had in the previous 12 months," said ASIC international relations director Rose Webb.

"In two weeks, 68 people contacted ASIC's Infoline, detailing hundreds of thousands of dollars in actual and potential investments going to these overseas promoters," she said.

"Some of the responses were good news. We had at least 10 investors who were about to send large amounts of money, from $5,000 to $28,000, when they heard our warning and stopped their investments.

"Unfortunately, the campaign also exposed a number of investors who lost large sums of money.

"Many lost at least $10,000 and two lost about $60,000 and $120,000."

Ms Webb said ASIC had been in touch with regulators in the US, Holland and Hong Kong to take action against unscrupulous investment promoters.

She said investors should follow simple rules if they received an offshore call offering a business opportunity: ask who you are speaking to, where they are from and if they are licensed by ASIC to deal in securities in Australia.

"If they are not licensed by ASIC, don't deal with them," Ms Webb said.

– ALEX MITCHELL

NEW LAWS: Queensland Fair Trading Minister Judy Spence.

A 21 POINT CHECKLIST MODIFIED FROM TOP AUSTRALIAN PROPERTY INVESTORS

1. Select properties within the $250,000 to $500,000 price range.

Properties priced below $250,000 will either be too small, not have the desired quality finishes, or not be in the best possible area.

- If the property is priced over $500,000, (in most cases) it will cease to become affordable to the vast majority of tenants. Most tenants will not be able to afford rental payments of $550 plus per week.
- It will also be difficult to obtain a 90% LVR finance option from most institutions.

2. Select properties within sought after "lifestyle" locations that will attract consistent rental demand by quality tenants.

- Select properties in established residential streets.

3. Select properties in areas within 15kms of the CBD but not the CBD or some CBD fringe areas.

4. Select properties within suburbs and streets where limited land is available.

- If there is limited land available for further development, you will have less competition for tenants.
- Property values will also increase at a greater rate.
- "Limited land" also means that the area is in demand — people want to live there.

5. Select properties in suburbs with proven capital growth over the past 5 years.

6. Select properties close to "water", e.g., beaches, oceans and rivers.

7. Select properties in suburbs which have a high rental demand.

- First call, then visit the "top" agents in the area and check their rental lists to assess the rental demand, e.g., check how many properties are on their For Lease list.

- Talk to the agent's rental manager in regard to "rental growth" in the area.

8. Select properties in areas which have "affluent" tenants with high disposable income.

- More and more people are now leasing residential property, and investing excess income into investments.
- The higher the tenants income, the more chance you have of raising the rental amount every year, and the less chance your property will be affected in the event of a recession or market downturn.
- High capital growth areas where gay individuals choose to live. Generally no kids and higher disposable income, i.e., Paddington in Sydney, etc.

9. Select properties which are located close to public transport.

10. Select properties which are "in demand" from corporate tenants.

- Corporate tenants pay more money, and are very secure tenants.
- You can call Relocation Agencies (listed in the Yellow Pages) to find out what suburbs corporate tenants most prefer.

11. Select properties close to educational facilities: universities, major public and private schools.

12. Select properties close to major sporting, dining and entertainment precincts.

- These days, people prefer eating out rather than cooking and eating in.

13. Select properties which have land content.

- The general "rule" is that land appreciates in value and buildings depreciate.
- In certain circumstances, specific high rise apartments might be worth more than houses in the same area, because they provide their occupants with fabulous views — water, city, mountains.

14. Select "townhouse style" properties.

- Townhouses should be a preference to apartments, flats and houses built on large land lots.
- Most Australians still prefer to live in a "house style" living environment rather than a high-rise apartment building, but because of the "shift" in our lifestyles people do not want to spend their free time watering the garden or pulling out the weeds.
- Apartment buildings do not provide the same level of security and privacy as does a townhouse property.
- There are far greater body corporate rates to be paid in relation to an apartment building than a townhouse property.
- Townhouses have the greatest appeal to corporate tenants because of their easy maintenance, increased security, extra privacy features and outdoor "lifestyle" areas.

15. Select properties which offer high depreciation and taxation benefits.

- Ask the property developer if they have a depreciation schedule for the property you wish to purchase, otherwise engage a quantity surveyor to perform a Depreciation Schedule Analysis on the property.
- The higher the depreciation allowance for the property the greater the tax benefit, the less money you will have to pay from your pocket towards the cost of maintaining the property.

16. Select properties within projects whose income potential is not based on "short term" or "holiday letting".

You are actually buying the tenant not the property.

- As you can now see, with the "holiday based" investment property such as serviced apartments, you are not purchasing the building structure, you are actually purchasing the tenant.
- If the tenant disappears, you can kiss your anticipated investment returns goodbye.

Competitors on your doorstep.

Furthermore, if your apartment is one of 50 or more, you will have 50 to 100 competitors who will want to sell or lease their apartment at the same time as you.

The old rule of property is that the balance between "supply and demand" dictates the price. If the property market takes a downturn and 50 or more "competitors" try to sell or "liquidate" their properties at the same time as you, it is very likely that your hard earned investment will be worth no more than 40% of its original value.

17. Select properties that are located within smaller low-rise "boutique" style properties.

- Select boutique properties, rather than high rise multi storey developments — less than 35 units in the project.
- Exactly the same problems associated with serviced apartments as per the above scenario also stand true for any high rise apartment blocks — 35 apartments or more. Especially the new warehouse shell based projects.
- If the property market takes a downturn and given the fact that you will have so many potential competitors on your doorstep, what do you think will happen to your property's rental earning potential or capital gain potential?
- If your neighbours panic and sell their property (which is similar to yours) at a lower value than their original purchase price, your property will automatically be devalued. Remember that property is worth only what a similar property last sold for. You will obviously have less competition for rental in a development of 15 units than a development of 150 units. The less units in the development means the less chance you will have of having multiple neighbour "competitors" discounting their rental price, thus reducing your property's rental potential.
- If similar apartments in your building get sold for prices below your purchase price, your property will automatically be valued at the same price, making it impossible to "re-value" the property and release extra equity in the future.
- In the event where the same financial institution financed most of the units in the same building and purchasers start "falling over", the bank may chose to re-value your property and ask you to inject extra equity needed to "top up" your loan.

18. Selecting a property where the price of the property offers at least a 5% gross rental return based on the "long term" rental guarantee the real estate agent is willing to provide.

- Ask the agent to provide you with a rental price which they are absolutely sure is achievable in the worst case scenario.
- If the "promised" and agreed to rental is not achieved by the rental agent after two weeks of trying to lease the property, the agent will receive no "marketing money" and will have to make up the difference between the rental guarantee and the actual rental price of the property.

19. Select properties within projects which are guaranteed to be built and completed.

Avoid the following types of off-the-plan projects:

- That may present a risk of not satisfying bank pre-sale requirements. If the developer can not obtain the funding, the project will never get built.
- Which are built by "amateur developers" who can not obtain the right funding or building price to complete the project. Ask the real estate agent to name other projects completed by the same developer, and go and inspect them personally.
- Where the project does not have a builder "attached" at the time of your purchase.
- Professional developers will have finalised the builder and construction contract price within the first three months of entering the marketing phase of the project. If they have not engaged a builder, you run the risk that a rise in the construction price will make the project too risky or unprofitable for the developer and the project will never get built.
- Which are not marked to being constructed within eight months of commencing the marketing phase.

Even large developers can run into problems and decide not to proceed with their project.

- If the project does not get finished, you will lose money due to the transaction costs (e.g. solicitor, accountant fees, bank guarantee fees, etc.) spent on purchasing the property.

20. Do not purchase off-the-plan property which is being sold "subject to permit".

21. Select properties which have 3 bedrooms, to increase rental income.

- You must only purchase properties that contain 3 bedrooms or a minimum of 2 bedrooms.
- One of your goals should always be to increase the rental price of your property every year as much as possible.
- Achieving the highest possible rental returns is far easier with a 3 bedroom property, 4 bedrooms is an overkill, as you are unlikely to get tenants requiring 4 bedrooms consistently renting the same property at the same time.
- One of the only reasons to overlook the above criteria is if the property is sold at an EXTREMELY low price.
- The only legitimate reason this could happen is as a result of dealing with a desperate vendor.

HOW TO OBTAIN 100% FINANCE

1. To obtain the ideal finance, you will have to make numerous calls and phone most of the various financiers who currently lend money towards residential property. I use good finance brokers who work on performance only. Do not pay upfront fees as they may not get you a loan but may keep your fee. I also now have my own finance broking company to service our clients called *21st Century Finance. 21st Century Finance* guarantees to get virtually anyone a loan and I have asked the team to offer every reader a free portfolio review valued at $195.

Email finance@21stcenturyacademy.com.au

- You can obtain the list of these lenders through the newspaper, through the Internet, through various mortgage based magazines available at any newsagent.
- What valuer does the lender use and will they accept the valuer who recently valued your property for "another" financial institution?

- – Will the lender accept the fact that you purchased the property at a wholesale price due to your skill?
- – Will they take market growth into account when evaluating the LVR?
- – **Will the financier lend you monies based on the Contract Price or Valuation, whichever is the HIGHER?**
- – Will the lender provide you with 100% LVR (loan to value ratio) or only 80%?
- – Will the lender provide you an Interest Only investment loan rather than principal and interest?
- – Will the lender provide you a 5 or 10 fixed interest facility versus variable rate?
- – Will your current financial status (income and assets) fit the financier's lending criteria?
- – Will the financier be willing to lend you monies for multiple properties?

2. You will need to call as many financiers as required, until you are able to "secure" at least two lenders.
   - – Have all the financial information the lender requires prepared, neatly arranged and ready for "show".
   - – Prepare a Professional Financial Proposal which will include:
     - • A valuation of the property and its rental potential.
     - • All the market research which you have performed, neatly bound in a presentation folder.
     - • A professional financial analysis (prepared by an accountant or an accredited consultant) in regard to the property and your particular financial situation. This analysis should include the following information:
       - * All the taxation benefits associated with the property and their effect on your overall holding cost.
       - * The property's depreciation schedule.
       - * The estimated rental income the property should achieve. You can obtain this estimate from the local real estate agents. They will be more than happy to provide you with

the estimate you need, as long as they have an opportunity to lease the property.

* **The bank will take 75% of the rental estimate into account and add this amount to your overall yearly income, sometimes 80%. This will help increase your borrowing capacity.**
* A longer term financial projection for the property (a minimum of 20 years).
* Show the bank that you are prepared for the worst case scenario. "Prove" to them that you are not a risk.
* Tell the lender your intentions to take adequate insurance coverage, including income loss insurance, trauma insurance, term life insurance and landlords insurance.
* Relationships are CRUCIAL in regard to property finance.
* Show the lender the bank valuation.
* Try to establish rapport with your lending manager.

- All the supporting media articles.
- Pictures of the property and all relevant information relating to your property.

3. Otherwise, get a firm time when you will have this approval.
   – Get the approval in writing.
   – The approval must be irrevocable.

4. You might need to approach more than three financiers to obtain the deal you want.
   – Approach as many lenders as required to get WHAT YOU WANT but be careful you do not sign the Privacy Act until they can give you a fair idea you will be approved to avoid marking your CRA, as every time you apply for a loan, it is recorded on your CRA, whether you receive the loan or not.
   – Just because one bank will not give you the money does not mean another financier will not. You must have the attitude you will get finance if you are absolutely committed as it is possible if you do not take no for an answer.
   – In the current market conditions, lenders are virtually

"throwing" money at potential borrowers. All you need to do is spend the required time and approach enough lenders as a Finance Professional, and you WILL get the deal you WANT.

INTEREST ONLY OR P & I LOAN?

–"Interest Only" loans are the best type of loans for investment property.

–Your property does will still in value whether you "inject" any extra equity into the property or not.

CAN I BORROW MONEY TO FINANCE PROPERTY IF I HAVE VERY LITTLE INCOME (LESS THAN $20,000 pa) OR NO INCOME AT ALL?

– If you have equity in your house or an investment property, you can use this equity as "buffer income" by establishing a Line of Credit Facility.

– You can use the Line of Credit to pay for the difference in cost between your overall property expense and the rental income you will receive.

– Approach the financier as a Professional Investor and clearly explain your intentions to use your equity as "Line of Credit Income".

– If all your other information is in order, most lenders will lend you the monies required to purchase your investment property.

  * Remember, the lender will take 80% of your potential rental income into account when assessing your loan "servicing" ability.

– If you have no equity and you have a low income, you can still obtain a loan but you will have to convince another party (a potential investor with the correct income requirement) to co-guarantee your loan.

  * The investor could be a family member, friend or a business colleague, etc.
  * You might have to share some of your profit with them, as an incentive for them to co-guarantee your loan.

WHAT HAPPENS IF I CAN NOT OBTAIN 100% FINANCE AND I NEED TO COME UP WITH EQUITY MONEY?

If you can not obtain 100% finance because you could not achieve a large enough discount, or you could not obtain enough leverage from the financier, you can still purchase the property with none of your own money.

You can borrow the equity required (which has not been financed by the lender) through the following means.

1. You can use the equity in your own home or in your other assets — commercial and investment, property, business, etc.
2. You can take out a personal loan from lending institutions. If you have a steady job most financial institutions will lend you up to $35,000 to $50,000 without the need for any security except your personal guarantee.
3. You can obtain a "business partner" in the property. You can approach family, friends or any other potential investor and ask them to "put up" their assets as security to borrow the equity money required. If there is no need for people to provide "hard cash" and if the investment is sound, it should be very easy to find investors.
4. You can borrow money from second mortgage lenders. Many solicitors lend second mortgage money for residential property but charge a higher interest rate. 1% to 4% above the current variable market rates.
5. You can borrow cash money from private investors, and offer them a higher interest rate or equity in the property. You can ask the vendor from whom you are purchasing the property to provide you with vendor finance for a small component of the purchase price. Meaning that if you are short $50,000 on a $250,000 settlement, you will still provide the vendor with $200,000 (obtained from the bank) and you will still owe them $50,000, secured by a caveat or second mortgage over the property and personal guarantees.

If you pay the vendor a high enough interest rate, they should in most cases agree. Again, it is just a matter of money.

SHOULD I GET A FINANCE BROKER TO ARRANGE MY LOAN?

- The process of obtaining a loan will teach you how you can do it yourself in the future and you will be able to establish your own relationships with key lenders for your future finance needs.
- Most finance brokers are incompetent.
- No result, no payment. Be careful because most finance brokers will ask you for an up-front fee. The problem with this is that if they do not get you the right deal, they still keep YOUR money so do not use a broker if they want payment upfront.
- If you do engage the services of a broker, make sure that you do not "screw" them on their fees. You want the best and they do not work for peanuts. If the broker provides you with the result you want and guarantees their performance, they should be paid a reasonable fee.

RATES DEFAULT PROPERTIES

This is another strategy that is very effective if done correctly and is a way to get properties up to 90% discount, revalue them and use as equity to purchase other property.

What is a Rates Default Property?

When an entity has defaulted on their annual rates payments to the local Council over a period of time, i.e., 3 to 5 years, the Council has the right to sell the property through a Public Auction. The purpose of the auction is to sell the property to another entity, which will not only be able to pay the rates in the future, but also pay out the outstanding rates to date.

When do Rates Default Auctions occur?

Generally rates default auctions occur when Councils are balancing their books, usually every six months. This is common around March–May and October–December.

How do I find out about these Auctions?

Lists of the registered Councils within Australia are available showing fax and telephone numbers. Call the Council and ask to speak to the Rates Clerk. You can utilise the script included or design your own. By law, when a property is coming up for Public Auction, it must be advertised to the public (e.g. in newspapers or the *Government Gazette*).

How much will it cost to purchase a Rates Default Property?

The cost of a Rates Default Property is dependent on how much is owing on that property's rates and also whether the Council decides if there will be a Reserve Price for the auction. This varies between States and also between Councils.

The formula used to estimate the Reserve Price or the possible cost of the property is:

Cost = Rates owing (3–5 years) + 10% Council Charges + Advertising Fees + Stamp Duty

You can ask what the rates are per year. Advertising is usually equivalent to what a local newspaper advertisement would cost. Council charges 10% of rates owing. Stamp Duty is the amount applicable in that State.

What you should know before attending a Rates Default Auction

Depending on different Councils and States, you may be required to lodge a 10% deposit on the day of the auction and then have 30 days to pay the remainder. Other Councils require the property be paid in full on the day of the auction. The successful bidder will also need to pay legal fees and stamp duty. So it is important that you have your monies organised before going to the auction. Councils usually accept bank cheque, cash or electronic transfer. Clarify all these details with the Council before you leave for the auction, and definitely before you start bidding.

Your Final Check

Ring the respective Council before you actually leave to go to the auction. The two reasons for this are:

1. The entity may pay their outstanding rates at the last minute and the property is withdrawn from auction.
2. The date of the auction can be changed.

Script — for enquiring about Rate Default Properties

Secretary

Hi my name is .... I am calling from .... Could you please put me through to your rates clerk?

Rates Clerk

Hi my name is .... I am calling from .... I was just enquiring whether you had any rate default auctions coming up within six months?

You do!!! That is great could you please fax or mail the details of the property / properties to me?

Thank you very much ....for your time and help.

Bye

If no

You do not, that is okay, I appreciate your help and time, would it be okay if I were to contact you in another six months. Y / N

Thanking you again

Bye

Going to the Auction

Land/Lot No	Rates Owing/Year	Reserve Price	What will You Pay?	General Notes

KYOGLE COUNCIL

Local Government Act 1993, Section 713

Sale of land for Overdue Rates

NOTICE IS HEREBY GIVEN to the persons named hereunder that the Council of Kyogle has resolved in pursuance of section 713 of the Local Government Act, 1993, to sell the land described hereunder of which the persons named appear to be the owners or in which they appear to have an interest and on which the amount of rates and charges stated as at 18 December 2000 are due.

Owners or persons having interest in the land	*Description of land (Lot, section and DP Nos. street & c)*	*Amount of rates (including extra charges) overdue for more than five (5) years*	*Amount of all other rates (including extra charges) due and in arrears*	*Total*
(a)	*(b)*	*(c)*	*(d)*	*(e)*
Forwood I	Lot 20, Sec G, DP 10036	$25.34	$2027.41	$2052.75
Francis MW & GD	Lot 1, DP 605611	$106.39	$1995.82	$2102.21
Guffogg MK & JA	Lot 1, DP 801665	$102.44	$2388.66	$2491.10
Collins Estate RN	Lot A, DP 392198	$248.06	$4231.36	$4479.42
Phelps GT	Lot 16, DP 17479	$665.00	$2115.61	$2780.61

In default of prior payment to the Council of the rates due and in arears, the said land will be offered for sale by public auction by Matt Dougherty Real Estate at the premises of Matt Dougherty Real Estate, Summerland Way, Kyogle, on Saturday, 6 May, 2001, at 10.00am. KEN DAVIES, General Manager, Kyogle Council, PO Box 11, Kyogle, NSW 2474.

[0052]

RYLSTONE SHIRE COUNCIL

Local Government Act 1993

Sale of land for Overdue Rates

NOTICE IS HEREBY GIVEN to the persons named hereunder that the Council of the Shire of Rylstone has resolved in accordance with sections 713 to 726 of the Local Government Act, 1993, to sell the land described hereunder of which the persons named appear to be the owners or in which they appear to have an interest and on which the amount of rates and charges stated as at 22 January 2001 are due.

Owner	*Description of land*	*Amount of rates (including extra charges overdue)*	*Amount of all other rates and extra charges due and in arrears*	*Total*
(a)	*(b)*	*(c)*	*(d)*	*(e)*
Mr L. J. Merrett	53 Rodgers Street, Kandos Lot 9 Sec 14 DP 8955	$256.14	$8514.95	$8771.09

In default of payment to the Council of the amount stated in column (e) above, together with any other rates (including extra charges) becoming due and payable after publication of this notice, the said land will be offered for sale by public auction at Rylstone Memorial Hall, Louee Street, Rylstone, on Saturday 12th May 2001, at 10.30am. JOHN A. SUMMERS, General Manager, Rylstone Shire Council, PO Box 42, Louee Street, Rylstone NSW 2849.

[0050]

ESTATE NOTICES

NOTICE of intended distribution of estate.—Any person having any claim upon the estate of BETTY IRENE ROBINSON, late of Fairfield West, in the State of New South Wales, Sales Lady, who died on 8th August, 1999, must send particulars of his claim to the executrix, Diane Patricia Pilotto, c.o. J. P. Gould, Solicitors, of Commonwealth Bank Chambers, 2/268 Canley Vale Road, Canley Heights, within one (1) calendar month from publication of this notice. After that time the executrix may distribute the assets of the estate having regard only to the claims of which at the time of distribution she has notice. Probate was granted in New South Wales on 20th December, 2000. J. P. GOULD, Solicitors, Commonwealth Bank Chambers, 2/268 Canley Vale Road, Canley Heights, NSW 2166 (D.X. 25110, Fairfield), tel.: (02) 9727 2888.

[0042]

NOTICE of intended distribution of estate.—Any person having any claim upon the estate of PETER SUI LUN LUI, late of Waitara, in the State of New South Wales, Retired Gentleman, who died on 20th June, 2000, must send particulars of his claim to the executor, Raymond Wai Ming Wong, c.o. Raymond W. M. Wong and Co., Solicitors, 18 Woodville Avenue, Wahroonga, within one

CHAPTER 15

THE BABY BUCKET PRINCIPLE

As we draw this book to a close, you will need to look at which strategy best suits you out of all the strategies we have covered. I am giving you a range of strategies because everyone is different but you will need to choose one or two to focus on, master them and then you can expand your strategies from there. Do not try to do a bit of everything. I do not use all the strategies. I focus primarily on two strategies, i.e., renting and selling insurance for example, but I do not do them all because you do not need to. With property I also usually focus on one or two strategies.

Determine which strategies you should do, and your investment strategy will change as you grow. You may move from one strategy to another, depending on your current goals.

I call the following strategy the "Baby Bucket principle" and it is designed to turn risk into your friend as it can ensure you can profit from risk, and can not lose your entire wealth. To do this, you divide your big bucket into some smaller buckets. I call it the baby bucket principle because I like to keep things simple.

Remember your big bucket.

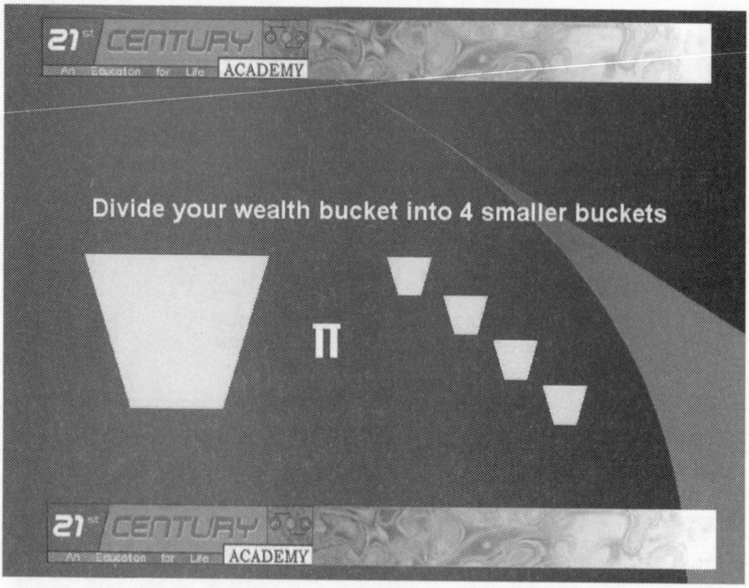
21st CENTURY
An Education for Life ACADEMY
Divide your wealth bucket into 4 smaller buckets
21st CENTURY
An Education for Life ACADEMY

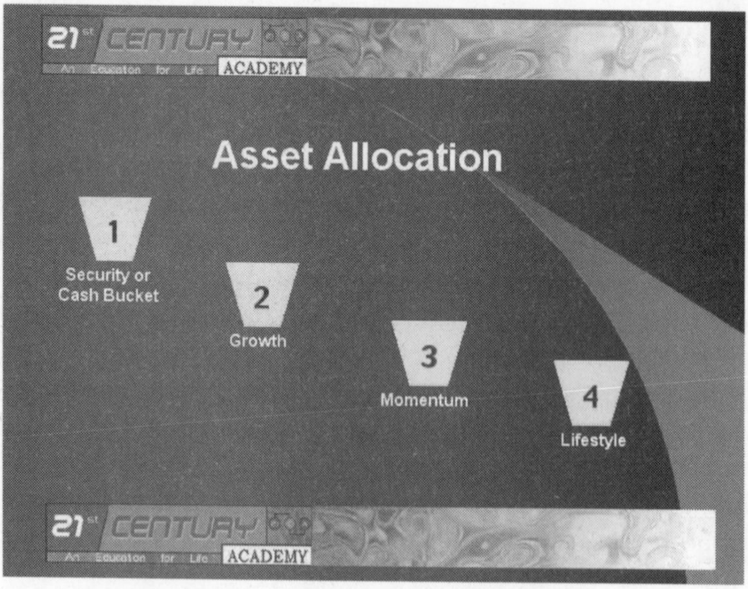
21st CENTURY
An Education for Life ACADEMY
Asset Allocation
1
Security or Cash Bucket
2
Growth
3
Momentum
4
Lifestyle
21st CENTURY
An Education for Life ACADEMY

You have got four buckets to fill up but which one do you fill up first? We will start on the first bucket. Let us name the buckets.

The first one we will call our security bucket.

Our second bucket we will call our growth bucket.

The third bucket is our momentum bucket.

The fourth bucket we will call the lifestyle bucket.

With the security bucket, do you think that it is a really high risk investment or low risk? Obviously low risk.

This principle is important as **the fastest way to become wealthy is determined by the speed at which you get yourself into a position where you can afford to lose money.** That is why high level investors can make an absolute fortune because they have plenty of money put aside that they can afford to lose. When you can do that, investing is so simple. You may say that is alright for high level investors but what if you are starting out, can you afford to lose anything? The answer is yes

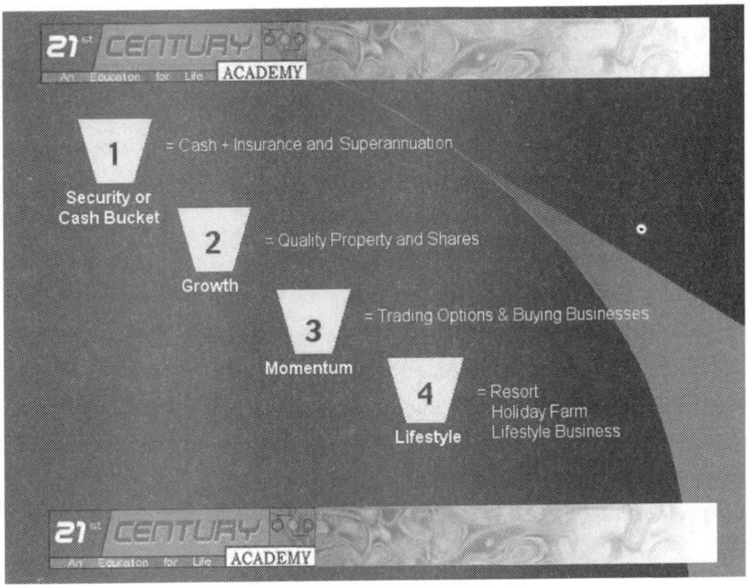

if you apply this strategy. The intention is not to lose but be able to afford to lose, so this is less likely to happen, as I will explain.

The Security bucket is low risk investments. These include your cash management trust accounts, i.e., physical cash. You would include insurance. You may require a good insurance broker if you intend to invest in property, etc. It is best to use a broker rather than an agent for insurance. An agent is more biased and will sell you their products, whereas a broker will sell you the best products that suit you as they are not generally controlled by one company.

I suggest income protection, disability, and health, you need to consider those sorts of insurances if you become an active borrower for investing to lower your risk in case you lose your job while building your wealth or suffer illness.

Growth investments — residential property and quality companies, renting, etc., are investments that belong in this bucket.

The Momentum bucket would cover renting, commercial property, traditional business, etc. This would help you understand why many people go broke. They get sick of working for a boss so they decide to become the boss and start their own business. They borrow against their house to start a business, and a traditional business for a 96 percenter is one of the highest risk strategies as they risk losing everything. If you are going to borrow against your house, here is a golden rule. Do not borrow for business until you can afford to lose the money. People who have suffered a business failure often say they wish they had known that 5 or 10 years ago.

Lifestyle bucket — what is a lifestyle investment? If you want to buy a hobby farm, are you buying it for the investment return or for the hobby? For people who own a place in the snow, it is mainly bought for the lifestyle element rather than investment return. An example is a restaurant. We were considering buying a restaurant in Noosa, one of the favourite places we always go. I thought with the amount we spent there for breakfast, lunch and dinner, we would probably own it by now. If we buy it, it is not really to make money but more for the sake of owning one, i.e., lifestyle choice. That is the difference. A lot of people make the mistake of not doing any growth investments or momentum but they want lifestyle and they jump straight into an investment for lifestyle, a place in the snow or a farm that maybe they can not really afford, rather than build up their investments first where that could fund a place in Aspen, or a chalet in Switzerland, out of their profits.

If you are smart, you can turn lifestyle investments into growth investments, i.e., we have two properties we bought mainly for lifestyle. One is a beautiful winter home in Queenstown, New Zealand which we use three to four times a year, plus allow family and friends to use. The rest of the time it is holiday rented and is still highly positive geared as we get very high rentals. So it makes us money, plus we get a free holiday home that pays itself off. However, this is often not the case for holiday homes in Australia where there is often an oversupply of holiday homes with high vacancies and poor capital growth.

The same applies with a farm. With rural property prices rising, it is becoming a much better investment plus a cash cow (excuse the pun), especially when cattle prices are good, but primarily it is for lifestyle — the joy of having a farm to escape to and enjoy the healthy rural lifestyle.

The reason we use these buckets is to prevent people from jumping into momentum investments straight away. What you need to do is divide your investment into levels of risk. So we are going to understand psychology, which is the fact that fear and greed drive people emotionally with investing. Fear will cause people to do nothing, place all their money under the pillow or just put it in the bank and leave it there. Many people are driven by fear. Fear of losing money so they just keep it in the bank. Obviously if we are too fearful nothing is going to happen. That will cause people to just put it in the bank and banks do not mind that because they make a lot of money. They make money out of nothing. That is all money is, it is an idea that too many people take too seriously.

The opposite to fear is greed. Some people are not fearful any more, they want to get rich quickly, so they jump into investments they can not really afford, lose money and put themselves in a difficult situation and as a result they never get rich quick. They stay broke longer. They will jump into a momentum investment, put all their eggs into that one basket which is not smart either. So what we want to do is learn about being financially intelligent and we also have to be emotionally intelligent. One way to do that is to be detached from the outcome, which means you will not be so driven by fear and greed. Or, do you want to be more cool, calm and collected? Being cool, calm and collected and not panicked requires you not to be attached to money. My millionaire mentor always said life is too short to be stressed over money. He said, "Be detached from money and be in a position where you do not have to worry too much about it." If there is a crisis, you should not panic. Another word for crisis is opportunity. Just like if the market is plummeting, people panic. We know we do not have to panic. You have learned how to make money when the market goes down and how to protect yourself if the market goes down so you can respond intelligently.

Remember, crisis is opportunity. You want to be cool, calm and collected. If you meet someone very successful financially, you will often notice someone very calm about money. Money is just an idea and they do not get hung up on it.

I will tell you an interesting story. I lost my wallet not that long ago. It had $1,000 cash in it. I was about to get upset about it and then I thought life is too short to get upset. I could be upset for a day or a week and I know some people who could get upset for a month about it. Some people get upset for a decade. I thought life is too short, it is a nuisance losing all the cards in it but it does not really matter. It obviously means someone else needed that money more than me. I consider this a donation to the universe, write it off and there is no point worrying about it. Eight years ago, if I had lost $20 I would have been upset. Imagine losing a thousand dollars, I would have been depressed. The only thing is that eight years ago there would not have been $1,000 in my wallet. The point is that you do not want to be too attached to money.

What we want is to be in between fear and greed, and control our emotions, i.e., being cool, calm and collected. That is why these buckets work from a psychology viewpoint. We spread the risk. The technical term for this is asset allocation. I am not talking about just diversification. A strategy many financial planners will teach you is that you should diversify. That usually means they do not really know what is going to work so they put it in different baskets and hope something works. That is really what diversification is to 96 percenters. It is not what I am talking about. We are being smarter with our money to allocate it so we can afford to take some higher risks on a portion of it to get higher returns, and low risk on some to give us peace of mind and security.

Let us say you had only $100,000 to invest. Out of that $100,000, you can deposit it all into momentum or you can spread it. I believe you should put a large percentage of it in security first as security is necessary in the beginning. You need to build your buffer zone. In the beginning, that is all you should build. You may build up your cash management trust. It may seem slow in the beginning but you will get yourself prepared. It will be like a snowball. When you start it down the hill it is a small snowball. It takes a bit of effort to get momentum but once it hits critical mass as it picks up speed, you can not stop it. Then it becomes easier. It is not difficult for me to become wealthier now. I just go to sleep to become wealthy but in the beginning it took discipline, it took sticking at something even when I had doubts.

Let us say you were to invest $15,000 of your $100,000 into your momentum bucket and put the rest in security and growth. That $15,000, if you put it into investment at high risk but also high return and if you were to lose the $15,000 would you be wiped out completely? The answer is no. In that example, you could potentially lose that $15,000 because now you are in a position where you can afford to lose some money as you are in a position to take advantage of some risk which gives you the chance to make higher returns.

Let us work out what percentage to put into each of these buckets. If you apply the baby bucket principle, you will be in a position to take advantage of opportunities. Let me break that down further. You need to determine your risk profile, whether you are aggressive, conservative or fearful. If you have just started investing, you could be conservative or maybe fearful. As you learn more you may start to be more aggressive, however you do not ever have to be aggressive. You just have to be honest with yourself and become clear whether you are a conservative or more aggressive investor.

Depending on that, let us work out what percentage to put in each bucket. This is not advice, it is just a guideline which you can modify to your own psychology. Seek financial advice for determining your risk profile and exact percentages you should adopt. If you are aggressive, you look at the aggressive column and select your age group.

	AGGRESSIVE	CONSERVATIVE
Under 45		
Security	20%	30%
Growth	45%	55%
Momentum	35%	15%
45–55		
Security	25%	30%
Growth	50%	60%
Momentum	25%	10%
Over 55		
Security	30%	40%
Growth	55%	55%
Momentum	15%	5%

Select your age group and jot down the figures for your age group. These are guidelines only and must not be construed as advice as every individual investor is different.

It is a guideline for you. Let us say you are younger than 45 and you are fairly aggressive. Out of every $100,000 you invest, you would consider putting 20% into security, 45% into growth and 35% to momentum. However, if you are conservative you can see you are only going to put 15% into momentum, and the older you get the less you are going to put into momentum as a percentage generally because you have less time on your side and you have different outcomes.

If I am young and conservative, I can put in 35%. If I am really aggressive I can put in more than 35%. That is up to you and you have to relate it back to your psychology. A lot of people get excited about options trading and rush to buy options. I believe there is nothing wrong with that if it is appropriate to you but would you borrow money to trade the options market? My answer is no because you are not in a position where you can afford to lose that borrowed money as you have no fallback position. (You could borrow against the net worth you already have, which is different because you are just transferring money out of say equity into another form of investing.) You may get away with a percentage of that but you would not rush out to get a personal loan and trade the options market using Simon's strategies. (However, renting companies you own, is a growth bucket investment and more people would be comfortable putting a larger percentage of their portfolio into this, especially if they insure their position, than to buy options (Simon's strategy) which is a momentum bucket strategy with higher risk.)

The reason you would not borrow money for buying options if you are just starting is that it is a momentum investment and you can not afford to lose that money. Simon used more of an aggressive approach where he could get a few thousand aside from savings that he could afford to lose as he had not borrowed the money. His psychology was that he did not want to lose but he accepted that this could happen and was prepared for it. So he was detached. As soon as you become attached, it affects your trading and that is why very few people long term make consistent profits in options trading because they do not go to work on their psychology. If you talk to Simon and people who have done his options training who have also developed their mindset through emotional intelligence training, i.e., received at *21st Century Academy*, they totally outperform the people who have gone straight into options and do not have the emotional intelligence training to create the ideal mindset.

The trained participants understand the baby bucket where other people generally get caught up with their ego and just want to make money to get rich quick. They are the sort of people who tend not to follow rules, do not listen and have to learn the hard way. That is why I teach strategies to minimise the risk so you can protect yourself. This explains why you may hear some horror stories about options trading. People with the wrong psychology who do not follow the rules, and get caught up in greed, lose as a result. That is why your psychology affects everything. You are playing with money, so it is important to be financially intelligent. Be smart with your money, not too fearful and not too greedy. You want to be balanced, intelligent and detached so you can enjoy it. **In closing, remember it is just a game, a game that you can learn to win and enjoy the process. Maybe life was never meant to be a struggle but just a beautiful stroll through a valley on a sunny day.**

It has been an honour to have shared this journey with you through this book and I sincerely would look forward to meeting you some day if our paths were to cross. I have attempted to give you a lot in this book, as my philosophy is to always give more than expected and it comes back tenfold. The way I receive is to hear your success stories, feedback and comments and you are welcome to email me at customerservice@21stcenturyacademy.com.au. I can not promise you a personal response due to the large number of emails I receive but you never know as I do personally respond to many.

Remember to take intelligent action with what you have learned as this book has removed a lot of excuses you may have had, as now you know how to do it. I encourage you to continue to develop your 21st century education as this is just the beginning of an exciting new world you can create for yourself.

On one last note, if I was to sum it up into one word, the most important thing that turned my life around and made my dreams a reality, that word would be COURAGE and lots of it! I wish you a lot of courage as you will need it but remember it is worth it. It is up to you to make that decision to live the life of your dreams or settle for a life of regret! As the famous advertisement says, "JUST DO IT" and then celebrate your success.

TESTIMONIALS

To see more, go to www.21stcenturyacademy.com and click on Discussion Forum and Success Stories.

First of all I have to thank Jamie and his team of licensed share speakers for teaching and sharing the strategies with me (and others out there). My only regret is not having learned these strategies earlier. It has changed my life dramatically and it definitely looks like I am well on my way to retiring at a ripe old age of 30! – I am 30 now...

I won't go into specific transactions I have made in the last 2 months, but suffice to say, that by renting shares I have now cleared $3500 per month. Would have been more this month but I used some of my premiums to insure myself against a fall. Otherwise my income would have been $4100 per month (double my current salary). If I am exercised, I will be happy to own the shares anyway, which I believe is an important factor when renting shares. You must be willing to buy the shares at that price you rented at – and it saves alot of angst and worries later on.

All the above was achieved with an initial $80k of my own money and $80k from a share loan but...remembering that I haven't yet had to use the share loan, I therefore haven't had to pay any interest! Also all the extra 'income' I have accumulated and will continue to receive, is being saved towards the following month/s, to allow me to rent more shares (assuming that I am not exercised) and to generate even more cashflow.

I have also shown my mum (who was initially sceptical of share renting and didn't believe that it could be done with such well managed risk) that it was possible! The upside of all this is that I will be receiving $500k from her in the next 2-3 months to invest towards my future as a show of her faith in me and in Jamie's strategies! I can't wait to see the returns with that added to my already fast growing capital! I guess she wanted to know that she could trust me with my 'inheritance' in a manner of speaking.

Also friends are now wanting to board the bandwagon and are constantly seeking help. I have provided them with Jamie's introductory DVD/video and it looks like they will be joining up soon and well on their way to financial freedom as well.
What can I say to finish except — THANK YOU JAMIE!
I owe you a dinner at the very least to show my appreciation! Look me up if you are ever in Brisbane. — Declan

Just thought that I would share with you the success of my first trade, in the hope that it may encourage some of you. I know that I was probably one of the most sceptical when I first came across these strategies, but I can honestly say that I am now converted, and looking forward to a very different future. Here's the trade: On the 30/08/2004 I rented shares with an expiry date of 23/09/2004, Exercise Price of $6.25 and premium of $0.245. Return was $1960 or 3.92% which is 47.04% pa (assuming I was exercised). Since it looks like I won't be exercised the return will be higher than that. And it only cost me $44 to place the trade. The rest of my money sat in the bank the remainder of the time. While my shares currently trading at $7.20, there is no sign of being exercised on or before Thursday when the contracts expire.
Thanks Jamie! Tim Wilson

It was great to catch up with fellow graduates and meet Jamie on Tuesday night, especially the Q&A Session with Jamie, prior to the commencement of the Seminar. I would like to get some feedback from fellow graduates as to the success of the evenings and whether it would be beneficial in the future if we could have a "refresher seminar/meeting" say once a year for Homestudy Graduates to use as a "think tank" or a Forum to express their ideas.
I recently rented shares @ $5.00 strike for August (0.11c) and received $1650.00 in the bank.
Tony – *Melbourne Seminar*

Well everybody... until I had a chance meet at an investment expo in Brisbane a few months ago I would never have even known about 21st Century *nor the renting shares that we all know now...*
To tell you the truth it was the nice girls Jamie had handing out the packs that got me. Jamie was there and now I wished I had talked to him but any way… Doing the course I have now a company structure in place… just like the vid. super fund .. trusts etc etc. I have done my 1st trade and received a cool $3400 in rental and if I do get sold I will gross $9900. Not bad for my 1st time out (for 1 month). That's without leverage which I will be doing in the near future… I challenge you out there to get off your butts and loose the fear… just do it!!! When I get fully under way I will be on $10,000 a month just in premiums alone (without leverage). I want to hear of anyone who is up to the challenge... come on I dare you!! THANKS JAMIE... GOgetter

Hello again… well another good month. Thanks to 21st Century this month I have received $4,000 in premiums. I did get exercised and bought back the shares which I gained on paper $6500 plus the $3400 ($9900) not bad for 5 min phone call hey...!!! This month I rented shares for $15.50 for 0.40c ea +$4,000 bought back at $14.55 … gain if exercised $9500.00 I may get sold so for the month I should receive $13,500.00 so that means $3375 gross per week. What a good idea!!!!!!!!!!!!!!!! I am now on track to retire within the next 12 months. YEA BABY this is the best cash generator around.
GOgetter

Hi Jamie, How's this for my very first trade? I decided after talking with my Broker that I wanted to buy shares to rent. I put $10k into my account and arranged a share loan of $10k. At the time, around mid March, the shares were trading at $4.83 so I was looking to buy 4,000 shares, a total of $19,320.

I decided however to buy them wholesale by selling insurance, i.e. 4 contracts of $4.75, and for this I got 23c, a total of $827 net of brokerage. So if I'm exercised at the end of April I'll effectively buy them at $4.52, minus brokerage. My shares are currently trading at $5.10 so with 3 weeks to go until expiry it's looking like I won't get exercised so I'll just keep the $827 and do it again next month. I didn't even have to draw on my share loan so I don't have to pay any interest. Not too bad. Thanks heaps.
Rich

Just thought I would drop you a line on one of your home study grads. In my first month renting shares I have made $1900 with little or no risk and already this month I have made another $500 renting shares and $360 selling insurance. The moment I started watching the videos I knew there was more to life than the daily grind. Thanks to you Jamie, I am going to make share renting my main source of income. Once again MANY THANKS…
Craig Thompson

Hi Michael here, I just did my second trade. I rented shares @ $14.00 and received $0.45c per share. I did 2 contracts (1 leveraged) and received $820.00 after fees, that's approx 3.5 %, same as last month, EASY MONEY, that's one month's home loans repayments for nothing, I love it.
Michael

My wife and I are currently half-way through the Homestudy program, and I thought I'd share some of our successes so far, although all non-financial yet, successes to us nevertheless:
1. We have decided to take up meditation, something I would never have thought of doing — this is a big change in my mindset and I'm more than willing to take it up!
2. We have planned our holidays for next year. I cannot take 1 week in every 4 (yet), but 1 long weekend in every 4 is more than good enough for me. There is a lot of Victoria we have not visited and it's now time to do so. My boss is more than happy for me to do this rather than taking more than 2 weeks in one go.
3. I have received a pay-rise already, just showing a more positive and proactive mindset has pay dividends (so to speak) in my workplace.
4. We have committed to give 10% to the Royal Children's Hospital in Melbourne. They have looked after our kids and we want to give something back. When we received the introductory video, we were very sceptical, which was good. We did some research on other 'wealth education' courses, but Jamie's was the only one we ever really considered as Jamie makes it simple to understand. Thank you to all who contribute to this forum and congratulations to those who have taken action, as having like-minded people around made our decision to do the Hometudy course so much easier. Life has never looked so much brighter! Regards, Carlos.

After lots of research, studying, doing the homestudy course and attending the Brisbane Conference we finally jumped in and rented shares this month on shares in October @ $0.46 giving us $920. Hopefully we are on our way and looking forward to doing another few next month and the next month and the ....
GavNic

I watched the free DVD that this site handed out. I found it very helpful and made $15,000 on a property in only 2 months. This is a truly inspirational DVD and I recommend it to all. Thanks.
Charlie
"After attending the initial 3 Day program, I realised just because I didn't have

'Big Bucks' didn't mean that I couldn't invest. Jamie's strategies on trading shares (taught by licensed share speakers) inspired me to take action and I bought shares for an outlay of $1,000. I closed out that position 6 days later for $2,000. That's an incredible 100% return on my first ever investment! I'm now saving like crazy and my whole energy for life has sky-rocketed. I now have the strategies and courage to start investing straight away instead of in 10 years' time."
Fiona Hill

... I have learned more about myself than I could ever have imagined... You are the most amazing and genuine individual I have ever had the pleasure of meeting and I only hope I can go on to make a difference in the lives of others in the future. Thank you for everything.
Sue Borg

I would like to begin to show my appreciation for allowing me to take part in 21st Century *3 Day Seminar, it has given me the insight of life and that anything is possible if you focus on what you really want in life. I consider myself very lucky to attend the intro night (I was forced to go to the seminar by my mother). The reason you had such an impact on me was because I too love giving to charity and the church too, but I have never known how to do it, since I couldn't even control my financial problems. But when your first words were: "The techniques that I will show you will gain you wealth, but I ask only one thing in return, and that is to give 10% of your earnings to charity", that really touched me. The 3 Day Seminar was different (in a good way) to what I expected... not only did you* SHOW ME THE MONEY, *but you also taught me a valuable lesson about life and how to control my emotions. That part of the seminar helped build on the relationship with my girlfriend and also my family.*
Jundill Orilla

After being dragged to the seminar by my husband much to my dismay, I have since achieved some great things in saving a large amount of money in 3 months, paid off our debt using the debt reduction strategies and also bought our house.
Margie Ponton

Since doing the 3-Day at the end of March, 2001 I have planned our cashflow for the next 12 months. Have consistently paper traded shares whilst waiting to draw down from our Line of Credit account, opened my Wealth accounts, accessed other peoples' money through a loan and met with our accountant to look at our tax situation.
Steve Dew

As owner of an Accounting Firm since doing Jamie's course we have improved our client education in helping and assisting them to build wealth through alliances with stock brokers and finance brokers. Personally I am currently sourcing finance for a shopping centre valued at $5 million which I can purchase for $4.2 million.
Craig Stowe (Accountant)

Since doing the December 3 Day I have managed to create enough Cashflow from our investments to take my family on a long overdue 5 week trip to visit my son in Switzerland. We will travel around Europe through our investments. It's great to have this new mindset that allows us to do that.
Annetta

Since attending the 3 Day with Jamie I have taken the ways to increase my active income to the maximum. I have given all my customers guarantees for my computer programming service, doubled my fees and my customers keep coming back.
Johnathon Field

We have borrowed other peoples' money, paying them a great return and making an even better return from renting shares. We are earning about $1,500 per month for free, and also borrowed money to add value to our property for a gain of $120,000 in 12 months. Borrowed against that, spent $500 on it and made $40,000 gain in 6 months!
Darren & Suzie Hague

I am over 60 years and have been taken to places I didn't know. This has helped me to have the confidence to take the first step to help me to retire. Thank you Jamie and 21st Century.
W G Fitzgerald

Gary was a full time student who was cleaning toilets to fund his university studies. By attending the seminar, Gary made enough money to quit his part time job. Gary migrated from South Africa and using the strategies taught at 21st Century was able to create a $50,000 share portfolio. He generates 5% returns per month, which equates to nearly $2,500 per month without the need to work. Money while you sleep. A dream come true.
Gary Lake

Great Seminar. Jamie gives you more strategies to create wealth. No matter how much I am in debt, I can still build wealth.
Ken Lau

"Young Couple makes $74,000 from thin air"

Young couple makes $74,000 from thin air. When we completed the seminar 18 months ago, we began searching for an investment property in Brisbane. After looking for a few months, we purchased a house within 5km of the CBD for $281,000. To improve our rental income, we renovated the bathroom (for only a couple of thousands dollars) which increased our rent by over 10%. Three months later, the property was revalued at $305,000, nearly $24,000 in thin air profits. After building a rapport with our real estate agent, she offered us two houses on one sub-dividable title for $450,000. Six months later the property has been revalued at $500,000 and is renting for $600 per week. Positive cashflow—that's great, plus another $50,000 in money out of thin air.
Jock and Amy Mitchell

...thank you for everything. I was one of the graduates from the weekend seminar in Melbourne and it has already changed my life drastically... I work one full time job, and another part time on the weekends. I've managed to get a pay rise from both employers on Monday. Part time job has gone up almost 50%, the other I'm still waiting for an exact figure but it is most likely going to be around a 33% increase. I've figured it's all or nothing, and I've made a serious life change, making the hard decisions and doing it quickly. I've already restructured my pay so that now I automatically save 80% of my GROSS income. That's right, before I have to pay my tax, car and jet ski.
Glenn Gillen

As a student, my life is only beginning. This has given me many more options to how I approach my goals. A very enlightening and enriching experience. Thank you.
Nusreen Ispahany

As a female I thought investing was only for men. Within 4 short weeks of doing Jamie's program, I bought my first investment for a discount of 7.5% under the valuation, which meant a profit of $19,000 in equity straight up! With the confidence of that experience I used some of the 'add value cashflow strategies' and negotiated my salary package from a measly $28,000 per year to $48,000. You can do the sums. In just 4 weeks I literally made $39,000 out of thin air - I'm stoked.
Sue Alympic

Since doing the course I have found a residential investment property at $15,000 discount with a 100% finance. I have also renegotiated my partner's loan and released $200,000 in equity to use the renting of shares strategy.
Lorraine Christian

My life has completely changed since completing the 3 day course with you Jamie. I had a few lessons on the way but I got through the tough time with just a few bruises and a whole heap of experience that money can't buy. I now have a company which rents shares, buys property and concentrates on businesses and projects that we want to concentrate our time on. We are financially free. I don't work a job anymore, but develop business ideas from home and spend the rest of my time finding properties and strategizing with our broker. It's so great. We have made more money in the last 2 months than I would make in a year. We have to pinch ourselves but it is real and getting better all the time. But best of all, I listened to Stuart Wilde and read his books as a result of attending your course. Ever since then my life really transformed itself. The money has started to flow, but more significantly I managed to remove myself from the wrong relationship and into the best one ever. We are now married and on the same path emotionally and financially. I have not 1 but 4 step kids too. They are just the best and I couldn't be happier. If I can do this in 18 months the hard way, then just see what will happen in the next 18 years! Thanks Jamie.
Julian Thornton

It has been a wonderful, full-on weekend. I especially felt the personal development part of the seminar was beneficial, as I need to get control of my emotional states. I had previously learnt about shares/share renting but I learnt a lot in the property sections. I discovered more about my potential personally as well as financially. I look forward to having a fantastic life now and in the future.
Roslyn Hartwig

Thankyou for the sensational weekend in Melbourne. I went there to pick up some tips on investing, but was shown how much more there is to achieving my goals than just the financial strategies. The weekend may have turned my life. Thanks once again.
Scott Haynes

The priority and focus given to the mindset portion of achieving financial and overall success. This is the first thing I'm going to share with my wife as soon as I get home and the thing that has impacted me the most.
Dwight Veenman

I would just like to thank Jamie and everyone at 21st Century. *The seminar was probably one of my best investments in my future and will prove to be invaluable. Being only 18, the seminar taught me so much in so many areas. After only 2 days I have noticed a big difference in the way I feel emotionally through the personal development aspect of the seminar. The strategies Jamie presented have given me the answers to gaining financial success in life. The property investment strategies were unbelieveable, instead of wasting my money on a new car, I am taking the first steps to purchasing my first investment property, I'm sure there are not too many people my age that have even thought of investing. Thank you so much for providing the information that will give me the ability to enjoy all aspects of life.*
Daniel Peters.

Jamie became a 21st Century *Graduate in 2001 and used the Debt Reduction Strategy taught at the 3 Day to eliminate nearly all his debts within 18 months of attending. He is now aggressively implementing his investment strategies.*
Jamie Morgan

I was particularly impressed with the first day on mindset, especially the idea of ENJOYING THE PROCESS as an affirmation for achieving something, e.g. attaining and maintaining a slim, healthy figure. Also how to change your state of mind in an instant.
Shirley Mundt

We have always known there was more to life than just working hard. We had our own business for some ten years, and boy did we work hard. We had tried all sorts of investments, read all the books, but without a mentor. Thank goodness we have never stopped looking for more. After finding Jamie's advertisement in the newspaper, we ordered his tape, attended his seminar in Adelaide in September 2002. From that we immediately set up a line of credit with our bank, re-valued our house, (we already had a CMT with an existing broker) had some monies in the bank, and started trading immediately renting shares. We have since established a share loan account and have started utilizing it with a 50% margin (likelihood of a margin call is minimal) plus we have security (extra monies in the bank waiting further opportunities). We have also established our own Self Managed Superannuation Fund, and we intend to trade this for renting shares. We have put a twelve month limit on our dreams, and firmly believe this is achievable using just some of Jamie's strategies. Properties are the next step for us, and the renting will take care of itself. All we need now is a like minded group of people to join our MILLIONAIRES CLUB as we are in a rural area. Where are you all????
Thanks a million Jamie
Andrew and Sandy Schutz

JAMIE McINTYRE
Co-Founder
21st Century Academy

Jamie McIntyre is an extraordinary young Australian making a big difference to the quality of other people's lives in this nation. He is a sought after Success Coach (Life Coach) and has travelled the world meeting and learning from some of the very best teachers and leaders on the planet including Anthony Robbins (Unlimited Power), General Norman Schwarzkof (Desert Storm), and Paul Zane Piltzer (Unlimited Wealth), Jay Abrahams (Fortune 500 Marketing Consultant), Robert Kiyosaki (Rich Dad, Poor Dad), and many others.

He became a self made millionaire in his twenties, an entrepreneur, a sought after public speaker, and author. He is founder of *21st Century Group of Companies*, including *21st Century Accounting* and *21st Century Finance.* He is also the founder of *21st Century Academy*, an education organisation that has provided a 21st century education to Australians and New Zealanders, and has received a Highly Commended Award from the Australian Achiever Awards. He was several years ago nominated as a Young Australian of the Year and has been responsible for educating over 95,000 people through his DVD courses and live seminars.

He is a leading advocate for real life education including financial literacy to be implemented into high schools nation wide. He believes this will give teenagers the most important skills they will need to excel in the 21st century, and improve what many say is an inadequate and flawed education system. He is also an advocate to change the bias practices of the financial planning industry, and wants to see financial planners have to produce real life investment results in their own life before being allowed to advise others in financial planning.

He is lobbying for improvements to superannuation to ensure Australians can fund themselves in retirement and is critical of the lack of transparency, competency and accountability of regulatory bodies such as ASIC.

ACKNOWLEDGEMENTS

Neither a book nor the creation of a concept known as a 21st century education could come about without the assistance of numerous people.

I would firstly like to thank the Stokes sisters, Sheena and Cherie for getting this project off the ground when it sat there idle year after year. Also thank you to Janet, my PA, for countless hours of typing and adjustments, and the ability to read my writing, Yasoda for taking part in completing the project, and Jana and Kim for the endless hours of editing, and Russell from *Emigraph*.

I would also like to make a big thank you to the entire team at *21st Century*past and present, including Warren Stokes — General Manager, Brett Gartner — Head Coach, Linda Barraud — our Logistics Event Organiser, Brock Hamilton — IT, our coaching team headed up by Derek Adams, Lea Tidy-Russ — Head of Customer Service, our entire external team of Licensees and our team of ever expanding agents throughout Australia and New Zealand, past promoters Jon and Connie Giann, and all past and present employees.

I would also like to thank my partners in business and all those who have been involved in some way with *21st Century Group*. Big thanks also go to all the graduates of *21st Century Academy* for making the dream of creating a superior educational system a reality. Your success stories prove that what we set out to do is occurring and that it has been worth it. Keep them coming.

A big thank you to my mentors and teachers, some of whom I will not name for privacy reasons but a big thank you to others such as Anthony Robbins who kick started me on the dream to self improvement, Jay Abrahams for his brilliant marketing skills, Michael Gerber for his business concepts, Robert Kiyosaki for making a complex subject so much simpler for me to understand, Stuart Wilde for his humorous way of looking at the concept of money and success, Robert Kirby for his passion and commitment to helping people heal emotionally and all the teachers whose books, seminars and tapes have played such a big part in guiding me to my success and helping other people emulate that success.

Most of all a big thank you to my family, especially my parents, my Dad for his extreme generosity and fair minded thinking, my Mum for her never ending support, love and care through my ups and downs. To my brothers and sisters for always being there, keeping me honest. Thank you for everything.

21ST CENTURY ACADEMY
ONLINE FORUM

"21st Century Graduates communicate from all over the world, offering each other support and encouragement"

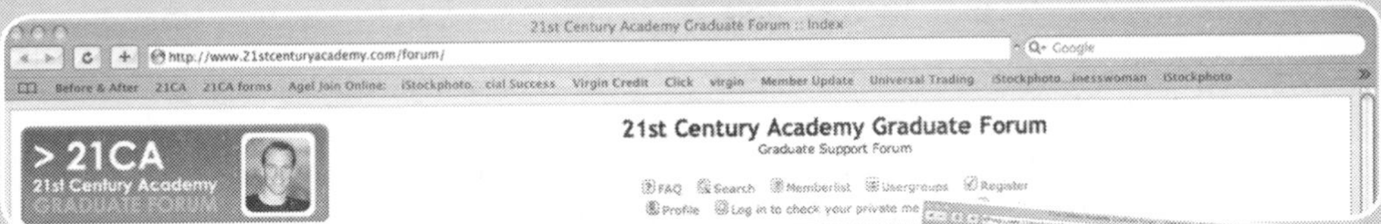

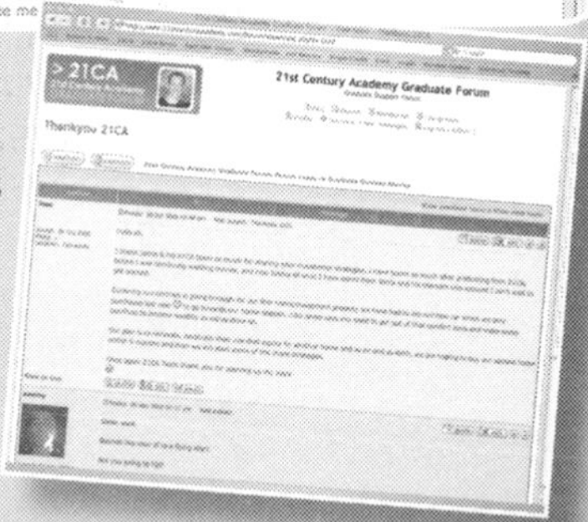

"21st Century Academy has a forum for Graduates seeking help and support. It's a place where Graduates from any where in the world can communicate with other Graduates in a positive and educational environment to encourage and support each other "

Some of the topics covered in the 21st Century Academy Graduate Forum include:

Special Announcements, 21st Century Blue Ribbon, Graduate Success Stories, General Discussion, Stock Market, Property, Internet Marketing, Finance, Business Structure, SMSF & Taxation Discussion, Academy Seminars, Questions & Answers, Free Public Discussion Area - Welcome to New Visitors, Testimonials, Homestudy Kit Questions & Answers, Free DVD & E-book Questions & Answers, 21st Century High School Forum, Parents & Teachers, 21st Century Internet Summit, Anthony Robbins and many more topics.

Go to www.21stcenturyacademy.com/forumdisclaimer.htm for more information.

GRADUATES

GRADUATES - SEAN & SHEREE RASMUSSEN

GRADUATES (FAR RIGHT - BILL STACY)

GRADUATES

GRADUATES

GRADUATES

CONTACT US:

Mail:	21st Century Academy	PO BOX 352, Tewantin, QLD Australia 4565.	
Fax:	Australia: (07) 5474 3006	New Zealand: (09) 358 7332	**Email:** enquiries@21stcenturyacademy.com
Phone:	Australia: (07) 5455 4800	New Zealand: (09) 358 7334.	If outside Australia dial (617) instead of (07). **Free call:** 1800 999 270

www.21stcenturyacademy.com/forumdisclaimer.htm

21ST CENTURY ACADEMY

GET JAMIE'S FREE E-BOOK & DVD

JAMIE McINTYRE

As a special gift, we would like to provide you and your friends and family with a free copy of Jamie's updated book (retails for $34.95) plus, a free DVD by author, Jamie McIntyre.

JAMIE McINTYRE
Co-Founder
21st Century Academy

The key topics covered in this E-Book and DVD are the following.

- How smart investors are replacing their income in 90 to 180 days or less by using the unique cashflow strategy.
- How to cut your mortgage in half and how to eliminate debt in 3 – 7 years.
- How some Australian's have become millionaires in the last 6 years, some who started with very little.
- How to put your kids through college starting with a $10,000 investment.
- **REVEALED**: How smart investors sell insurance in the market for a small fortune, and why your financial planner doesn't know about it.
- **EXPOSED**: The myth that it takes money to make money – 8 ways investors raise money to start investing immediately, even if they have no cash.
- How to instantly add tens of thousands of dollars to the value of your property for as little as $400.
- A step-by-step process on how to buy an investment property... with virtually no money down!

WHAT I DIDN'T
LEARN AT SCHOOL
BUT WISH I HAD

Please inform your friends you have arranged for a FREE E-Book and DVD to be sent to them so when it arrives they know you asked for it to be sent as a FREE gift. An email address is required to send them a FREE E-Book or they can download it for FREE from www.freedvdoffer.com.au and also order the DVD.

You can also email your friends this link **www.dvdoffer.com.au** *for them to access the free E-Book and DVD offer. Or you can join the online Affiliate Program at* **www.21stcenturyacademy.com/affiliate.htm** *and email your coded link to people and we will track this for you and pay you $600 referral fee per every new 21st Century Homestudy Member we receive from your recommendation as a thank you or credit to our program.*

YOUR INFORMATION - Please **PRINT** all information in the spaces below.

First Name:______ Last Name:______
Address:______ State:______ Postcode:______
Phone (H):______ (W):______ (M):______
Email Address:______

Referral 1 Name:______
Address:______ State:______ Postcode:______
Phone (H):______ (W):______ (M):______
Fax:______ Email Address:______

Referral 2 Name:______
Address:______ State:______ Postcode:______
Phone (H):______ (W):______ (M):______
Fax:______ Email Address:______

Referral 3 Name:______
Address:______ State:______ Postcode:______
Phone (H):______ (W):______ (M):______
Fax:______ Email Address:______

FAX BACK FORM TO 21ST CENTURY ACADEMY

Mail: 21st Century Academy PO BOX 352, Tewantin, QLD Australia 4565.
Fax: Australia: (07) 5474 3006 New Zealand: (09) 358 7332
Phone: Australia: (07) 5455 4800 New Zealand: (09) 358 7334. If outside Australia dial (617) instead of (07). **Free call:** 1800 999 270

www.21stcenturyacademy.com

21ST CENTURY ACADEMY

HIGH SCHOOL BOOK DONATIONS

Passionate Teachers Required PLUS...

Book donations to every High School in Australia & New Zealand

JAMIE McINTYRE
Co-Founder
21st Century Academy

Jamie McIntyre

Australia's leading 21st Century Educator, Co-founder of 21st Century Academy – a multi-million dollar Education Organisation, and creator of the revolutionary 21st Century Education system, also nominee for Young Australian of the Year, investor, entrepreneur, author and a consistent giver to charities.

The author's commitment is to donate at least 20 copies of his best selling book which retails for $34.95 in all leading book stores, plus the **High School Seminar DVD** series (valued at $497) recently filmed of Jamie educating High School students on many of the topics covered in his best selling book — to every High School library in Australia and New Zealand. If you would like to nominate your local High School to receive a complimentary set of the book and DVD, then please complete the following:

YOUR INFORMATION - Please **PRINT** all information in the spaces below.

❑ **Do you think this type of information should be added to the school curriculum?** ❑ **Yes** ❑ **No**

School:__________

Address__________

First Name:__________ **Last Name:**__________

Address:__________ **State:**__________ **Postcode:**__________

Phone (H):__________ **(W):**__________ **(M):**__________

Email Address:__________

❑ **Yes, send me a free 3 Hour DVD of Jamie's Seminar.**

What would you like to have been taught at school?

❑ **Yes, I'm a School Teacher or Head Master and would like to implement 21st Century Education books or DVD Programs into my school.**

FAX BACK FORM TO 21ST CENTURY ACADEMY

Mail: 21st Century Academy PO BOX 352, Tewantin, QLD Australia 4565.
Fax: Australia: (07) 5474 3006 New Zealand: (09) 358 7332
Phone: Australia: (07) 5455 4800 New Zealand: (09) 358 7334. If outside Australia dial (617) instead of (07). **Free call:** 1800 999 270

www.21stcenturyacademy.com

21ST CENTURY ACADEMY

3 DAY SEMINARS

"OUR 3 DAY EVENTS ARE HELD IN LUXURIOUS LOCATIONS AROUND THE WORLD"

MILLENNIUM HOTEL, QUEENSTOWN NZ
28th - 31st July, 2006

ROYAL PINES RESORT, GOLD COAST
22nd - 25th September, 2006

HAWAII HILTON WAIKOLOA RESORT
1st - 4th December, 2006

SHERATON RESORT, FIJI
TBA 2007

LONDON
TBA 2007

LAS VEGAS
TBA 2007

DUBAI
TBA 2007

GOLD COAST
TBA 2007

JAMIE McINTYRE & SOME GRADUATES
2006 GOLD COAST, AUSTRALIA EVENT

I would like to invite you to consider developing an ***EDUCATION FOR LIFE*** *by joining myself and my mentors at 21st Century Academy. If you are absolutely committed to improving your quality of life, being at your best to ensure your dreams become a reality and to take charge of your financial future, then I challenge you to enrol into a 21st Century Academy 3 Day live event and/or also join the Elite Platinum Partnership. Do not wait or delay because if you're like most people you will have good intentions but you'll get caught up in making a living instead of designing a life and fail to produce a fraction of what you are capable of. I can assure you that I won't betray the trust placed in myself or the entire 21st Century Academy team. I guarantee that I will share with you and give you more than you'll expect. You'll thank me greatly at the end of the 3 Day Seminar, not only because of what you'll receive immediately but also because of the tools and strategies you will have for the rest of your life. I look forward to connecting with you in person if you choose to join this exciting journey with us.*

Jamie McIntyre - Co Founder and Head Facilitator of 21st Century Academy

YOUR INFORMATION - Please **PRINT** all information in the spaces below.

☐ Yes, I would like to attend a 3 Day Event. Please send me information or go to www.21stcenturyacademy.com for more information.

First Name:______________________ Last Name:______________________

Address:______________________ State:__________ Postcode: __________

Phone (H):__________ (W):__________ (M):__________

Email Address:______________________

FAX BACK FORM TO 21ST CENTURY ACADEMY

Mail: 21st Century Academy PO BOX 352, Tewantin, QLD Australia 4565.
Fax: Australia: (07) 5474 3006 New Zealand: (09) 358 7332
Phone: Australia: (07) 5455 4800 New Zealand: (09) 358 7334. If outside Australia dial (617) instead of (07). **Free call:** 1800 999 270

www.21stcenturyacademy.com

21ST CENTURY ACADEMY 24 MONTHS

HOMESTUDY MEMBERSHIP

"WHAT I DIDN'T LEARN AT SCHOOL BUT WISH I HAD" HOMESTUDY PROGRAM

JAMIE McINTYRE
Co-Founder
21st Century Academy

LIMITED DISCOUNT OFFER...

YES, ENROL ME NOW!

*I want to be one of the exclusive group of people who discovers how to make their dreams a reality through discovering the investing strategies of the rich. I can't wait to watch these amazing events; to hear how it is possible for investors to earn significant profits starting almost immediately. And hopefully, I'll be in the first 34 registrations, so please also set aside my **11 SPECIAL BONUSES** valued at $10,735 and send my **Homestudy** and **Advanced Fiji Homestudy** to me for only $3,995 or $49 per week* plus, include my 24 months of support.*

Also include the 3 Day Bonus Seminar Ticket for myself and 1 Teenager, if I'm enrolling inside the next 21 days.

****If you select a payment plan you pay more than the early bird upfront payment plan.***

This program currently covers the Australian, New Zealand, UK and US Markets and is suitable for most clients worldwide.

OVER 60 HOURS OF DVD'S & AUDIO WITH OVER 18 SPECIALIST SPEAKERS. INCLUDES THE LATEST UPDATED INFORMATION COVERING AUSTRALIAN SHARES, US STOCKS, AUSTRALIAN, NEW ZEALAND, UK AND US PROPERTY, BUSINESS & INTERNET MARKETING AND CUTTING EDGE PERSONAL DEVELOPMENT.

21ST CENTURY HOMESTUDY MEMBERSHIP- Please TICK your selection

Become a 21st Century Homestudy Member. Includes the **Homestudy Program** and **Advanced Fiji Homestudy**, plus access to 24 Months Ongoing Support Services. **BONUS:** If you enrol in the next 21 days you also qualify for the **3 Day Seminar Ticket,** plus 1 Teenage 3 Day Ticket as part of this package. Plus a ticket to the **Internet & Business Mastery Seminar Ticket** (valued at $1,997).

Go to www.21stcenturyacademy.com for more information.

100% 90 Day Money Back Guarantee

PAYMENT OPTIONS: From AUD$49 a week (AUD$1 = approx US$0.75cents)

- ❑ **$3,995 x 1 Full Payment (Save by paying in full)**
- ❑ **$199 x 27 months + $199 deposit ($5,572) (Less than $49 per week)**
- ❑ **$398 x 11 months + $398 deposit ($4,776)**
- ❑ **$1,145 x 4 months ($4,580)**

Plus, a **$45 P&H fee** will be added in addition to your payment for delivery anywhere in the world. Allow 10 to 21 days for delivery.

YOUR INFORMATION - Please PRINT all information in the spaces below.

First Name:______________________ **Last Name:**______________________

Address:______________________ **State:**__________ **Postcode:**__________

Phone (H):__________ **(W):**__________ **(M):**__________

Email Address:______________________

❑ **HOMESTUDY PROGRAM** – ❑ DVD Format ❑ Audio – ❑ MP3 CD's or ❑ Audio CD's

❑ **ADVANCED FIJI HOMESTUDY PROGRAM** – ❑ DVD Format ❑ Audio – ❑ MP3 CD's or ❑ Audio CD's

(Note DVD's and MP3's will be sent unless Audio CD's are requested).

❑ Please charge me **Total AUD$** __________ from my credit card

❑ MasterCard ❑ Visa ❑ Bankcard ❑ American Express ❑ Diners Club (tick one)

Enter Credit Card Number ❑❑❑❑❑❑❑❑❑❑❑❑❑❑❑❑

Expiration Date ❑❑❑❑ ❑❑❑❑

3 or 4 Digit Credit Card Security Code (Located on Back of Card)

Name of cardholder:______________________ **Signature:**______________________

❑ Enclosed is my cheque made payable to 21st Century Academy: PO Box 352, Tewantin, QLD Australia 4565

FAX BACK FORM TO 21ST CENTURY ACADEMY

Mail: 21st Century Academy PO BOX 352, Tewantin, QLD Australia 4565.
Fax: Australia: (07) 5474 3006 New Zealand: (09) 358 7332
Phone: Australia: (07) 5455 4800 New Zealand: (09) 358 7334. If outside Australia dial (617) instead of (07). **Free call:** 1800 999 270

www.21stcenturyacademy.com

21ST CENTURY ACADEMY

PRODUCTS

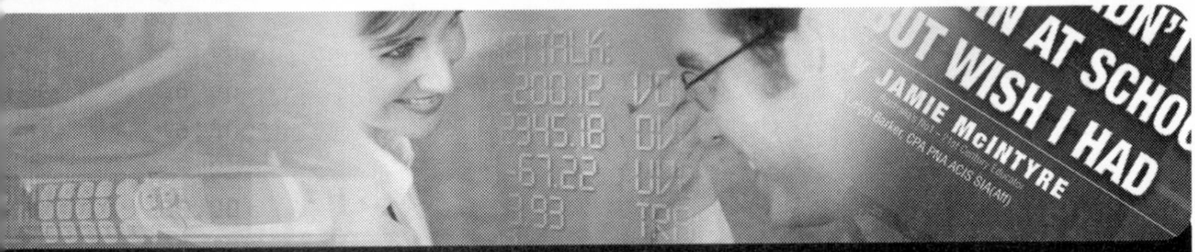

"21st Century Academy have a variety educational products for everyone"

- ❑ Jamie McIntyre's Book, "What I Didn't Learn At School But Wish I Had", *Retails for $AUD34.95 in all leading Bookstores.*
- ❑ 21st Century 24 months Homestudy Membership.
- ❑ **3 Day Live Seminar Events** *(Held in Australia, New Zealand, Hawaii, Fiji and future events in London, Las Vegas and Dubai). (Must become a 21st Century Homestudy Member to attend).*
- ❑ Million Dollar Sales & Marketing Homestudy
- ❑ Public Speaking Seminar & Homestudy
- ❑ Tax Minimisation & Asset Protection Seminar & Homestudy
- ❑ 21st Century Women's Academy Seminar & Homestudy
- ❑ Leadership Academy
- ❑ Business & Marketing Homestudy
- ❑ High School Homestudy for teenagers
- ❑ Selling Insurance E-Manual and Hard Copy Manual for instant cashflow.
- ❑ Platinum Membership *(For exclusive Networking & Advanced Workshops limited to 50 members per year, held in Exotic Locations around the world with Jamie McIntyre and selected speakers and mentors, 3 times a year. The ultimate Peer Group.*
- ❑ Fast Track Property Homestudy by Warren Borsje
- ❑ Kim Reilly's Options Homestudy, *including* Simon Martin's Advanced Options Course & Bourse Data Software.
- ❑ Rick Otton's Positive Cash Flow / Property "Wrap Pack" Homestudy
- ❑ Rick Otton's Rent Pack
- ❑ Anthony Robbins Live Seminars and Personal Power II Program
- ❑ Nik Halik Share Trading MSMI
- ❑ Nik Halik Share Traders Pack
- ❑ 5 Year Support Extension for 21st Century Homestudy Memberships
- ❑ Premium One-on-One Coaching
- ❑ Internet & Business Mastery Seminar or Homestudy
- ❑ 21st Century Internet Software
- ❑ Bourse Data Software

21ST CENTURY SERVICES INCLUDE:

- 21st Century Accounting
  www.21stcenturyacademy.com/21st_century_accounting.htm
- 21st Century Finance
  www.21stcenturyfinance.com.au
- 21st Century Share Broking
  www.21stcenturyacademy.com/sharebroking.htm
- 21st Century Insurance
  www.21stcenturyacademy.com/21st_century_insurance.htm
- 21st Century Property Sourcing
  www.21stcenturyacademy.com/property_sourcing.htm
- 21st Century Equity Funds
  www.21stcenturyacademy.com/equityfunds.htm
- 21st Century Web Services
  www.21stcenturywebservices.com
- Share Trading Diary Subscription Service
  www.optionsforaliving.com

YOUR INFORMATION - Please PRINT all information in the spaces below.

❑ Please send me information about the products I have selected above or go to www.21stcenturyacademy.com for more information.

First Name:______________________ Last Name:______________________

Address:______________________ State:__________ Postcode:__________

Phone (H):______________ (W):______________ (M):______________

Email Address:______________________

FAX BACK FORM TO 21ST CENTURY ACADEMY

Mail: 21st Century Academy PO BOX 352, Tewantin, QLD Australia 4565.
Fax: Australia: (07) 5474 3006 New Zealand: (09) 358 7332
Phone: Australia: (07) 5455 4800 New Zealand: (09) 358 7334. If outside Australia dial (617) instead of (07). **Free call:** 1800 999 270

www.21stcenturyacademy.com